PN
1991.3
.U6
F6

Fornatale, Peter.

Radio in the
   television age.

DATE			

=RADIO=
IN THE
TELEVISION AGE

PETER FORNATALE

JOSHUA E. MILLS

The Overlook Press
Woodstock, New York

First published in 1980 by
The Overlook Press
Lewis Hollow Road
Woodstock, New York 12498

Library of Congress Cataloging in Publication Data

Fornatale, Peter.
  Radio in the television age.

  Bibliography: p.
  Includes index.
  1. Radio broadcasting—United States—History.
I. Mills, Joshua E., 1947-   joint author. II. Title
PN1991.3.U6F6   791.44'0973   79-67675
ISBN 0-87951-106-0

RADIO IN THE TELEVISION AGE

CONTENTS

PREFACE   ix

INTRODUCTION: How and Why People Use Radio   xiii

1 THE GOLDEN AGE ENDS   1

2 ADAPTING FOR SURVIVAL   9

3 THE EMERGING TEEN CULTURE   35

4 FORMATS   59

5 RADIO NEWS   93

6 FM   117

7 THE SEVENTIES   137

8 NONCOMMERCIAL RADIO   165

9 WHITHER RADIO?   187

BIBLIOGRAPHY   197

INDEX   204

ACKNOWLEDGEMENTS

This project could not have been completed without the support of dear friends and the cooperation of total strangers.
We are grateful to:

First of all, Stephen R. Labunski, executive director of the International Radio and Television Society, who brought us into his home at a time when we were discouraged, and inspired us to go on.

And to Kevin L. Goldman of *The New York Times,* whose early support and subsequent research helped bring this project to fruition.

Carmela Seidel of APRadio (who asked our questions of Gordon McLendon), Robin Kardon, Marci Baker, and Richard Lorenzo for their valuable research assistance.

Irene Mularchuk of the Radio Advertising Bureau, who never wearied of answering our questions, helped us unearth invaluable materials, and cheered us on. Jay Francis of Group W, Peter Hamilton of NBC, Connie Anthes of Arbitron, and Richard Spring of National Public Radio, for their prompt responses to our queries, and Robert Alter and Ken Costa of the Radio Advertising Bureau for opening doors.

David Rubin, Mitchell Stephens, John Kochevar, William Burrows, and the other members of the New York University Department of Journalism and Mass Communication for their support. And Roger Jones and the staff at the NYU libraries for their assistance. We gratefully acknowledge the financial assistance of NYU's Graduate School of Arts and Science Research Fund.

The staff at the Federal Communications Commission, especially in its offices of Consumer Assistance and Minority Enterprise and its Broadcast Bureau, who helped us unravel knots and proved that some bureaucracies can function well.

To all those who granted us time to talk with them about radio: Lou Adler, Dr. Morton Bard, Chuck Blore, the Honorable Tyrone Brown, Dean Burch, Dan Daniel, Sam Cooke Digges, Joe Durso, Jr., the Honorable Charles Ferris, Jim Gordon, Richard Harris, Samuel Holt, Ellen Hulleberg, Dan Ingram, Mel Karmazin, Donald McGannon, Gordon McLendon, Robert Meyrowitz, Tom O'Brien, the Rev. Dr. Everett Parker, Nan Rubin, Jim Schulke, Tony Schwartz, Frank Seitz, Warren Somerville, Emerson Stone, Jeff Tellis, Jack Thayer, Ed Wakin, Alan Walden, Maurie Webster, and Robert Wogan. And all those who preferred to talk with us "not for attribution." We're also grateful to Dr. John Bardeen and to Daniel Kops for their detailed correspondence.

In addition, we are deeply appreciative of Erik Barnouw for *A History of Broadcasting in the United States,* and of Sydney W. Head for *Broadcasting in America: A Survey of Television and Radio,* two epic works that must remain the foundation of all studies in broadcasting.

Without our good friend and editor, Mark Gompertz, whose enthusiasm for this project never dimmed his insight, we would have struggled even more.

We owe much to the friends whose patience we pushed to the limit—where we found understanding and compassion, and energy: Bill Ayres, Lisa de Mauro, Dennis Elsas, Steve Leeds, Tina Press, Don Thiergard, and Julie Wolf.

And finally, we cannot offer sufficient thanks to Susan Fornatale, who in sharing a husband gained a friend, and whose support is a rib of this book.

PREFACE

On July 13, 1977, we gave a lecture at New York University on radio since the arrival of commercial television. A large part of the discussion focused on the great Northeast blackout of November 1965. We said then, as we do in this book, that the blackout was radio's grandest hour since World War II, and that its performance that night had reminded people of just how valuable a tool radio is in nearly everyone's life.

An hour after the class ended, power went out all over the New York metropolitan area. The students, we later learned, were very impressed with our timing! Perhaps they would have been less impressed if they knew that Mills, for all his praise of radio, had not learned the lesson of the first blackout: He did not own a transistor radio and spent much of the evening seeking news from Fornatale, whose suburban home was not affected. In between news reports, the commitment to this book was reaffirmed (and the next afternoon, Mills bought a transistor radio).

Everybody listens to radio. They listen at different times, for different reasons, in different degrees, but...they all listen. Radio's penetration into American life is truly staggering: There are nearly twice as many radios in the United States as there are people. More than 95 percent of America's cars have radios, and the average household has 5.7 sets. Radio, then, is the most ubiquitous of the mass media.

Yet despite its overwhelming presence, radio's impact on us goes largely unexamined. In its 60-year history, radio has so entrenched itself in our lives that it has become nearly invisible. In *The Responsive Chord,* Tony Schwartz says that less than two percent of the population acknowledges radio as a vital source of information— about the same percentage of people who remember to acknowledge air as one of the ingredients they consume in life. It doesn't surprise us. People rarely think about radio, and talk about it even less. And the public is not alone in failing to take note of contemporary radio.

We were amazed, when we began the research for this book, to discover how little had been written in popular publications about radio's past 30 years. Much of the material we unearthed was in the trade press. Even the very best broadcast histories seem to lose interest in radio when televison arrives on the scene.

Our purpose was to remedy this. To use a favorite phrase of Gordon McLendon, a radio innovator whose presence vibrates throughout these pages, we have tried to "fill a void." We think this is the first book about radio in the television age for fans and students, as well as for people in the industry. What's more, we think this is the first book about radio written by people who, for better or worse, are children of the television age. Most books and articles we have seen reverberate with a fondness for the Golden Age of radio, which ended with the coming of television. We admire much of what was on the air during the Golden Age, and indeed we return to it again and again to find roots of contemporary radio. But we never listened to *that* radio. We have no memories of it. And so our view of radio is utterly contemporary. We know it only as it is and has been for the last 30 years. That point of view informs this work, and will provide, we hope, a complement to the many excellent histories of the Golden Age.

What's more, we are part of the generation that grew up listening to rock 'n' roll. From our preteens to the present, this music has been part of our culture and part of our lives. We accept rock 'n' roll as natural, honest, and lively (even as our enjoyment of it moves through crests and troughs). We find that too many books on broadcasting, whether they be tolerant, bemused, or scornful of rock 'n' roll, seem to yearn for the "old days" of a different popular music.

First and foremost, this is a history of radio in the 1950s, 1960s, and 1970s, told in chronological order, with two major facets—radio news and noncommercial radio—treated separately within the text. We have learned a great deal in the course of this study, and it has increased our excitement about radio's services and its untapped potential. It is our hope that this book will provoke a greater awareness of how and why people use radio, and how they might seek to improve it in the years ahead.

P.F. & J.M.
July, 1980

INTRODUCTION:

HOW AND WHY
PEOPLE USE RADIO

It wasn't so bad. We had couches to lie down on and lots of nice people. Luckily, we had a radio, a transistor radio, and we lay around and listened to it, and the time went pretty fast.

—An office worker,
immediately after the great blackout,
November 1965

I listen to the radio from the time I get up until I go to bed. It regulates my day and it keeps me company. I can do other things at the same time, cook, clean, and still hear it all the time. I do everything with it and because it's in the kitchen I'm in there with it almost all day. Also, when you're home with children, the day seems to have no beginning and no end, and radio really helps to break it up a little.

—A housewife

THE story of radio in the television age is more than the story of stations, networks, formats, operators, and regulators. It is the story of listeners. They live in cities, towns, and villages, rather than "markets." And they have needs as well as "buying power."

Over the last 30 years, listeners made a transition that the prophets of doom had not anticipated. They began listening to radio differently. They listened to *stations* rather than *programs,* and they tuned in at more times during the day. Among the habits that evolved were:

bedroom radio: About 71 percent of America's bedrooms are equipped with radios, and 60 percent of all homes have clock radios. It has replaced the rooster as the medium by which most Americans awaken.

kitchen radio: About 56 percent of American's kitchens have a radio. Over breakfast it spews out valuable information: weather, traffic patterns, school closings, sales. Throughout the day it provides companionship, and most people agree it is easier to dry wine goblets or cut vegetables while listening to radio than while watching television.

car radio: In 1952, just over half of America's autos had radios. With the figure now at 95 percent, it is estimated that auto radio reaches seven out of ten adults within the course of a week—in an environment the other media scarcely touch. Radio draws its largest audiences of the day during commuting hours; and on longer trips, it offers both companionship and an intriguing sampler of regional culture. Radio is used to instruct and advise drivers at Los Angeles International Airport, inside the Baltimore Harbor Tunnel, and at Great Adventure in New Jersey and Disney World in Florida. Signs advise entering motorists where to tune their radios for these special broadcasts.

office radio: Many firms pipe radio through their factories or offices to provide low-key background, an "environmental wall-paper," that is considered good for morale. Many workers will tune in desk radios to check the weather before making lunch-hour plans or going home.

outdoor radio: Its great mobility allows radio to go anywhere, from deep forests to mountaintops, from the beach to the street corner. This has proved both a blessing and a curse. Many municipalities have banned radio playing on public transportation, and debates are frequent on whether to ban it from beaches. One person's much-needed electronic companion in the woods is another's unwanted reminder of a civilization left behind.

ballgame radio: Fans often bring radios to ballgames to follow another game in progress. (The annals of sportswriting are rife with anecdotes of crowds bursting into cheers at seemingly inappropriate times, because many in the stands are listening to another game.)

More peculiarly, many fans bring radios to games in order to listen to the play-by-play broadcast of the game they are at! These fans seem to have grown so dependent on a media interpretation that they cannot get by without it. At the Forum in Los Angeles, before each basketball game, the announcer intones on the public-address system, "For those fans following the game on radio, we ask them to respect those sitting around them and to keep their radios at moderate volume."

TV radio: Remarkably, more than one million people in the last few years have bought radios that pick up television sound. They are used mainly by housewives, who listen to their favorite soap operas as they do the chores. The sets also are popular with sports fans, who are able to take advantage of all the televised sports that radio doesn't carry. TV-band radios come in automobile and portable models.

In the last three decades, as radio listening habits changed, surveys were commissioned—most often to help identify listeners for stations and their advertisers—that sought to find out not just where people listened to radio, but why. A major study was conducted in 1962 by Harold Mendelsohn for the Psychological Corporation, on behalf of

WMCA, New York. He found that listeners liked the wide variety of radio stations because they could find programs that either corresponded to their moods, or that could help change their moods. "Generally speaking," he wrote, "radio functions as diverting 'companion,' and it helps to fill voids that are created by, one, routine and boring tasks and, two, by feelings of isolation and loneliness."

This element of radio-as-companion has at least three dimensions. Mendelsohn described radio as a "human surrogate" to those workers—such as truck drivers and toll collectors—cut off from social contact during working hours.

It can also serve to connect individuals who are alone, by making them feel as though they are part of a group. Mendelsohn termed this element of radio a "social lubricant," and found it among adults and teenagers. "Radio news and information shows," he wrote, "allow the listener to participate vicariously in the great events of the day... radio allows him to share with others a wide variety of events of common interest and concern. The listener uses radio to bind him closer to other listeners like himself merely by virtue of having been a witness to the same happenings." Anticipating what Marshall McLuhan called "the tribal drum"—a resonant signal reverberating through the environment and tying a tribe together—Mendelsohn observed, "To the teenager who is often particularly in need of approved social cues, radio's role in providing him with such cues is significant...." Consider teenagers alone in their rooms, doing homework, while their families watch television in their living rooms. Listening to a favorite show, on some level he or she is aware that all over the listening area, other teens are in similar circumstances. Each alone, they are brought together by radio. And when they go out, they take their transistor sets to provide a blanket of sound that keeps them apart from the world they walk through—hooked into their peer group. The only change in this phenomenon in the last 20 years is that the tiny transistors, once valued for their compactness, have given way to massive "personal entertainment centers" that have extraordinary fidelity of sound, as all-too-many passersby will attest. These contemporary models, unlike the tiny transistor radios that could be held up to a listener's ear, now must be looped in the crook of the arm, or worn on a shoulder strap. Quality of sound has come to be treasured more than compactness but the motive is the same: to be with your tribe whatever the surrounding crowd.

Finally, to the deeply troubled, radio-as-companion can be a source of help. Most radio stations keep a list of counseling services near the studio telephone, for listeners who might need referrals, whether their problems are emotional or drug-related.

One late-night disc jockey had this story to tell of a harrowing phone call received while on the air:

"A hysterical young girl called me on the phone early one morning and claimed that her boyfriend, in Paramus, New Jersey, was about to commit suicide. Since he was a devoted listener to our station, she thought there might be something I could do.

"I told her to calm down, and walked hesitantly back to the studio. When the mike came on, I ignored the scheduled commercial, and talked about all-night radio as an antidote for loneliness, despair or even suicide. I ended with the line, 'So whether you're in Hartford, Connecticut, Brooklyn, or Paramus, New Jersey, don't cop out. We can't afford to lose you. Get involved. It's up to you to build a brighter tomorrow. Or at least to try!' Then I played a record.

"When I returned to the record library, every phone line in the place was lit up. Each call was just about the same: 'Hey, man, how did you know?' "

Perhaps the most bizarre incident of this sort in recent years occurred on October 6, 1975, when a young man walked into a bank in downtown Manhattan and took ten hostages. He carried a pistol—and a radio! As news leaked out and police mapped plans, an enterprising reporter, Mike Eisgrau of WNEW, telephoned the bank. The young man, Ray "Cat" Olsen, answered the phone himself and recognizing the station's call letters asked that the disc jockey then on WNEW-FM, Scott Muni, play records by Bob Dylan and the Grateful Dead. Muni complied, as Olsen was able to verify on his radio. He called up to talk to Muni, and large portions of their lengthy dialogue were broadcast live. The siege lasted more than eight hours, during which time WNEW-FM continued to play Olsen's requests. Some time after hearing a tape of himself on the radio proclaiming the Grateful Dead the greatest band in the world, Olsen dozed off. Police moved in and seized him. No injuries were reported.

Dr. Morton Bard, a psychology professor at the City University of New York, commented about the Olsen incident, "Radio has a great value to us in cutting through the sense of aloneness. It's like touching someone without actually having that other person there.... The information that comes through the radio, whether it be music or words, distracts one from being with oneself, from experiencing what many of us have begun to feel as the pain of aloneness, and I think that's why radio is so important. The person on the radio is a person with whom one can be close without having to tolerate all of the disadvantages of closeness. And then you can have your fantasy, you see, without having to experience whatever pain there is in being close to someone else."

Muni later reflected: "It's strange. In this business people hear my voice; it comes into their rooms, they grow up with it. I was a friendly voice, someone Olsen could talk to."

Olsen, of course, was by no means the ordinary radio consumer. But one communication theorist, Ed Wakin of Fordham University, asserted, "You had a member of the audience experiencing the extreme version of the normal experience—which is a very intimate contact with the radio. And he didn't want to leave it behind. The symbolic act that Cat Olsen performed was that he came into the bank with a gun in one hand and a radio in the other, and, as it turned out, happily, he used the radio instead of the gun."

A 1968 survey for the National Association of Broadcasters found that a significant number of listeners valued radio for its companionship function. Fifty-five percent of those questioned said they turned on the radio as a release from boredom; fifty-nine percent said they used radio to keep from getting lonely. These figures were not as high as the categories of "news and information," where more than 85 percent said they used radio to keep abreast, or the 88 percent who said they relied on radio for "pleasure and relaxation."

Radio—and the ingenious people who work in the medium—have produced in recent years a variety of services that don't show up on surveys and are less easily classified. Among the most unusual:

—An on-the-air dating service in Baltimore, in which the evening deejay took calls, in between records, from people who said they were having a hard time meeting people and wanted help.

—A disc jockey in San Diego who provided answers to high school students' homework problems along with rock 'n' roll music. Dozens of students from more than 20 local high schools donated their answers for use on the air.

—An "adult book hour," sponsored by the Radio Information Center for the Blind in Philadelphia, provided readings of explicit books not easily accessible to the blind, such as *Fear of Flying* and *The Joy of Sex*.

—A New York announcer who drank himself into a stupor one July 4th, on the air, to demonstrate to holiday drivers the effects of drinking. As he consumed a fifth of scotch during his show, his speech grew slurred; colleagues said he was seriously hung over the next day.

—"Religious" broadcasts on WOOK, Washington, D.C., that proved to be tips on numbers to bet in lottery rackets. A typical sermon: "The first three figures is 547... My God, my God. And take the mysterious two that was blessed through last week, if you place it on the five you'll see it's still working for you, and the 74th and the seventh verse was a blessing to Washington, D.C." The station lost its license in 1975.

All these uses of radio—from the far-reaching and dramatic to the silly—have been formalized by media theorists into "functions of the mass media," which apply not just to radio but to all mass media. These functions include entertainment, information (sometimes called surveillance of the environment), transmission of social heritage (sometimes called enforcement of norms), and serving the economic system by creating a demand for goods.

Children become radio users at an early age—although not as early as they turn to television—and from it learn group values and language, picking up a broad vocabulary. As they grow into preadolescents, programming is designed to attract them, and radio listening helps confirm a group identity. It may be based on "hipness" (radio acceptance of *hype, hassle,* and *rip-off* helped make them, for better or worse, common English). It may be based on ethnic pride. Or it may be based on civic responsibility or sophistication. Sometimes the enforcement of norms is explicit, like "be sure to vote," "drive carefully" or "don't miss this sale!" Other times it is subtle; the patter of deejays or the latest commercials can condition a listener by reflecting changing attitudes about what behavior is acceptable. Radio, like other media, begins to let children know that it's OK for women to ask men for a date or for girls to want to be doctors.

Radio's role in the economic system is just as powerful. Unlike television, which thrives on mass audiences and lowest-common-denominator programming, radio segments the market into identifiable groups. It provides programming for ethnic groups, for teenagers, for housewives, and for commuters. Advertisers have found these "target audiences" a cost-efficient way to reach potential buyers. Radio advertising, at lower rates than television, also has proved an excellent complementary reinforcement to television advertising campaigns. And according to the Radio Advertising Bureau, avid radio listeners are more receptive to new products than avid television viewers or avid newspaper readers. Western Union officials, for example, credited radio with the public's acceptance of the Mailgram.

Nothing better illustrates how radio fulfills most of these mass-media functions than its performance in a crisis. For instance, during the record cold winter of 1976, WOWO, Fort Wayne, Indiana, suspended regular programming for two days to serve as "weather central" for its 51-county listening area. It broadcast 1,100 weather bulletins and information on closings of 1,800 schools.

On an afternoon in April 1966, when tornado warnings were issued for the vicinity of Kansas City, Missouri, four reporters were dispatched from WDAF in radio-equipped cars to cover the story. As the storm neared the city, WDAF, a middle-of-the-road (MOR) music station, suspended all regular programming. A staff announcer reviewed take-cover procedures frequently for listeners, while the news staff—broadcasting live—conducted interviews and reported damage. For two hours and seven minutes WDAF stayed with its tornado alert, until the storm had passed; during that time no commercials were broadcast. Dozens of other stations have provided similar aid, comfort, and information to listeners during hurricanes, floods, winter storms, and the nuclear accident at Three Mile Island in Pennsylvania. But for sheer impact—and the enormous number of people affected—nothing better defines how radio can serve its listeners than the great blackout of 1965, which thrust much of the Northeast United States into darkness for nearly a dozen hours.

"The lights flickered out," said a man trapped in an elevator in Manhattan for several hours. "We tried ringing the alarm, all three of us took turns, but no one came, and we had no idea what was happening. We heard nothing." They had no radio.

Among the many radio stations that were knocked off the air, a fair number were able to switch to emergency transmitters and return within a few minutes. They abandoned all advertising and regular programming. Listeners searched in the darkness for their transistor radios, then rushed out to buy both candles and batteries, settling down to hear what was going on.

"This is a temporary situation," said one radio anchorman to his listeners. "Don't be alarmed. Please don't call us—and don't call the police, don't call the hospitals. Keep the phone lines free. They aren't meant for mass emergencies and can overload as well. Listen to the radio; go to sleep, relax...."

Another announcer reported, "We can't reiterate this too often: traffic is at a standstill, where it's moving it's barely moving, bumper to bumper, the expressways, the streets are clogged, so stay off the roads, stay in your house, keep close to your transistor radio...and a brighter day will dawn."

Millions of Americans heeded the advice. Apartment dwellers had spontaneous cocktail parties around transistor radios. Posh hotels turned them on in their lobbies so that guests and walk-ins off the street might keep informed.

Any streetcorner with a radio became a focal point of neighborhood activity.

In Albany, New York, college students crossed the city block by block, carrying radios, calming residents with information. Throughout the affected areas stations broadcast pleas for off-duty police officers and fire fighters to report to work. Experts phoned in advice on how listeners should protect their appliances against power surges when electricity was restored; their advice was put on the air. Listeners were warned about food spoilage. Suburbanites were given available traffic information to let them know where family members might be stalled on the way home.

In the blackout hours, radio pulled people together. Dan Daniel, a veteran New York City announcer, was working at WMCA, the first station back on the air with a backup transmitter.

> We went into a jingle, [Daniel recalled] and all of a sudden stopped dead...all the lights went out. We groped our way through the dark and the engineer set up a makeshift microphone and turntable, and he put me in this little engineer's maintenance shack, and all of a sudden we started to touch people's lives....
>
> After all, it hadn't been that long since the missiles of October [the Cuban missile crisis of October 1962]. It hadn't been that long since the [President] Kennedy assassination. And once we realized the magnitude of this thing, being primarily concerned with the 18 million people in the metropolitan area, I wanted to be a calm voice in the storm.
>
> I received over 18,000 pieces of mail, over half of which were from people who had never heard me before. There will never ever be another moment like that for me on radio.

The stations had plenty of airtime to fill, and their largest captive audience ever. Reporters were given ample opportunity to provide colorful detail and some made the most of it. Witness the report of Stewart Klein on WNEW, as a police siren yowled faintly in the background:

> It's an eerie sight here in Times Square. The Great White Way is dark. The only lights are the headlamps of the cars, and it's hard to recognize this now-darkened corner. The flashing news sign on the Times Building—it's still tonight. That Accutron sign that ticks off in flashing bulbs the minutes and the seconds and the tenths of seconds—well, time stands still tonight. The Chevrolet sign that you've seen in every

picture postcard view of Times Square—right now it's just a shell of black neon tubing.

There's a corny old song about a broken heart for every light on Broadway—well, tonight there are no lights on Broadway.

What made radio's performance all the more striking was the absence of alternative sources of information: The other media were out of service. Television sets were chained to the power system by their electric cords. (Network broadcasts originating in New York City were interrupted by the blackouts, then were resumed from elsewhere in the country; but of course they could not be received in the affected areas until power was restored.) Newspapers couldn't print, and even papers like *The New York Times* that rushed to out-of-town printers to produce blackout editions didn't reach their anxious readers until hours later. The teletype machines of the Associated Press and United Press International were silenced. Ironically, the other media had to rely on radio to find out what was happening and where to deploy their staffs.

George P. Hunt, managing editor of *Life* magazine at the time, told readers in the November 19, 1965, edition, "A few minutes after [the blackout] the report came in by transistor radio that the blackout embraced most of the Northeast, and the implications of our predicament dawned on us. Here was an astonishing news story unfolding around us, and here we were, the New York editorial staff, trapped in a skyscraper with no lights, jammed phones, and stalled elevators."

Just as crowds had gathered outside Wanamaker's department store when the wireless began delivering first details of the *Titanic's* sinking in 1912, so did thousands and thousands of people in the dark gather round the radio. It was soapbox and public address system, companion, and servant to millions of people. In 1938 Orson Welles' "War of the Worlds" broadcast proved that radio had the power over people—presumably rational, sensible people—to create panic. Nearly 30 years later, radio proved beyond any shadow of a doubt that it could soothe the troubled breast of a public faced with an emergency the scope of which it could barely perceive.

Quite simply, it was radio's grandest hour since the advent of television.

Yet for all its penetration into and interaction with American lives, for all its effectiveness as a news and entertainment medium, contemporary radio seems to have earned too little respect in communications circles. How else to explain the short shrift it gets, once television comes along, in even the best histories of broadcasting? Or how little space it is accorded in many textbooks? Radio fares no better in the competing media. Newspapers hardly report what's on radio beyond skeletal listings and perhaps a semiannual feature story. Popular magazines only occasionally carry an article about radio. (Trade magazines such as *Broadcasting* and *Television/Radio Age* report on it regularly, but they are generally read only by people in the broadcasting industry.) You could watch television 100 hours a week and never hear or see a word about radio, with two exceptions: Some local stations buy time on television to advertise, and CBS in 1978 added a situation comedy about radio, "WKRP in Cincinnati." (In early 1980 the show was one of the top-rated in the country.) Radio has fared slightly better in films and a good deal better—not surprisingly—in popular music. But news of contemporary radio rarely appears in other media.

Three philosophers have analyzed this void. Their work is highly controversial. Some regard it as brilliant and others as self-indulgent pap. Their names are Marshall McLuhan, Edmund Carpenter, and Tony Schwartz. About one thing they all agree, that radio is not studied or appreciated enough.

"The power of radio to retribalize mankind, its almost instant reversal of individualism into collectivism...has gone unnoticed," McLuhan writes in *Understanding Media*. "The transforming power of the media is easy to explain, but the ignoring of this power is not at all easy to explain." He ascribes this ignoring of radio to "some essential numbing of consciousness such as occurs under stress and shock conditions."

Where McLuhan's theorizing is abstract, Carpenter is a bit more specific. McLuhan was one of the first to call attention to the impact of media regardless of their content; Carpenter was one of the first to seek to measure that impact in primitive cultures. He concluded, in *Oh, What a Blow That Phantom Gave Me!*, based on studies in North Africa and New Guinea, that radio was potentially dangerous, as it broke down tribal consciousness and then retribalized populations, "building nationalism to a fevered pitch and creating unreasonable national goals and consumer hopes." He complained, "Those who control the content of radio take such arguments lightly. To them, what matters is what radio *says*. To me, what matters is what radio *does*. They regard radio as a neutral instrument and place full responsibility for its use on people. I see nothing 'neutral' about my technology."

Both McLuhan and Carpenter agree that if the "proof" of radio's impact is clear in primitive cultures then it has a similar if muted effect on sophisticated cultures. Carpenter wrote, "In New Guinea, when villagers ignore their leader, the government may tape record his orders. The next day the assembled community hears his voice coming to them from a radio he holds in his own hand. Then they obey him." An echo of this occurred in 1978 in Passaic, New Jersey. Dozens of music lovers had lined up outside the Capitol Theater, hoping to buy tickets to a Bruce Springsteen concert about which they had heard rumors. Some of them carried radios. The concert had not, in fact, been scheduled, and no tickets were on sale. The crowd refused to leave. The theater operator called a radio station known for its concert bulletins and asked that the same information that he had been telling the fans in person be broadcast. As soon as the radio carried news that no concert had been set the crowd began to disperse.

Incidents like this draw little attention. McLuhan and Carpenter ascribe the neglect to radio's "magical" properties.

"Radio is provided with its cloak of invisibility," McLuhan wrote. "It is really a subliminal echo chamber of magical power to touch remote and forgotten chords." Carpenter agreed, "By concentrating on content and ignoring effect, adminstrators remain oblivious to one of radio's principle achievements: it promotes magical systems...."

What separates the work of Tony Schwartz from that of McLuhan and Carpenter is that he practices what he preaches. If, as McLuhan and Carpenter suggest, radio is a "magical" medium, then Schwartz is a magician. Schwartz accepts the "retribalized global village" of McLuhan and Carpenter, but what chiefly concerns him is the question: How do people determine what they hear? "People don't have earlids," he says. Schwartz's theory, which he spelled out in *The Responsive Chord,* published in 1973, is that rather than receiving messages from the medium, people receive a signal that causes to reverberate within them some information they already have. "The content of radio is us," he said in 1979. "The content of radio is the interaction between the stimuli on the air and the stored material in our brain." Schwartz contends that radio is so widely misunderstood because people try to analyze it as though it delivered a message—the movement of information across space.

"People don't remember radio as a source of information because they do not consciously listen to it," he said. "Rather, they bathe in it and sit in it. Just as we are not conscious of breathing, we are not actively aware of radio-mediated sound in our environment. Yet we are deeply involved with radio, and we are strongly affected by radio programming that allows us to participate. . . .

"When you ask some people if they listen to radio, they say, 'No.' Then you ask them if they drive to work and they say, 'Yes.' Then you ask them if they drive to work with the radio on and they say, 'Yes.' They don't listen to it, they sit in it."

The proof of Schwartz's theory may indeed be the effectiveness of his work. He has created more than 5,000 media campaigns for clients; he advised Gerald Rafshoon, who directed Jimmy Carter's media campaign for the presidency in 1976. While Schwartz works in both television and radio, he calls the latter "an ideal medium for affecting attitudes through evoked recall communication."

One of Schwartz's favorite radio techniques—and an illustration of "the responsive chord" at work—is what he calls "mnemonic speech." He designs radio spots to use rhythmic patterns that suggest more than is actually heard and help trigger the listener's recall. "In a commercial for the movie *Woodstock* I designed the names of rock groups in the film into mnemonic speech. For many adults the names were imperceptible, because the full names were not sufficiently isolated for them to hear and *learn*. For teenagers or those who knew the rock groups' names, the design was both pleasant to the ear and clearly perceptible.... Another commercial, for a bank, produced exactly the opposite result. Here, a list of bank services was compressed even more than the rock groups' names.... Adults had no difficulty perceiving all the services mentioned, but teenagers, who have less familiarity with banking, could perceive only some of the items mentioned."

If Schwartz is right—and we think he is—then Carpenter may indeed be right: radio can be a dangerous instrument in irresponsible hands. Schwartz acknowledged this when he met with members of the Senate Communications Subcommittee and the Federal Trade Commission in 1977. He told them, "I can avoid any ruling [about advertising]...it's hard to make regulations about quicksilver." He also told them that the question of truth-in-advertising was not so important in broadcast advertising, because even if claims were regulated, what was more significant was their impact—which could not be regulated. The officials left Schwartz's studio scratching their heads.

So there stands radio today. Its receivers nearly double the population. It lives in nearly every room of every home and in nearly every car. Its breadth of coverage and depth of penetration is unmatched by any other medium. It can send out signals that trigger responses in our brain. Yet 30 years ago no one would have guessed how powerful a media force it would become; in fact, many did not think radio would survive.

1

THE GOLDEN AGE
ENDS

A typical weekday evening in 1947: The family is gathered in the living room, Dad in the rocker, Mother in the armchair, the kids sprawled on the floor in front of the radio. It's 7:00 PM, time for CBS Radio's "Mystery of the Week." At 7:30, the dial is turned to ABC, and the familiar background music of "The Green Hornet" fills the room. At 8:00, on NBC, a new star, Milton Berle, hosts a variety show. At 8:30, the family has to choose among "The Falcon," "A Date with Judy," or "America's Town Meeting."

1

S O it went across America. Radio dominated the evening in nearly every home. The most popular entertainment in the world was a twist of the dial away—and free. It was the Golden Age of Radio.

But that age was ending. Although 1946 and 1947 were profitable years for radio, at the highest levels—the networks—plans were being made to use radio's profits to build the television industry. In June 1946, the NBC research department prepared a memo that predicted an $8 million loss from television in the next four years. It suggested that radio should be made to finance that loss and estimated that $3.5 million in federal taxes could be saved by applying radio profits to television development costs. In effect, the radio networks would be made to finance their own burial.

The following year, NBC chairman David Sarnoff urged radio network affiliates to get into television. Many of them heeded his advice and applied for construction permits from the Federal Communications Commission (FCC). So 1948 emerged as a year of transition. The number of cities with television stations grew from eight to 23, and the number of stations on the air from 17 to 41. Production and sales of television sets also grew, but the FCC applied the brakes. On September 29, 1948, it ordered a freeze of all pending television licenses while it studied the likely impact of the new medium. The freeze was extended because of the Korean War, and lasted until June 1, 1952. Nonetheless, large-scale television programming began in 1948. The national political conventions were televised, and variety shows like "Toast of the Town" (hosted by Ed Sullivan) and "Texaco Star Theater" (with Milton Berle) debuted. Initially, radio held its own, despite the excitement over television.

Because of the freeze, many cities had no television. While New York and Los Angeles had seven stations each, cities as large as Houston, Pittsburgh, St. Louis, Milwaukee, and Kansas City had only one station. This shortage of television outlets kept national advertisers dependent on radio. Network radio advertising declined, but not drastically.

1948 :	$134 million
1949 :	$129 million
1950 :	$125 million
1951 :	$114 million
1952 :	$103 million

The erosion in national advertising was to some extent offset by a growth in regional and local advertising, so that overall industry revenues rose between 1948 ($417 million) and 1952 ($473 million). The handwriting was on the wall, nonetheless, for any radio network executive who looked at television's figures. The infant industry had network advertising worth $2.5 million in 1948. By 1953 it had leaped to $172 million! And with good reason: advertising agencies were learning that television worked. (Erik Barnouw, the broadcast historian, cited the Hazel Bishop cosmetics firm as an early example of television's power. It was doing a $50,000 annual business, he said, when it bought its first television commercials in 1950. By 1952, its income was $4.5 million.)

The trends did not permeate the radio networks' programming departments, however. On the one hand, no funds were allocated from above to develop new programs. On the other hand, too many radio executives could not believe the Golden Age was over. So radio tried to meet the challenge of television with programming that was remarkably similar to that of the mid-1930s. A dozen network shows had been on the air for more than 20 years, and 108 had been on for more than ten. Programmers thought the continuity was a virtue. Many of them had been in radio since its inception, and they had seen the Great Depression and World War II come and go, each leaving radio stronger. Why, then, should they fear television? They thought they had the strongest mass medium in America—and in 1947 they were right. They failed, however, to understand either the potential of television or the excitement it aroused.

Radio had gained strength during the Depression because many people already had home sets, and listening to the radio cost them little, indeed less then buying the newpaper each day. Radio grew during the war because it could provide bulletins and dramatic reports more quickly than newspapers, which were also handicapped by a shortage of newsprint. With the end of the war, radio's promise seemed enormous. In 1946 alone, 500 new stations went on the air, and in 1947, 400 more. Only insiders who had followed television's early history knew what was about to happen.

The popular perception of television is that it was spawned after World War II, a full 25 years after the invention of radio. In fact, they were born in the same era. As early as 1879, a drawing in *Punch* showed a couple sitting at home, watching a tennis match on a screen above their fireplace. In 1884, the German physicist Paul Nipkow devised a rotating disk with perforations that was a breakthrough in broadcasting pictures. By 1927, a periodical, *Television,* was being published and Commerce Secretary Herbert Hoover (elected president the following year) appeared on an experimental telecast in New York City. The broadcast industry thought that commercial television was just a few years away.

Those few years proved fateful. The crash of the stock market in 1929 and the subsequent Depression dried up funds needed for development and refinement of television sets. And unlike in the 1920s, no hordes of eager consumers, cash in hand, were lined up to purchase the units. Experimentation continued on a modest level; in 1939 Allen Dumont had a home television receiver ready for marketing, and RCA demonstrated television publicly at the New York World's Fair. But the Federal Communications Commission had not decided which television system should be standard and delayed commercial broadcasting. With the outbreak of World War II, licensing, production, and experimentation came to a halt. Thus radio enjoyed two decades of prosperity with television lurking just behind a closed door.

When the war ended, the large broadcast corporations were ready to develop and market television. A strong economic outlook, a widespread demand for consumer goods, and the return from the armed forces of scientists and trained electronics personnel assured television's success. The radio picture was less clear. Throughout its glory years, the industry leaders had been the networks. Now those networks were committed to promoting television at the expense of their own radio operations. They saw that the public, especially the middle class, which could afford sets, was showing an enormous enthusiasm for television. When Milton Berle, one of television's first stars, began his Tuesday 8:00 PM show on NBC, New York City theater and restaurant owners noticed a dip in business. (Twenty-five years earlier, the new medium, *radio,* had produced a similar phenomenon with its most popular shows.) The public went TV-happy and so did many sponsors.

Network radio began to take a beating, and three headlines from *Business Week* summarize the sad story: "Radio Rates Start to Crack" (April 28, 1951); "TV Is Hot on Radio's Heels" (May 24, 1952); and "Network Revenue: Down, Down, Down" (July 17, 1954). Morale plummeted and many employees feared the future. With diminished revenue, the networks were not able to bid effectively against television for talent. The dual impact resulted in a stampede of radio personnel into television.

Much has been written about how the major stars of radio drama, comedy, and musical entertainment jumped to television. The effect behind the scenes was just as dramatic. "Radio stations had a terrible time keeping personnel," recalled Jack Thayer, a former president of NBC Radio, in 1979. "Everybody wanted to get into television. They would leave and go do anything—sales people, sales managers, program people. They would go to school to learn about television. They were trying to find out what the different ways were to do things, how to run a camera, anything. . .everything. It was like vaudeville when films began. Management left, technicians left. It was like rats deserting a sinking ship."

The defections, and their impact on morale, made it even more difficult for network radio to wage the good fight. Front-line officers were not attuned to how conditions had changed, or were inexperienced. Some were bitter and wouldn't have anything to do with people who expressed the slightest interest in television. The networks flailed about. They tried cutting rates to lure the advertisers back. But the rate reduction cut their potential revenue and led to warfare with affiliate stations.

The affiliates were fighting battles on several fronts: They had to contend not only with television but the enormous proliferation of independent stations that had been licensed after the war. (As the war ended, fewer than 1,000 AM stations were on the air. By 1953 there were 2,391.) This meant many more stations were dividing the audience and the advertising pie. For example, in 1947 total radio advertising was $374 million; in 1953 it was $464 million. But divided by the number of stations on the air, the average station revenue dropped from $246,000 (in 1947) to $194,000 (in 1953). When CBS cut its nighttime radio rates as much as 50 percent in 1952, affiliate stations felt betrayed. They saw their revenue dropping even more.

By the end of the freeze on licenses in 1952, television had won the battle for the lucrative evening audience. Radio's prime-time ratings had fallen close to daytime levels, about one-third what they had been before television. The number of television stations on the air tripled. With the advertisers behind it and the viewers in front, television became the most important entertainment medium in the country.

The radio networks, through trial-and-error, tried to cope by cutting corners. They simulcast the audio portions of some television shows (usually by former radio stars, like Jack Benny), or they taped the audio and broadcast it at different times. Comedians who no longer commanded massive radio audiences were asked to work without live orchestras and staffs of writers. Some comedians became the hosts of radio quiz shows: Groucho Marx on "You Bet Your Life," Eddie Cantor on "Take It or Leave It," and Herb Shriner on "Two for the Money." Increasingly, where once they had used live performers, radio turned to records, and to disc jockeys who introduced the recorded songs. Some were big names: Frank Sinatra and Paul Whiteman in 1951, and later Tennessee Ernie Ford and Amos 'n' Andy.

By 1954 many of the top-name shows from the Golden Age had been switched to television. The affiliate stations began to give up the fight. Why beat their heads against the networks, they reasoned, when they could draw more local advertising while playing records suited to their local audiences, following the lead of the independent stations. The defections began. As they lost affiliates, the networks became weaker still. What the networks could have done—if anything—is not clear. Perhaps their diminished stature in the face of television was inevitable. Certainly more vigorous leadership and the search for more imaginative programming would have helped morale and buttressed radio's image. The climate and the radio networks' ownership by the same corporations that owned the television networks made that hard. But the prophets who thought that the fascination of watching pictures at home would kill radio entirely proved shortsighted indeed.

The four-year freeze on television licenses provided a transitional period: TV laid grand plans and radio, consciously and unconsciously, learned to cope. Eventually, as television blossomed economically, pioneers of a new radio were blazing trails. Television did indeed lower the boom on network radio. It replaced radio in the living room as the conduit of evening entertainment. With the end of radio's prime-time dominance came a staggering loss of prestige and morale to those in the industry.

Even as the *enfant terrible* muscled into the spotlight, the seeds of the new radio had been planted. Socially, culturally, and technologically the remedies for its ailments were at hand. It was simply a matter of time. Many of those who had labored through the Golden Age and reaped its rewards felt they did not have that time, and they jumped ship for television, went into other lines of work, or retired. And a new generation came forth and flourished.

ADAPTING FOR
SURVIVAL

In the late 40s there was a feeling that radio towers would be scrap steel within five years. But Todd Storz and Gordon McLendon came up with new approaches, and went into format radio, which is taken for granted today, and it gave them a device for targeting in on audiences and proving the viability of radio.

—**Sam Cooke Digges**
President, CBS Radio

RADIO jokes abounded in the early 1950s: one cartoon showed a young boy dusting off a radio in the attic and asking his dad, "What's that?" Americans had seen icemen put out of work, ice chests discarded for refrigerators, and silent pictures give way to talkies. It was against memories like these—recent memories—that many people gauged radio's chances against television. Radio was rapidly becoming something else, but what that was, no one could say. It is no wonder that so many people, in discussing radio's imminent death, confused the networks with the industry as a whole. The networks were certainly crippled, but independent radio thrived; the little talking box was a long way from being ready for the attic. At first, the young pioneers of radio's second coming did not attract as much publicity as the network moguls. Many of the most innovative labored in the Midwest, far from the media capitals. Because they often worked by trial-and-error, they could not always articulate their plans and strategies. But they were succeeding.

Even in the winter of radio's greatest discontent, 1954, when total advertising revenues dipped for the first time since 1938, industry revenues still grossed more than $450 million. Television had given radio a chill and a bad case of the shakes—but there never was any stoppage of vital signs. Station owners, investors, manufacturers, and all their employees had a vested interest in finding a new way to make radio work. What these people had to do was to determine how to change, and then explain to their audiences how they were changing.

There were several crucial components to local radio's success. One was the widespread reliance on records, and on the disc jockey (or deejay), the announcer who played the records, read the advertisements, did promotion for the station, and sometimes read the news as well. (The term "disc jockey" first appeared in the July 23, 1941, issue of *Variety,* replacing an earlier term, "record jockey.") Disc jockeys had their antecedent in early announcers like Reginald Fessenden, the distinguished inventor and pioneer, who on Christmas Eve 1906 broadcast a reading of passages from Luke (astonishing and startling a great number of wireless operators accustomed to hearing only Morse code and static on their sets; some undoubtedly thought the Lord had come calling for them this Christmas). Frank Conrad, who produced informal broadcasts of news, weather, and recordings from his garage in Pittsburgh in 1920, was another hero. But the modern disc jockey did not emerge until the playing of records on radio became widespread, and that practice was frowned on for many years.

Because the custom in radio had been to broadcast live performances of music, the conventional wisdom in the industry was that it was demeaning for a station to play recordings. There were legal obstacles as well. It was common practice during the 1930s for record companies to stamp on their releases "not licensed for radio broadcast." They feared that airplay would cut into record sales and the concert fees of performers (a view that is the exact opposite of current theory, which holds that airplay is critical to promoting sales). And the FCC insisted that stations playing records remind their listeners constantly that they were not hearing live performances. Nonetheless, some announcers experimented with recordings.

An early pioneer was Al Jarvis, who thought he could use records to offer listeners a more diverse program, a panorama of stars, night after night. He went on the air at KFWB, Los Angeles, in 1932 with a program called "The World's Largest Make-Believe Ballroom." Although the show was locally successful, it did not attract any attention outside its listening area. Los Angeles at the time was not yet a major market in the eyes of network leaders and owners of major East Coast stations. But Jarvis's program came under close scrutiny by a KFWB newsman, Martin Block. Block moved to New York City and joined WNEW, an independent station, where he gained prominence by playing records in between news reports on the trial of Bruno Hauptmann, who was convicted in 1935 of kidnapping the Lindbergh child. Block eventually broadcast a show he called "Make Believe Ballroom" and earned his reputation as the first modern disc jockey.

In 1940 the age of the deejay won legal relief; the courts ruled that broadcasters, once they had purchased a record, could play it on the air as they liked. And the FCC eased its requirements for identifying recorded material to once every half-hour. Legal skirmishing persisted on another front, however, in negotiations with the American Society of Composers, Authors and Publishers (ASCAP) over royalties. Broadcasters were sufficiently dissatisfied with ASCAP to fund the development of a second licensing organization, Broadcast Music, Inc. (BMI), in 1939. The ASCAP-BMI disputes would have a significant impact on radio in the 1950s. (See Chapter 3.)

It is easy to appreciate the bonanza that disc jockeys proved to be for local stations. Deejay shows required no orchestras and no writers. Gone were actors and actresses, directors, and most of the support staff. One critic contemptuously labeled the deejays' product "gypsy radio" and noted: "It is ludicrously cheap. . . only a license, a transmitter, and a subscription to *Billboard* [for its charts of best-selling records] are essential." With deejays at the microphones, station managers developed a new strategy that became a major component of local radio. It originally was known as "formula radio," and later as "format radio." The most familiar type is Top 40—which means playing only songs drawn from the 40 best-selling records. But Top 40 is only one formula. The concept, as it emerged in the late 1940s and early 1950s, involved methodology rather than content. Stations no longer left things to chance, nor to the disc jockey's whims. They developed rules that would give each station a definable personality to its listeners. These rules might include: playing X number of songs an hour, identifying the station X number of times by its call letters, and specifying where to do the commercials. What formula radio postulated was that listeners appreciated consistency: no matter who the deejay or what the time of day, the station would be recognizable among its competitors. This was a radical bit of thinking.

The goal became to hold the audience. Broadcasters believed that listeners drawn to a station wouldn't turn the dial as long as the station's "sound" remained consistent. Thus radio's eclectic programming gave way to formulas.

The networks eventually began experimenting with stars as disc jockeys. Their reputations, personalities, and patter were supposed to draw an audience. But records and deejays worked better on local radio for several reasons. Stations could play songs that were regional hits, if they conscientiously surveyed shops to see what people were buying. They could offer deejays who were familiar with the community—and who worked, through live appearances, at meeting their listeners.

This local emphasis, of which the deejay was only one facet, became the single most important element in radio's success during the television era. By accepting that it would not be prime-time entertainment, radio was free to offer different things to different people. A network—radio or television—could bring the world into your home, but it couldn't tell you which roads had flooded on your way to work. Local radio could not only play regionally popular music, it could provide more local news than the networks, public service announcements (vaccination programs, church bazaars, school closings), hometown sports results, and, through advertisements, news about local merchants. It sounds so simple and obvious, it's hard to imagine that anyone ever thought that radio could die. But operators had to learn to provide this new material, and the public needed to learn that it would be there.

In 1954 the National Association of Radio and Television Broadcasters issued a report that noted, "Stations are participating more and more in community activities. They originate campaigns for new libraries and better highways. They make their microphones available to clubs, schools, church groups, business associations. The report of local news and doings has assumed major proportions and now makes up about 40 percent of all news broadcasts on the average station." New technology helped: with tape recorders and editing equipment, local stations were able to provide in-depth coverage that national networks had no time to duplicate.

On the heels of localization came specialization: seeking out and catering to special interest audiences. If television, like radio of the Golden Age, sought to provide its advertisers with the largest audience possible, radio was now able to fill the cracks and find the people not watching television or not served by television. Where only a few years before radio had offered a standardized, coast-to-coast sound, it now spoke in a variety of voices to specialized audiences. This breakthrough in radio programming had been suggested as early as 1947 by an FCC report, "An Economic Study of Standard Broadcasting." The FCC suggested that "a small segment of the listening audience carefully selected as a minority group, may, if it is loyally attached to the station, give it a unique fascination for advertisers."

Even before television flourished, independent stations, especially those competing with network affiliates, had begun to carve out specialized audiences because they couldn't compete with the networks' high-priced star system. One of the earliest studies of targeting a special audience was conducted by the NBC Radio Network in 1948. The project examined teenagers' listening habits in New York City, Philadelphia, Pittsburgh, and Chicago, and found that 64 percent of the adolescents had their own radios. NBC released the report, "Urban Teen-Agers as Radio Listeners and Customers" the following year, and noted that this audience had a buying power of $6 billion. The report found that "Your Hit Parade" was the favorite show among 18- and 19–year-olds, and that it also did well among younger teens. It is ironic that NBC could have commissioned this study, and then could ignore its findings while independent stations trampled its affiliates by going after the teen market.

The FCC report on specialized audiences had suggested cultivation of "minority groups" for *expansion*. With television's arrival, the motivation became *survival*. One of the first groups so cultivated was the black audience. Television, like the radio networks before it, provided no material specifically for blacks. "Amos 'n' Andy," a long-running and immensely popular radio show, had made a successful transition to television in 1951. For many years it was the only television show, however misinformed and prejudiced its stereotypes, about black family life. (In the early 1960s, the growing power of civil rights groups convinced broadcasters to take the show off the air.) Television not only failed to reach out to black audiences, but because blacks had a lower median income than whites and purchased fewer televisions in the early 1950s, they were a natural target for radio. Studies in city after city showed that a majority of the black population listened to the radio station that seemed most aware of black interests.

Some radio stations responded by designing shows for black audiences, with encouraging results. Albert Abarbanel and Alex Haley discussed the phenomenon of "Negro radio" in *Harper's* magazine in 1956 and suggested that it served several functions by:

—helping black businessmen, and whites serving black areas, to target their audiences.

—helping listeners discern through the ads where they were welcome to shop (particularly useful in segregated areas).

—providing highly visible, prestigious jobs within the community for blacks.

—providing community service announcements about black civic groups, church groups, and recreational facilities.

Most of the stations were white-owned. And they drew white audiences as well, particularly because the music, whether gospel, rhythm 'n' blues, or jazz, was more interesting than most music available on other radio stations. Negro radio, Abarbanel and Haley concluded, "seems to have satisfied almost everybody. It has brought American businessmen enormous, previously untapped profits. It has rejuvenated small radio stations and added new income to large ones. . . ."

"Negro radio" had other ramifications for the radio industry; if other special interest groups could be identified, they too could be serviced by radio. Programming spread that was directed at teenagers, farmers, ethnic groups, religious denominations. Most of these groups found little programming of special interest to them on television. Between localization and specialization, radio escaped direct competition with television and found it could profit without the evening audiences.

In *Understanding Media* Marshall McLuhan observed: "With TV accepting the central network burden derived from our centralized industrial organization, radio was free to diversify, and to begin a regional and local community service that it had not known, even in the earliest days of radio 'hams.' Since TV, radio has turned to the individual needs of people at different times of the day, a fact that goes with the multiplicity of receiving sets in bedrooms, bathrooms, kitchens, cars and now in people's pockets. Different programs are provided for those engaged in diverse activities."

It seems so obvious: People could be doing something else and still listen to radio. The status of the radio in the Golden Age—and its position in the living room—must be recalled to appreciate how innovative this concept was. Radio became liberated from the living room. It was free to penetrate other rooms of the house, seeking those not watching television. It moved to the kitchen, out to the patio, into the car, and its programming reflected that change. Radio offered service, entertainment, and companionship; it became an omnipresent medium.

Radio's penetration into American life was enhanced by new technology: the discovery of the transistor, the development of more sophisticated car radios, and the invention and marketing of the clock radio.

The vacuum tube had served the industry well from its refinement by Lee DeForest in 1907 through World War II, but it was relatively inefficient. Large and fragile, it had a high power consumption and limited life expectancy. As early as 1924, researchers sought an alternate method of power amplification. Not until after World War II did they find it. On December 23, 1947, Drs. John Bardeen, Walter H. Brattain, and William B. Shockley, working at Bell Laboratories in Murray Hill, New Jersey, found a key that unlocked radio's future. They called it the transistor, a contraction of *trans*fer res*istor*. Like the vacuum tube it could conduct, modulate, and amplify electrical signals. But it moved electrons through a solid, not a vacuum. The transistor had many advantages over the vacuum tube: it used less power and created less heat; it was durable and had a longer life; it was less expensive; and it was miniscule. The transistor made possible the miniaturization of electronic devices and became a major weapon in radio's struggle against television.

While military applications of the transistor were examined, news of the breakthrough was suppressed until June 30, 1948. It was refined for several years and then tested in consumer equipment. The first commercial transistor radio, the Regency, made by Texas Instruments and priced at $40, went on sale in 1953. At first it was marketed—and perceived by the public—as a novelty. "The world's smallest radio—small enough to fit in the palm of the hand—was demonstrated yesterday afternoon in Times Square," Jack Gould wrote in *The New York Times*. "The populace took the coming of the 'Dick Tracy Age' with disconcerting calmness." But consumers quickly grew excited about the transistor radio, and sales took off. Between 1953 and 1956 the number of portable radios sold annually doubled to 3.1 million. By 1965 more than 12 million transistor radios a year were being sold.

Dr. Bardeen recalled, in 1977, "We felt that the first commercial applications of the transistor would be to hearing aids and portable radios, because people would be willing to pay a premium for the small size and very low power consumption as compared with tubes....None of us in our wildest dreams thought that development would proceed at the pace it has over the years....I did not envisage the worldwide impact of portable radios which bring people in the remotest villages in contact with the outside would, whether they are literate or not." In what Bell Laboratories termed a tribute to Alexander Graham Bell (a teacher of the deaf as well as an inventor), hearing aid manufacturers were granted licenses for the transistor without charge. By 1952 the first transistorized hearing aids were commercially available. In 1956 Drs. Bardeen, Brattain, and

Shockley shared the Nobel Prize in physics for their work on the transistor.

Even before the Golden Age of radio dawned, David Sarnoff (the broadcast visionary who rose from office boy with the American Marconi company to direct the Radio Corporation of America) was predicting the widespread use of automobile radios and other unlikely devices. "It is reasonable to expect [radio's] eventual application to automobiles, and in some cases to individuals," he wrote in *The New York Herald* on May 14, 1922. A year later he expanded his prediction to include airplanes, railroads, steamships, and motorboats. His vision of car radio did not take long to prove accurate.

It was invented by William Lear, perhaps better known as the designer of the Learjet (a small private airplane) and the Lear car stereo systems. "In the fall of 1928 I placed the first car radio ever built on Paul Galvin's desk," Lear recalled in an interview in *Billboard*. Galvin was a battery manufacturer in Chicago. "It created some interest around the plant, but the general feeling was that radios in cars would never go over. The chief concern was that they would be legislated out of existence for driving safety reasons." Lear's fears were not as ridiculous as they seem today; Sarnoff's prophesies about car radios had generated heated debate about whether people could drive safely and listen to the radio at the same time!

Lear continued, "It was a year later—Black Friday, the day the bottom dropped out of the stock market—while Paul and I were en route to a radio manufacturers' convention in Atlantic City that we came up with a name for our auto radio. We decided to call it Motorola." The Galvin Manufacturing Company became Motorola, Inc.; Lear held a one-third interest. Despite the stock market crash, the car radio was soon available and selling well. Veteran New York broadcaster Frank A. Seitz vividly recalled the car radios of 1931: "They were monsters. Enormous. Reception was spotty and they didn't have the sensitivity of today's radios. They were subject to a lot of ignition interference and the antennas were slung under the running gear from the front of the car to the rear shock absorbers.

They were cumbersome and unreliable. Most of them operated from separate B batteries under the floorboards that had to be replaced quite often." After the war, new technology greatly improved car radios. By 1946, nine million automobiles had radios; by 1963, 50 million. In 1979, a total of 110 million American cars had radios—95 percent of all cars on the road. In the wake of television, the automobile gave radio its new prime time: the commuting hours of 6:00–9:00 AM and 4:00–7:00 PM. They came to be known as "drive time," a term coined in 1957 by Gerald Bartell, who owned a group of Midwest radio stations. These hours continue to provide radio's largest audience.

Radio penetrated another corner of American life when the clock radio was put on the market in 1946, first manufactured by General Electric. The clock radio was developed not in GE's broadcasting division but rather in its "telechron" section, where electric clocks were produced. One GE official described the invention as "the search for a better mousetrap. The clock people were expanding their product area and decided to attach a radio to this timing device." GE transferred the device to its radio division; the new product was a big hit with consumers. With some ingenuity, clock radio manufacturers soon developed additional options and extras. Among the innovations of the time: a battery-run, portable model; drowse bars and snooze alarms, which permitted a sleeper to reset automatically the alarm for 10 to 20 minutes after it first sounded; built-in night-lights, calendars, barometers, and outlets for other home appliances (It became possible to hook a coffeemaker into a clock radio.), and the "slumber switch," which allowed listeners to set their radios to turn off after they fell asleep. Despite the obvious technological capacity and despite their popularity over radios, television sets have never been marketed successfully with built-in clocks or shutoff devices. Television industry representatives have offered no explanation.

These were all major components of the new mobility of radio, and part of a large and pretty picture that was evolving. Rather than waiting for the audience to gather around the set, radio was tracking down its local listeners—and advertisers knew it. In 1947 local time sales passed network sales for the first time. From 1948 to 1953—the first five years of television's impact—as network sales fell from $134 million to $93 million, local sales climbed from $171 million to $250 million. And in 1953 the radio industry received an encouraging confirmation of its life expectancy in a massive study of radio released by the Arthur Politz research organization. Its results were exceedingly optimistic about radio, an unexpected view that generated some skepticism. The Politz study laid out on paper what the new radio could do and why:

—Forty-three million American homes (96 percent of the families in the United States) had radio, including 19 million homes that also had television.

—In addition to radios at home, 13 million Americans owned portable radios, and 26.5 million cars had radios (71 percent of all passenger cars).

—The study also found that 65 out of every 100 people said they listened to radio every day, and 88 out of 100 used a radio at least once a week.

The Politz report broke the day down into seven listening periods:

listened to radio	
Between waking and breakfast	29%
During breakfast	28%
Between breakfast and lunch	27%
During lunch	15%
Between lunch and supper	25%
During supper	17%
Between supper and bedtime	29%

The consistency of radio listening throughout the day was startling and its showing during the evening hours seemed to indicate that prime-time television, while dragging radio down from the glory of the Golden Age, had not rendered it obsolete. The Politz report concluded, "The fact that radio can and does serve and entertain almost everybody almost everywhere at any time without interfering with their other activities is an exclusive and distinguishing characteristic of the medium."

The growth of the suburbs—with more people driving to work, and more multi-car families—offered local radio a natural target for many of Politz's predictions, and confirmation of some of his findings. Suburban listeners and their impressive demographics were much sought. They found themselves the targets of advertising wars. As they moved in, local merchants would greet them, only to find stiff competition from the emerging shopping centers. Other media than radio attracted advertising, but between home and store these suburbanites traveled by car—and only radio could reach them there. The catchword of radio advertising salesmen became, "We can hit the consumer on the move."

Local stations, with a solid base of local advertising, began to attract both regional and national sponsors. The big national brands that had defected to television came back in search of these suburbanites on the move. Advertisers still made their television buys, but they knew it was radio that would find shoppers in the stores, in cars, on the beach, at the pool—anywhere except when they were in front of the television.

The novelty of television had obscured radio's ability as a sales medium. But once television was no longer new, advertisers could see past its glare, and they looked at radio in sharper focus. No doubt the rising cost of TV advertising helped clear their vision. Radio's lower rates permitted a shotgun approach of multiple buys in multiple markets, or on different stations in the same market, for the cost of a single television buy. And of course radio's specialization made it easier to target audiences. Few hemorrhoid ointment ads were broadcast on Top 40 stations; few ads for blue jeans were broadcast on classical music stations.

Another effective weapon in radio's advertising armory was humor. The comedian Stan Freberg broke new ground with offbeat, unpredictable commercials that worked best on radio because they were zany—too zany to be accompanied by pictures. A particularly memorable Freberg campaign for the Radio Advertising Bureau involved pretending to make the world's largest ice-cream sundae in Lake Michigan. (The Freberg tradition lives on in contemporary radio advertising, most notably in the work of Dick Orkin and Bert Berdis.)

Radio began to attract advertising attention as the most diversified and flexible of media. But that flexibility was on the local, not network, level—with one major exception.

In 1955, NBC introduced "Monitor," the only significant network experiment in radio between the onset of television and the late 1960s. It lasted nearly 20 years. NBC designed "Monitor" to try to rescue weekends, when audiences tuned in only for ball games. Weekend radio, the networks found, was hard to sell to advertisers. "Monitor" tried by offering a potpourri of interviews, comedy skits, remote pickups for on-the-scene reports, sports, and news, all planned around well-known anchormen (Ed McMahon, Gene Rayburn, Barry Nelson, Frank Blair). "Monitor" was initially on the air 40 hours each weekend, but was eventually cut back to 16 hours. It was hailed in the press on its tenth anniversary as a forerunner of talk radio, but "Monitor" never reached its 20th anniversary: It went off the air in January 1975. Its executive producer, Bob Wogan, blamed major-market stations—including the NBC-owned stations—for refusing to carry it. "They firmly believed that whatever you do Monday through Friday you have to do on Saturday and Sunday," he said. Much celebrated in its heyday, "Monitor" died a quiet death.

The mid-1950s was a fertile period for radio. The hopeful were confirmed in their optimism. But whatever the climate, however willing the advertisers, hardy pioneers were needed to till the fertile soil. Radio's recovery, we have seen, came amid massive turnover within the broadcasting industry. The exodus of personnel contributed to the misconception that all of radio was dying. But the turnover opened the door to a new generation of radio broadcasters, both in the front office and on the air.

They were eager, willing, and as one observer remarked, "They had nothing to unlearn."

These young, aggressive pioneers shaped modern radio. Many of its watchwords—Top 40, Beautiful Music, All-News—were invented by them. Most, in fact, were developed by one extraordinary man, Gordon McLendon. If modern radio has a father, it is indeed McLendon, who in 1979 sold his last station and turned his full attention to producing films, feeling—perhaps with some justification—that there was nothing left for him to do in radio.

Gordon McLendon was born June 8, 1921, in Paris, Texas, and raised, until the age of 13, across the Red River in Idabel, Oklahoma. Then his family moved to Cass County, in East Texas, where he starred on the high school debating team and edited a weekly paper. McLendon was a skilled linguist. He had learned Choctaw in Idabel, which was near an Indian reservation, and at Yale he majored in Oriental languages. He left college to join the Navy during World War II, and served in intelligence, translating Japanese documents, and interrogating prisoners. Returning home, he and his father Barton, who owned a multimillion-dollar chain of movie theaters in the Southwest, bought a 100-watt station, KNET, in Palestine, Texas. At the same time the family received a permit to build KLIF in Dallas, which went on the air in November 1947. The McLendons sold KNET, and Gordon actively managed KLIF and did much of the on-the-air work, assisted by a parrot that could shriek on demand, "KLIF! KLIF!"

His first innovation (after the parrot) was to bring daily major league baseball broadcasts to his listeners. It led to the first of many controversies McLendon was embroiled in. Texas had no major league baseball team at the time, but the Texas League was an affluent minor league operation. Team owners had a rule prohibiting major league broadcasts within 50 miles of a minor league game. McLendon defied them, but in a novel way. He didn't broadcast major league games from the ball park; he re-created them. McLendon sat in the KLIF studios, receiving running reports on the game by telegraph. In turn he would do a play-by-play, simulating crowd noises with recordings made at the various major league parks. He took pride in realism, and had a recording of the "Star Spangled Banner" as it was used at each ball park. For Boston games, he had crowd sounds with a Boston accent. His first sports re-creation was a football game in

November 1947; his first baseball game, a spring training exhibition between the New York Yankees and the St. Louis Cardinals the following March. McLendon's on-the-air persona was the "Old Scotchman," a comical, thickly accented announcer.

For some games, as McLendon did the play-by-play, he would have a staff member broadcast through an echo chamber announcements such as "Will the driver of New Jersey license number. . . " For other games Jim Kirksmith did the play-by-play while McLendon sat nearby, doing a running translation in Japanese, as though the game were being piped overseas—presumably for his own amusement rather than for any commercial reason. The games were extremely popular and McLendon formed the Liberty Broadcasting System to provide member station with the re-creations. Between 1948 and 1951, more than 400 stations signed up. "We originated the various things that the networks didn't do," McLendon said in 1979. "The major league game of the day, the first professional football ever heard on a regular basis, the only Friday night football games on a network basis —we bought all the Miami University games, the only Saturday night games—we bought the Louisiana State games. We had the college basketball game of the night." McLendon kept adding spin-offs, like his "Great Days in Sports" series, which offered re-creations of events from the past, including boxing and tennis matches (for the latter, he would have one employee click his tongue, to simulate the sound of the racket hitting the ball, while other aides stood around the microphone mumbling in English accents—for Wimbledon matches, naturally).

McLendon made his name in sports—in 1951, *The Sporting News* named him the top football broadcaster in the country—but he soon looked for other opportunities. "I thought that the only way that radio was going to stay around was through concentration on music and news and nothing else but," McLendon told *Billboard.* "Television was already usurping the major sports events." In 1952, major league baseball denied McLendon the rights to broadcast games, and the Liberty network folded.

In three aspects of local radio, McLendon immediately had an impact: local news, radio formats, and promotional gimmicks. McLendon was as imaginative in his news coverage as he was in his sportscasting. He outfitted radio cars to scour Dallas for news. He always looked for a local angle, a technique he outlined for the Georgia Assocation of Broadcasters in 1957:

> We localize a great many of our news stories. We have a list of 250 top citizens in each of our cities and we're expanding that list all the time. We subdivided the list into the top leaders in oil, banking, industry, society, business, education, etc. We use this list to get their names and voices on the air just as often as possible. For instance, when a story arrives concerning a development on the cotton market, we'll immediately call a top local cotton leader, record his comments, and localize the story around him.

Through innovations like these McLendon changed the sound of local news. Chuck Blore, a radio innovator himself and a former McLendon employee, said, "Gordon realized radio had the edge on television as far as news went. TV had those heavy cameras and couldn't move them around; they were shooting film. Gordon realized he was watching newsreels on TV, and did something about it." McLendon was not yet thinking all-news; that came later. But KLIF, with innovative news, local profiles and a variety of music, soon became a very popular station in Dallas, and McLendon started to expand. One of the tools of expansion was the Top 40 format.

There are almost as many versions of how Top 40 originated as there are broadcasters who worked in it. The confusion stems from the difference between the original Top 40, which simply meant that a station played the tunes from a chart of best-selling records, and the refined Top 40, in which the biggest hits were repeated over and over again—what the industry calls "rotation."

The list-of-hits concept had its roots in the famous "Hit Parade," at times known as "Your Hit Parade" and "Lucky Strike Hit Parade." The show started on radio in 1935 and closed on television in 1959. Each week it offered a countdown of the top ten (sometimes seven or eight) hits, interpreted by its cast, which at one time included Frank Sinatra.

In 1953, Bob Howard was a popular New Orleans disc jockey on WDSU, playing "The Top 20 at 1280." When radio magnate Todd Storz purchased WTIX, New Orleans, he and his station manager, George "Bud" Armstrong, decided to double the formula to "The Top 40 at 1450." But it was in *Omaha,* at KOWH, that Storz was credited with developing Top 40, in 1955.

Storz and his assistant at KOWH, Bill Stewart, were sitting and drinking in a bar across from the station. They had been there for hours and had noticed how often some songs were replayed on the jukebox. Near closing time, a waitress walked over to the jukebox, took change from her pocket, and played the same song three times in a row. Concluding from this that people liked familiarity, Storz and Stewart decided to reduce the number of songs played on the station and to repeat the biggest hits more often. Storz decided that one song each week should be designated a "pick hit"; it and the number one song were played once an hour. This was the genesis of sophisticated, modern Top 40. Storz later claimed that he first noticed the jukebox phenomenon during World War II, but Stewart insists he and Storz made the discovery in Omaha.

Into this format, McLendon—who always watched Storz closely—injected a new element: promotion. When McLendon hired disc jockey Johnny Rabbitt at KLIF, he overturned autos along freeways outside Dallas, and had painted on the bottom of each, "I just flipped for Johnny Rabbitt." To introduce the new disc jockey, he had Rabbitt broadcast from inside a glass booth in a parking lot. In another promotion, a man appeared on a Dallas street corner handing out cash, mixing an occasional $10 or $20 bill in with a lot of singles. He attracted newspaper and television coverage. When this "mystery millionaire" was interviewed live on a television newscast, he revealed that he was the new morning deejay on KLIF. McLendon also introduced the promotional jingle, that singsong repetition of a station's call letters.

McLendon was innovative in other formats as well. He aggressively promoted "Beautiful Music" at KABL, San Francisco, in 1959. He developed the first successful all-news station, XETRA, in Tijuana, Mexico, in 1961. (Its signal reached the Los Angeles area.) He tried an all-classified-ads format at KADS, Los Angeles, in November 1967. It went off the air the following summer, but McLendon said it was viable and that he hadn't devoted enough time to promotion.

McLendon was among the most inventive of station owners, and among the most widely imitated. Respected, but not loved, his feuds were famous, his gaffes legendary, his ego enormous. He ran for the U.S. Senate in Texas in 1964, and in the Democratic gubernatorial primary in 1968. He appeared in a swamp horror movie, *The Killer Shrews* (and distributed another, *The Gila Monster*). He got into trouble with the FCC for flagrant violations—such as changing programming he had promised to retain (See Chapter 5.)—and was thought to be arrogant and obnoxious by many of his competitors, even though he was admired for his success.

Sportscaster Lindsey Nelson, who at one time worked for Liberty, recalled McLendon in a *Sports Illustrated* memoir: "He had moved to a two-story building at 2100 Jackson Street in downtown Dallas. Its most impressive feature was a huge map of the United States on the lobby wall, with the cities linked together by lines criss-crossing each other. I made the same mistake everyone else did. I assumed it was a map of the Liberty network. Actually, it was an American Airlines map."

McLendon Broadcasting, based in Dallas, sold its last station in 1979. But Gordon McLendon had left his mark on contemporary radio.

* * *

Robert Todd Storz, born in Omaha on March 8, 1924, played with radio kits as a child and had a ham operator's license when he was 16. During World War II he served in the Army Signal Corps as a cryptographer. His first radio job was at KWBW in Hutchinson, Kansas. He returned to Omaha in 1947 and got an announcing job on KBON but was fired after he advised a complaining caller, "Madam, on your radio you will find a switch which will easily turn the set off." He then got a sales job with KFAB, Omaha. Like McLendon, Storz got his start in radio management when his father bought him a radio station, KOWH, Omaha, in 1949. He promptly terminated what he called "minority programming"—classical music and country music —to play "popular" music; he also introduced cash giveaways.

With his father's backing he formed Mid-Continent Broadcasting and Storz Broadcasting, acquiring WTIX, New Orleans, WHB, Kansas City, and WGDY, Minneapolis. The Omaha and New Orleans stations cemented Storz's reputation as a father of Top 40 and of cash giveaways. He was a direct competitor of McLendon in both promotional devices and Top 40 refinements. But when he died in 1964, he left less of a mark than the Texan. Storz never became, as McLendon did, an on-the-air personality and he didn't develop any other new formats. According to many associates, he was a sound businessman but a Midwestern, self-proclaimed lowbrow who didn't like New York. As a result he didn't know advertising agency people or network people; he was strictly small-town. McLendon labeled Storz: "A lone wolf. . . Todd was not a gregarious, garrulous person. He was quiet, reserved, highly intelligent. He knew what his listeners wanted, certainly."

McLendon said he and Storz were close friends, "So close we would not have thought of competing with one another. We had an agreement that we would not go into each other's markets. It was an unspoken verbal agreement." Nonetheless, they did compete, when Storz owned WTIX in New Orleans and McLendon was "consultant" to WNOE, owned by his father-in-law at the time, former Louisiana governor James Noe. Perhaps McLendon likes to deny that New Orleans pitted the two giants in competition because WTIX, then a feeble 250-watt station, was top-ranked in town. Not until after Storz's death did WNOE, with 50,000 watts of power during the day and 5,000 watts at night, topple WTIX from first place.

Storz was blasted in a 1956 portrait in *Time* magazine that labeled him "the king of the giveaway," and sneered, "His low estimate of listeners' intelligence is tempered only by his high regard for their cupidity." *Time* also criticized Storz's penchant for sensational newscasts, noting that he ignored the United Nations "for other international bodies—like Anita Ekberg." (One of Storz's former station managers said, "He thought of a lot of things that weren't socially useful. He really wanted a raunchy, slightly pornographic, bloody newscast.") But the *Time* article sloppily reported that Storz's flagship station was KOHW (it was actually KOWH), and Storz amused the broadcasting industry with a rebuttal advertisement in *Broadcasting* (on July 2, 1956) addressed to *Tiem* magazine.

Whatever *Time's* view of Storz, he ran a tight ship and a tough training ground for younger broadcasters. "I worked for him a year and a half as a salesman in Kansas City and a year and a half as manager in Minneapolis and I went from there to a network vice presidency in New York," said Stephen Labunski, president of NBC Radio from 1965 to 1969 and currently executive director of the International Radio and Television Society. "You can't do that just on charm. It had to be the organization I was with. We were hot. We were an industry model." Other graduates of the Storz operation include Jack Thayer, another former NBC Radio president, and Dick Harris, head of Westinghouse (Group W) Radio.

An example of Storz's innovative cash giveaways was the "Lucky House" promotion, developed in Omaha. Street addresses were broadcast over the air and if the residents called the station within a minute, they received a $500 prize. In another contest, Storz hid six checks in an Omaha public library, broadcasting clues to listeners, but had to call off the promotion when the library was overrun by treasure-seekers. In Kansas City, a WHB treasure hunt for $2,000 caused enormous traffic jams, and the police chief demanded, unsuccessfully, that such promotions cease. In Minneapolis and in Omaha, Storz sent listeners looking for cash prizes of $100,000. All this made the FCC unhappy; the commissioners wrote Storz and complained that the giveaways seemed both an attempt to purchase listeners and an invitation to competing stations to try similar inducements. This would lead to a reduction in public service broadcasting, the FCC suggested. Storz, who was seeking FCC approval for his purchase of WQAM, Miami, defended the giveaways as entirely legal, but he indicated a willingness to cease them entirely and immediately if his application for WQAM were approved. The FCC awarded Storz the license by a 4–3 margin after deciding it didn't have the right to interfere in program content.

After Storz died on April 14, 1964, Storz Broadcasting went under the control of his father, Robert, assisted by Bud Armstrong, who later became president.

Much of what we take for granted about modern radio is the legacy of Storz and McLendon. At a time when the traditional leaders, the networks, had rolled over and played dead, these two broadcasters gave the industry energy, fresh ideas, and leadership. By actively recruiting young broadcasters, by hiring students out of college, they brought forth a new generation of radio personnel. Radio surely would have survived without them, but today it is more exciting and diversified because of them.

* * *

Gerald Bartell was another young, innovative broadcaster who termed his approach to radio programming "objective"—that is, he claimed that he would not impose his views on what he played, but would only give listeners what they wanted. "My ambition is to keep them glued. I just want them listening 24 hours a day," he told *Fortune* magazine in 1958. "There's nothing I'd like better than to run a commercial station producing top jazz, classical music and good features. But outside of New York and Los Angeles there's simply no market for such a product...I'm not knocking my programming: I think it's wholesome, fast-moving, well-produced. But it's not a question of what I like to hear, or what my wife likes to hear: it's what I think most people like to hear." The Bartell Broadcasting Group was organized around WOKY, Milwaukee; it perhaps dramatized the gulf between these independent operations and the networks that McLendon, Storz, and Bartell were all based in the center of the country, far from network headquarters. From San Antonio, New Orleans, and Miami to the south, to Milwaukee and Minneapolis to the north, they forged a new kind of radio. For several reasons they avoided the fortresses of the Old Guard: New York, Washington, Philadelphia, Boston.

They were all from Middle America, enjoying their first success in the cities where they lived; they enjoyed the goodwill of their family names, as well as the connections, and knew their potential advertisers and their listeners. But McLendon noted (in 1979), "If you wonder why we weren't doing it in New York, San Francisco and so forth, it was because there were no stations in those markets available for sale at good prices. By the time any stations might have become available, someone else had copied the format, in New York, Boston, Philadelphia, San Francisco. . . . Before either of us could expand to the West Coast or the East Coast, we had been copied."

* * *

As the networks sagged and independent operators rallied their stations, network affiliates often remained stuck in the middle. They were accustomed to the prestige and the glamorous programming that affiliation provided them—and they all too often were accustomed to a strong network boss who would tell them what to do. They stagnated, while their local competition experimented and promoted itself. It's notable that when McLendon, Storz, or Bartell bought a station affiliated with a network, they usually cancelled the affiliation within a few months. This was the case with Storz's third station, WHB, Kansas City, purchased in mid-1954, and affiliated with Mutual. In September of that year, Storz announced that WHB would be an "aggressive and intelligently programmed independent station," and broke with Mutual. WHB's follow-up ad in *Sponsor* magazine was more explicit: "Big Switch! Unburdened by a lot of programs only *some* people want to hear." Similarly, in March 1955, WNOE, New Orleans, dropped its Mutual affiliation and switched immediately to a 24-hour format of music and news. Five months later, KNOE, in Monroe, Louisiana, dropped its NBC affiliation; KNOE said, "It is no longer practical for a radio station to belong to a network." A week after Bartell bought KCBQ, San Diego, in 1955, the station severed its ABC affiliation. This trend continued in following years as Plough, a Memphis pharmaceutical firm that owned a group of stations, and Westinghouse also severed network ties. The aggressive, innovative stations were disaffiliating, but a lot of other network affiliates—especially the "old-line" affiliates from the early days of the network—staggered along, hoping some miracle, or some dramatic network leadership, would turn them around.

And so radio entered the mid-1950s. While the befuddled networks and their affiliates struggled, significant elements of the industry were making money. Radio had found a new niche in American life and unimagined riches were just around the corner. Along came rock 'n' roll.

3

THE EMERGING TEEN CULTURE

Okay now. To Beatrice and Eddie, who need each other more now than ever before. Also to Nick Barbane of the United States Navy from your girl Pat. To Gene from the Dell girls and to Jimmy Smotta love from Joyce of the Bronx.

And to Ellen and Jimmy, Peggy and Reno, Judy and Red, Joyce and Teddy, Marlene and Don, Yvonne and Buddy, Elaine and Billy, Fran and Tommy, Anita and Jackie, Cal and Rae, Maryann and Billy, Bootsie and Carol and Johnny Accacella, Mary and Jerry and Little Jerry, Jr., Antoinette and Dominic, Carmine Mangarelli and Ralph Renga, and especially to Charlie Accacella, going steady 15 months and Lucy says, 'I know I get you mad but I don't mean to, it's just love, that's all.'

For Kenneth Cook of St. Albans from Joan Harding, who still loves him. And for all the kids of Andrew Jackson High: Gail, Jackie, Helena, Dorie, Kenneth, Jerry, Billy, Shadow, Baby, Joan, Olga, Clifford, Connie, José, Slim, Mousie, and Tommy ... here's the record in the number 23 spot, Pee Wee Creighton and 'I Need Your Love.'

—**Alan Freed**
On *WINS,* New York,
circa 1955

35

ROCK 'n' roll was not just energetic music that teenagers loved to dance to; it was the lever by which they came to move the world. For the first time, their age group—larger and more affluent than ever before—gained a decisive vote in shaping popular music, becoming a significant force in the marketplace.

The rock revolution marched on two sturdy legs: the Top 40 format, and the rich heritage of black rhythm 'n' blues. Because stations based play lists on what the record stores were selling, as teenagers bought more records than adults, they determined what would be on the air. In the mid-1950s most of those records were rock 'n' roll.

Critics suggested that rock 'n' roll bubbled up from the nether world or was created by a conspiracy to corrupt youth. But in its earliest days, rock was no more than rhythm 'n' blues played for a white audience. ("Rhythm 'n' blues" was itself a marketing term coined to replace "race music"; *Billboard* changed the terminology in 1949. These records were marketed primarily to blacks, and were played on stations trying to attract black listeners.) In the early 1950s, deejays, who were polling record shops to see what was selling, sensed that rhythm 'n' blues records were attracting a substantial audience of white teenagers. One need look no further than the popular white music to see why: almost all the hits were ballads, not intended for energetic dancing. Among the Top 10 tunes of 1950 were "Goodnight Irene" by the Weavers and "Mule Train" by Frankie Laine. In 1951 the hits included Patti Page's "Tennessee Waltz," "How High the Moon" by Les Paul and Mary Ford, and "On Top of Old Smoky" by the Weavers. The next year's top tunes included "Cry" by Johnny

Ray, "Anytime" by Eddie Fisher, and "Doggie in the Window" by Patti Page. If teenagers wanted fast music to dance to, they could not find it in the Top 10 record bins. So they turned to black music.

One of the first men in radio to make this discovery (although it was presented to him on a platter) was Alan Freed. Freed was born December 15, 1921 in Johnstown, Pennsylvania. He grew up in Salem, Ohio, where his father worked in a clothing store. Freed was interested in both classical and swing music, and at Ohio State University, which he attended for two years, he played trombone in a jazz band called the Sultans of Swing, named after a popular Harlem band. After serving two years in the army, he was hired, for $45 a week as a disc jockey on WKST in New Castle, Pennsylvania, playing classical music. He switched to WAKR in Akron, Ohio, in 1946, where his "Request Review" was a popular show. In 1950 WXEL brought Freed to Cleveland, and the next year a competitor, WJW, hired Freed to host a late-night show called "Record Rendezvous," sponsored by and named for a local record store owned by Leo Mintz.

Mintz brought Freed to the shop one day to observe what he thought was an unusual but pronounced trend: white teenagers in great numbers buying rhythm 'n' blues records. Freed watched the teens dancing in the aisles and returned to WJW convinced he had seen the new day dawning. He got permission to follow his regular program with another show on which he would play rhythm 'n' blues. He first called the show "Moon Dog House," then "The Moon Dog House Rock 'n' Roll Party." From this title he claimed to have coined the term "rock 'n' roll." In truth, "rocking and rolling" was a common lyric in rhythm 'n' blues recordings, a euphemism for sexual intercourse. Freed was not the only white deejay playing black music; others included Hunter Hancock in Los Angeles, George Oxford and Phil McKernan in San Francisco, George Lorenz of Buffalo, New York, "Symphony" Sid Torin of Boston and later New York City, Zenas Sears in Atlanta, and Gene Nobles in Nashville. But Freed was the first deejay to promote rhythm 'n' blues to a white audience, and to build that audience systematically. He was both a master showman and a manipulator, promoting the music and himself. One vehicle for doing this was concerts: Freed hosted the shows and also was their promoter. His first concert was set for March 21, 1952, at the Cleveland Arena; he called it "The Moon Dog Coronation Ball" and contracted for a variety of black musicians and singers. It was to be the first time that Freed gained nationwide notoriety.

By Freed's on-the-air mentions alone, the concert drew nearly 25,000 fans. WJW was proud of Freed's clout and circulated handbills to advertising agencies and potential sponsors that noted, "Radio Alone Pulled 25,000!" There were two problems: the arena only seated 10,000, and nearly 20,000 tickets had been sold. Gate-crashing and general rowdiness marked the evening. Police and fire reinforcements were called in. Five persons were arrested for intoxication and at least one person was stabbed. The music was inaudible over the crowd noise. Midway through the evening fire marshals ordered an end to the concert. Charges of fraud, for overselling tickets, were filed against Freed and a partner; they were later dropped. Accounts vary as to the racial mix of the crowd, ranging from "two-thirds white" to "almost all Negro." But Freed had made his mark. *Billboard* began to report on his growing ratings in Cleveland, and other radio entrepreneurs began to switch to similar programming.

Freed soon made his presence felt just outside of New York City. WNJR in Newark, New Jersey, was bought by the Rollins Broadcasting Company in 1954 and was programmed to offer 19 hours a day of rhythm 'n' blues and spirituals, with some sports and news. The music featured three out-of-town deejays on tape: Hancock, Sears, and Freed. WNJR began to attract national advertisers for the first time since the dawn of television, and it began to draw local advertisers from New York City as well. As WNJR gained attention in New York, WINS was playing the type of popular music white teenagers didn't seem to care for. WINS program director Bob Smith heard a Freed tape on WNJR, called him in Cleveland and offered him the Big Apple. Freed was hired for a late-night shift at WINS, but was soon moved to the 7:00–11:00 PM slot, where he enhanced his reputation as the "father of rock 'n' roll." He went on the air September 8, 1954, and the station's ratings started to climb. As before, he began promoting concerts. (He had already staged a show in Newark on May 1, 1954, to capitalize on his popularity there.) Freed's first New York concerts, called "Alan Freed's Rock 'n' Roll Party," were held on January 14 and 15, 1955, at the St. Nicholas Arena in Manhattan. They went off without violence. With Freed's success in New York—media capital of the country, home of the advertising agencies and the networks—this new music and the culture it was spawning were constantly in the spotlight. Big money was involved. Concert promoters and record companies jostled for position in the marketplace. Six major record companies—RCA, Columbia, Decca, Capitol, MGM, and Mercury—dominated the market. Between 1946 and 1952, 162 records sold more than one million copies; 158 of them were released by the Big Six. But as white interest in rhythm 'n' blues began to grow, independent companies that had scratched out a survival income by serving minority markets—much as independent radio stations did— suddenly found their products in demand. Dozens of independent record companies struck it rich with the emerging popularity of rock 'n' roll. Among the most famous were Chess Records in Chicago, which recorded Chuck Berry and Bo Diddley, and Sun Records of Memphis, which recorded Elvis Presley and Jerry Lee Lewis. Increased competition among record companies seeking airplay led to aggressive wooing of deejays.

In their search for a mass market, both record companies and radio stations sought a wider acceptance for rhythm 'n' blues, which was viewed by many as raucous and overtly sexual. Record companies began to produce "cover versions" by having a white, clean-cut performer "cover," or interpret, a powerful rhythm 'n' blues song. In 1954, a classic case was "Work With Me Annie," by Hank Ballard. The "work" was sex, the song made clear, and the rhythm 'n' blues tune— covered by Georgia Gibbs—was released as "Dance With Me Henry," making it more suitable for white audiences,. the conventional thinking went. Later Pat Boone covered Little Richard's "Tutti Frutti" and "Long Tall Sally" and Ricky Nelson, Ozzie and Harriet's son, covered Fats Domino's "I'm Walkin'." These bowdlerized versions kept an important element of black culture from wider exposure.

Another type of cover simply involved copying the competition. As soon as a fast-selling record was spotted, other companies would rush out their own versions of it. Sometimes they sought to replicate the sound of the original; other times they recorded with whoever was available. Only speed mattered: throw the record, with a recognizable title and lyric, into the marketplace, induce deejays to play it, and some consumers would buy it. This led to a good deal of confusion at radio stations, where each deejay might play a different version of the same song.

As important as the songs were the discs on which they were recorded. A struggle, known as "the battle of the speeds," had been raging within the recording industry for six years over a successor to the 78-rpm record. The high-fidelity, long-play record was introduced by Columbia in 1948, following years of research by Dr. Peter Goldmark. Its speed was 33 1/3 rpm. A few years later RCA introduced the smaller 45-rpm disc, and began marketing low-cost phonographs that accommodated only 45s. LPs were obviously superior for classical music and show tunes. But the 45 had many advantages: it was lighter, less breakable, and cheaper to produce and to buy. Juke boxes could hold more 45s, and record companies could mail them to deejays around the country far more cheaply. Because the introduction of the 45 coincided with the marketing of this new music, many teenagers came to view it as a cachet of their generation.

A more important symbol was rock 'n' roll. It was a statement, an acting out of teen resentments by an inarticulate generation. It is no coincidence that one of the earliest serious films about adolescent rebellion and juvenile delinquency, *Blackboard Jungle,* in 1955, had as its theme song "Rock Around the Clock," the first rock song ever to hit number one on the charts. This adolescent revolt—against what, the kids often did not know, or at least not well enough to say—had as its heroes Marlon Brando, who starred as the motorcycle gang leader in *The Wild One,* and James Dean, who had the title role in *Rebel*

Without a Cause. And into their lives came Elvis Presley.

Presley looked aggressively sexual; as he sang, he strutted and postured and shook his pelvis (hence, he was dubbed Elvis the Pelvis). Already something of a legend in the South, his first national exposure was a television appearance (January 28, 1956) on the Dorsey Brothers' "Sound Stage." Presley created shock waves as he thumped his pelvis into his guitar. On April 3, an audience estimated at 40 million—a quarter of the U.S. population at the time—watched him on "The Milton Berle Show." Radio play of his records exploded as sales took off. On April 21, he reached the number one spot on the *Billboard* chart for the first time, with "Heartbreak Hotel." He remained there for 25 of the next 37 weeks, with seven smash hits. He dominated radio as no performer ever had (or would, until the Beatles in 1964).

On September 9, Presley appeared on the Ed Sullivan Show—one of those certifiably memorable moments in American popular culture—and pulled an astonishing 82.6 percent share of the television audience. The staff of the Sullivan show tried to placate the critics of Presley's style by showing him only from the waist up. Elvis, in tie and jacket, went on; his pelvis did not. Still, the critics were outraged. Jack Gould wrote in *The New York Times* that Presley "injected movements of the tongue and indulged in wordless singing that was singularly distasteful." The criticisms were nothing new.

Even before the arrival of Presley on the national scene, opposition had been mounting to the playing of rhythm 'n' blues for white audiences. Some leaders claimed that the music would inflame teenage passions and cause them to run amok. Addressing the Teachers Institute of the Archdiocese of Boston, the Very Rev. John P. Carroll said, "Rock and roll inflames and excites youth like the jungle tom-toms readying warriors for battle. Inject a word or misunderstanding and the whole place blows up. The suggestive lyrics on rock and roll records, of course, are a matter for law enforcement agencies." But Carroll's reference to "jungle tom-toms" illuminates the other objection to rhythm 'n' blues—a racist objection. Black music was not suitable for white teenagers. The transition from rhythm 'n' blues to rock 'n' roll came in the same days the U.S. Supreme Court was ordering school desegregation in *Brown* v. *Board of Education of Topeka.* But society was in many ways still segregated. Negro programming had always been kept off in a corner; "race music" as a descriptive term was only a few years out of date. To many white parents this sudden proliferation of music that either sounded black or imitated blacks seemed ominous. In some areas of the country it was not acceptable to discuss the music in terms of race, so complaints often focused on the sexuality.

Variety, the self-proclaimed bible of show business, took to describing the new music's "leer-ics." An official of the American Society of Composers, Authors and Publishers (ASCAP) told *Variety* that he considered rock 'n' roll not just "junk, but in many cases...obscene junk, pretty much on a level with dirty comics and magazines."

Some radio stations joined the fight as well. In October 1954, WDIA, Memphis, announced it would screen all incoming records for suggestiveness and said it had banned 15 records. The following March, Los Angeles deejay Peter Potter said he thought *all* rhythm 'n' blues records were dirty and detrimental to teenagers. In Mobile, Alabama, a station said it would throw out at least half of its rhythm 'n' blues records because "filth in both title and words makes their destruction a must." In Houston, the Juvenile Delinquency and Crime Commission began to compile a list of objectionable records it wanted banned from the radio. Campaigns were mounted in Northern cities, too, including Chicago and Boston. The alliance of anti-rock 'n' roll forces was to have enormous impact on the record companies and radio at the end of the 1950s; but for the time, the beat went on.

After McLendon, Storz, and Bartell demonstrated how successful Top 40 could be, stations around the country followed suit. Executives were hired from the Midwest chains, whose tapes were studied, analyzed, and copied. By 1956, Top 40 stations and "tight play lists" were common. If Presley were put into a straitjacket on the Ed Sullivan Show, radio welcomed him with open arms and more:

with nonstop Presley programming, look-alike contests, leather-jacket giveaways, and contests for tickets to his concerts and films. An unusual Presley promotion followed his induction into the army in early 1958. Chuck Blore—the program director of KELP, El Paso, Texas, a McLendon station—recounted, "Elvis had just been inducted, and he went to El Paso for his first haircut. Well, I knew a guy at the base who swept up a piece of Elvis's hair, and I put it in a gold frame and I gave that away. It was the first promotion I did without cash, and the biggest promotion that I've ever done in El Paso. There was more public reaction to this lock of Elvis's hair than to the $10,000 giveaway we'd done two months before." (What makes this promotion all the funnier is that army records show that Presley's crewcut was given to him at Fort Chafee, Arkansas.)

Rock and radio were made for each other. The relationship between record companies and radio stations became mutually beneficial. By providing the latest hits, record companies kept stations' operating costs low. The stations, in turn, provided the record companies with the equivalent of free advertising. Business grew unimaginably; record sales nearly tripled from 1954 ($213 million) to 1959 ($613 million).

Most radio stations and record companies were happy with the arrangement. But the advertising agencies were not. They were among the last holdouts against rock's presence on radio and were reluctant to place their clients' ads on rock stations. Many agency people did not like rock. They believed what they read in *The New York Times, Variety,* and *The Wall Street Journal*: that the music was dangerous. Another problem was that New York agency people were fairly isolated and didn't know what radio was like in other parts of the country. In 1957, many Top 40 stations had the largest audiences in their markets but this went unnoticed by the agencies. Sometimes the stations would send in falsified demonstration tapes to New York agencies, fearing that sponsors would not advertise if they knew the station played rock 'n' roll.

Typical of the resistance to rock audiences was one network's line to advertisers: "If you sell white buckskin shoes and bubble gum, by all means use a jukebox station." Mitch Miller (the bandleader was Columbia Records' director of artists and repertoire) complained to a convention of deejays, "You have abdicated your programming to the corner record shop, to the pre-shave crowd that makes up 12 percent of the country's population and zero percent of its buying power, once you eliminate pony-tail ribbons, popsicles, and peanut brittle." History has proved the power of the youth market, but the contempt and ignorance in Miller's remarks capture accurately some of the formidable obstacles that rock radio faced. Many Top 40 stations were forced to rely on local sponsors rather than national advertisers and their agencies. Nonetheless, Top 40 radio made money hand over fist in the late 1950s.

McLendon, Storz, Bartell, and Plough were joined in June 1956 by an influential ally, Group W, which had disaffiliated from NBC. Group W was led by Donald McGannon, highly respected in the business world—one trade magazine nicknamed him Dynamo Don—and his sweeping changes helped make the new rock radio respectable to the New York agencies. Before the disaffiliation, KDKA, the Group W flagship station in Pittsburgh, was broadcasting classical concerts every Wednesday night by the Pittsburgh Symphony, whose members were clad in tuxedos. It was enormously expensive compared to the cost of playing records. McGannon ended the concerts and also released most of the old announcers, whom he termed "sedentary."

But if McGannon made a favorable impression on the business world, other broadcasters rankled the Establishment. Storz and McLendon had always come in for criticism. The Bartell Group's flagship station, WOKY, Milwaukee, had as its motto "Let's make nothing but money." Critics were quick to point out what this had to say about Bartell's commitment to public service.

Meanwhile, Alan Freed was serving as a lightning rod for much of the criticism that rock 'n' roll accrued. If Elvis was reprehensible, the reasoning seemed to be, at least he was young, didn't know any better, and was manipulated by advisers. Freed, on the other hand, was perceived as one of the sinister manipulators. His hands were indeed everywhere: he reigned over the New York radio scene with his evening show on WINS; continued to promote concerts; hosted a syndicated radio program that was broadcast by local stations around the country (Radio Luxembourg carried his show for European audiences); packaged anthologies of records, with titles like "Alan Freed's Memory Lane"; appeared in rock 'n' roll movies, playing himself (usually in return for a percentage of the profits); and hosted television shows, including a short-lived CBS network program, "Rock and Roll Dance Party." It was short-lived because it came under fire on two counts: the show was sponsored by Camel cigarettes, so Freed was blamed for encouraging young people to smoke, and on one of the first shows Frankie Lymon, a young black singer, danced with a white girl. The show was broadcast live and the racial fires were fanned again: Rock 'n' roll not only would overstimulate teens' sex drive, it could lead directly to miscegenation and mongrelization of the white race. Preachers went wild in denouncing Freed. He was becoming a marked man, but not a cautious one.

On May 3, 1958, Freed was promoting a rock concert in Boston that starred Jerry Lee Lewis. Police received reports of disorders, heavy drinking and scuffling in the audience, and ordered the house lights turned on. Freed took the microphone and reportedly told the audience: "Hey kids, the cops don't want you to have a good time." In the ensuing commotion at least one person was stabbed, dozens were beaten, and Freed was charged with incitement to riot and anarchy. Months later the charges were dropped, but the rest of his New England tour was canceled and other cities banned the concerts.

An early warning signal of even bigger trouble for rock 'n' roll and radio came on Memorial Day 1959, when Storz convened his second annual Disc Jockeys Convention at the Hotel Americana in Miami Beach. Attendance was about 2,500, including a substantial number of prostitutes provided by the record companies for the deejays. This was not unusual; what set it apart from many other conventions was the press coverage it received. The continuing hostility to rock 'n' roll and incidents like the Boston riot had kept deejays in the spotlight. Newspapers had long ranked among the opponents of rock 'n' roll, and headlines about the Miami Beach convention referred to "Booze, Broads and Bribes." It was the "bribes," and the news reports about them, that signaled the payola scandals slowly unraveling in Washington.

"Payola" was a term coined by the media to indicate cash payments in return for air play. That is, record companies or their representatives would pay disc jockeys or program directors—whoever was responsible for selecting the records to be played—for putting songs on the air. The fee was based on how often the song was played and on the size of the market. In the earliest days record companies would present deejays with gifts simply as "favors." As the play lists grew more restricted and the competition among record companies more intense, cash payments developed. Often these were entirely aboveboard: the companies listed the deejays as consultants and paid them by check.

The exchange of favors and the use of consultants' fees (legal) and kickbacks (illegal) are not exactly strangers to contemporary commerce. It remains standard practice for radio personnel to receive free tickets to any concerts they wish to attend, and free copies of all records (which they often turn around and sell to record shops). Newspaper reporters who write about music receive the same favors, and record companies will gladly pick up the tab for a writer to fly anywhere to do any interview. Some newspapers object, but many others do not. The practice is hardly limited to music coverage. Sportswriters often receive complimentary tickets to events they are not covering, as well as "working press" passes to games they are; film critics are flown all over the world to do on-location interviews. So are travel writers. Consumer writers attending the annual shows of appliance manufacturers are often given "demonstration models" they can keep. Some media watchdogs, and indeed many writers, feel these situations are unethical; but by and large they are accepted as reasonable business practices. Ample accounts have been provided of favors done by and for businessmen and government officials, among military officers and government contractors and among captains of industry and labor leaders.

It is against this background—both the American way of business and the enormous antipathy toward rock 'n' roll—that the payola scandals must be measured. On the one hand, payola practices did affect— and restrict—air play, and thus influenced both record sales and the public's taste. On the other hand, it was clearly an attempt by many powerful elements of the Establishment once and for all to expose rock 'n' roll for the sham they thought it was. We already have noted many of the opponents of rock 'n' roll. Two other groups made notable contributions to the fight: newspaper publishers and the American Society of Composers, Authors and Publishers (ASCAP). Newspapers seemed to line up against rock 'n' roll for several reasons: they were generally conservative, with adult readers who didn't care for the music. Many newspapers owned "old line" radio stations that were slow to change and threatened by the raucous Top 40 competition. Press coverage of rock 'n' roll had never been balanced.

ASCAP's involvement in the fight was more direct. In fact, ASCAP triggered the payola investigations. Throughout 1959 the nation had been titillated by rumors, then investigations, and finally admissions of guilt in the rigging of television quiz shows. Contestants were coached and tipped off in advance about questions—and given the right answers. Producers decided which contestants would win and lose based on keeping the audience excited. "The $64,000 Question" was the best-known of the corrupt shows. In the course of the quiz show hearings, which were conducted by a House Legislative Oversight subcommittee chaired by Representive Oren Harris (Democrat, Arkansas), ASCAP officials called for a wider look at "corruption in broadcasting." They had in mind payola. When Harris agreed to expand his probe, ASCAP spokesmen gleefully took credit.

ASCAP's presence in the lineup of rock 'n' roll's enemies is not hard to understand. Its antipathy to radio dated back to the beginnings of commercial broadcasting. Before radio, ASCAP members earned their royalties principally through the sale of records and sheet music. ASCAP felt strongly that radio's use of records would reduce its members' royalties. When stations helped found Broadcast Music Inc. (BMI) in 1939 and urged songwriters and recording artists to sign with it, ASCAP and BMI became competitors, each seeking to bargain on behalf of composers, publishers, and authors. Through the 1940s a majority of blues, rhythm 'n' blues, hillbilly, and later rock 'n' roll artists signed with BMI. ASCAP, whose roots were in Tin Pan Alley, apparently was less concerned with the emerging music and concentrated on mainstream popular material. When rock 'n' roll exploded on radio's airwaves, and then, under the limited play list formulas, forced out other types of music (much of it ASCAP music), ASCAP officials joined the front against rock 'n' roll. They suggested that rock was palpably junk, and wouldn't be on the airwaves unless deejays were paid to play it. This was also the thinking of newspaper reporters who sneered at rock and denigrated the talents of its stars. Apparently it was the thinking of many government officials as well.

When probers turned their spotlight on the music business and on the relationships between record companies and radio personnel, they found ample evidence of collusion. Alan Freed, for example, had virtually unlimited opportunities to promote the records of artists he had under contract for concerts. He could provide free advertising for his own concerts simply through his record selection. Far worse, he was listed as a co-author on over a dozen rock songs, including Chuck Berry's classic "Maybelline." No one has come forward to suggest that Freed actually sat down with Berry and wrote the song, or that Berry, a prolific songwriter, needed to consult with Freed, but because the author of a song receives a royalty each time a song is played (so do the singer, the producer, and the publisher of the song) Freed could increase his earnings simply by playing songs he "co-authored" more frequently. These practices seem unsavory, but were, in fact, legal (unless Freed insisted on co-authorship before he would play a song).

Other variations—all legal—were practiced by Dick Clark of "American Bandstand" fame. He owned stock in record companies whose artists he would invite to appear on his show, and he also owned music publishing companies. In all, Clark was financially involved with 33 companies in the music business, including three record companies, a management firm, and a record-pressing plant.

His relationship with the rock performer Duane Eddy perfectly captures this wheeling and dealing: He managed Eddy, owned publishing rights to all his songs, and owned a share of Jamie Records, the label on which Eddy recorded. Clark invested $125 in Jamie Records and later sold the stock for $12,025. Between 1958 and 1960 Eddy released eleven records, and Clark played them a total of 240 times on his television show. When Congress eventually scheduled the payola hearings for early 1960, ABC ordered Clark to choose between "American Bandstand" and his music businesses. He agreed to divest himself of all music business interests. He later said the decision cost him at least $8 million. Clark also signed an affidavit swearing he had never received payola, and ABC then stood by him and provided lawyers for the hearings. Despite some acrimonious questioning, he was not charged with any wrongdoing. In his testimony Clark contended that all the seeming conflicts of interest were normal business practices in the music business.

Freed, meanwhile, had quit WINS after the Boston melee, claiming the station had not backed him up. He signed with WABC, the New York owned-and-operated station of the network, for an evening rock show, starting on June 2, 1958. That November he began a weekday TV show, from 5:00 to 6:00 PM on New York's Channel 5. A year later, with payola probes unfolding, ABC asked Freed to sign an affidavit like the one Clark had signed. Freed refused. He said he had not received payola, but that he would not sign the affidavit "on principle" and also because it was a slur on his reputation. ABC fired him. Within a few days, so did Channel 5. Freed later conceded that he accepted payments but maintained his innocence. "If I've helped somebody," he said "I'll accept a nice gift, but I wouldn't take a dime to plug a record. I'd be a fool to; I'd be giving up control of my program." Freed told gossip columnist Earl Wilson, "A bribe is when somebody says, 'Here is a $100 bill. Lay on our record.' But if I by myself, based on my 19 years of experience, decide a record should be a hit, and I help it, am I going to turn down a gift of a bottle of whisky or something?

"I've never taken a bribe....Somebody said to me once, 'If

somebody sent you a Cadillac, would you send it back?' I said, 'It depends on the color.' " These types of responses and his refusal to sign an affidavit set Freed up for prosecution. Nevertheless he may well have been right on target when he said, "What they call payola in the disc jockey business, they call lobbying in Washington."

The payola probes unfolded on three fronts. The Federal Trade Commission in Washington, in 1959, filed complaints against a number of record companies, charging unfair competition. Under FTC rules companies had 30 days to respond and either to agree to come before an examiner or to file a consent order, which meant the firm agreed to stop the practice in question without admitting any guilt. Most of the companies filed the consent agreements.

In Manhattan, the district attorney summoned a grand jury to determine if commercial bribery charges should be filed against deejays and record company personnel. While the jury was hearing evidence, the big ballgame got under way in Washington: the House hearings opened on February 8, 1960, before an attentive nation whose appetite had been whetted by the quiz show probe. The appetite was quickly satisfied: In the first week, deejays testified they *had* accepted payments to play records. Heads started to roll throughout the radio industry. Many deejays, including stars, quit before they were asked questions. Others were called in by station managers and owners. Some contracts were bought up; other deejays resigned. Station managers and owners in some cases were no doubt outraged by the allegations of commercial bribery on their property. They also knew they had to make the correct moves, for the FCC was watching how license holders responded to the payola situation. Others may have been disappointed that the payments slipped by them to their hirelings. One Storz employee said: "Todd used to sit and scheme for hours about how he could tap into this cash flow. It drove him crazy—and a lot of other station owners too—to know that all these payoffs were flowing right by them into the hands of deejays. He kept looking for a way to get a share, to get the record companies to channel money to the station owner...." Many of the displaced deejays switched careers; others migrated to different markets and went back on the air. Thus San Francisco's KYA added to its roster Tom "Big Daddy" Donahue, Bobby Mitchell, and Joe Niagara, all of whom had been stars in Philadelphia, and Peter Tripp, of WMGM, New York.

In May 1960 the Manhattan grand jury returned charges of commercial bribery against eight men, for accepting more than $100,000 in payoffs for playing records. The biggest name on the list was Alan Freed, who was charged with 26 counts of accepting payoffs. He went on trial in February 1962, and his supporters claimed that he was being made a scapegoat. To their dismay he pleaded guilty to two counts and was fined $300 and given a six-month suspended sentence. Freed by then was on the air in Los Angeles, at KDAY, and he seemed over the hump. But in March 1964 a federal grand jury indicted him for income tax evasion. The Internal Revenue Service charged that Freed had failed to report $57,000 in income from 1957 to 1959, and that he owed taxes of $38,000. While Freed was awaiting trial, living in Palm Springs, he entered a hospital, suffering from uremia. He died three weeks later, on Janurary 20, 1965. The self-proclaimed father of rock 'n' roll radio was 43; by all accounts he died broke.

Freed was egotistical, manipulative, strong-willed, and, it would certainly seem, to some extent corrupt. His explanation of accepting gifts are ingenuous at best. To his supporters, though, he died a martyr to rock 'n' roll. "Alan took the fall for a lot of guys," one colleague said. "It did shorten his life. He deserved better. He was the first major voice on radio, the first breakthrough for black artists. And probably that had something to do with his downfall."

The payola probers and their supporters thought that, aside from identifying crime, they would stamp out rock 'n' roll. Comments and questions from the probers make that clear. (One congressman asked Dick Clark why he hadn't played Bing Crosby songs on "American Bandstand.") History certainly proved them wrong. Some supporters of rock 'n' roll saw the probe as a conspiratorial attempt to deflect public attention from corruption at the television networks (Establishment and, therefore, good guys) to vulnerable independent radio stations (contemptible and irresponsible chain operators, and disc jockeys who were promoting vulgarity, sexuality, and miscegenation). The truth lies somewhere between these extremes. Many of rock radio's critics were ignorant. Some were racist. Others had vested interests to protect. The payola probes and the legal and rhetorical indictments of rock 'n' roll radio were certainly the result of years of resentment by Establishment institutions of an emerging teen culture. Nonetheless they served to focus on several corrupt aspects of the music business. Favoritism, cost overruns, consultants' fees, and lobbying do indeed permeate much of American commerce. In each case, including rock 'n' roll radio, the final product usually suffers and the public is the victim.

Two interesting footnotes to the payola probe amplify this point. One of the charges against deejays was that they permitted record companies to pay for their vacations. With the House hearings already under way, it was disclosed that John C. Doerfer, chairman of the Federal Communications Commission, had just enjoyed a six-day trip to Florida and Bimini, paid for by the Storer Broadcasting Company. President Eisenhower demanded—and received—his resignation. And it was discovered that Congressman Harris, whose subcommittee was probing these conflicts of interest in broadcasting, owned 25 percent of television station KRBB in El Dorado, Arkansas. He eventually sold the shares.

In September 1960 Congress approved amendments to the Federal Communications Act that prohibited the payment of cash or gifts in exchange for air play, and held radio stations responsible for their employees who accepted gifts. But payola did not go away. Investigations flare up every few years. The publicity and the convictions, however, forced record companies and broadcasters to change their operations. The music was strong enough and popular enough to endure, even if the probers didn't believe that. The radio stations set out to prove them wrong.

Station management tightened control over air play, continuing a trend in Top 40: before payola, stations already had moved toward central control, seeking a consistent sound no matter who was on the air and seeking to prevent different deejays from playing different cover versions of a hit. Management became increasingly reliant on the Top 100 charts of the trade publications, notably *Billboard* and *Cashbox*. The Top 40 format was not visibly damaged by the payola hearings. Contrary to the probers' expectations, young people continued to buy rock records, and not Bing Crosby's, and so the charts reflected those sales and the stations played what the charts listed. But between 1958 and 1962, a series of startling coincidences took out of action many of the more charismatic and talented stars of rock 'n' roll:

—Little Richard retired from the entertainment business to enter the ministry in 1957. (A decade later he returned to rock 'n' roll.)

—Presley was in the Army from 1958 to 1960.

—Jerry Lee Lewis was blacklisted when the news got out in 1958 that he had married his 13-year-old cousin. Promoters canceled his concerts.

—Buddy Holly (and two lesser lights, Ritchie Valens and "The Big Bopper") died in a plane crash in February 1959.

—Chuck Berry was arrested in 1959 and charged with transporting a 14-year-old girl across state lines for immoral purposes; she was a prostitute in Mexico whom Berry brought back to St. Louis to work in his nightclub. The case dragged on for three years; Berry finally went to jail in 1962.

—The Everly Brothers served in the Marine Corps in 1961 and 1962.

With these stars out of the lineup, the music industry tried to fill the gap with rock by formula, creating "stars" by marketing alone. It was a slack period for radio's partner. Sales dipped in 1960, and climbed very, very slowly in subsequent years. But Top 40 radio proved that its strength was greater than the quality of the music; stations continued to make money, and more stations converted to the format. In New York City, Top 40 once and for all became entrenched, wooing and winning the advertising agencies and national sponsors into the rock 'n' roll camp. Two stations played a major role in the battle for respectability.

The first was WMCA, a small and relatively weak station owned by the Straus family that founded Macy's department store. R. Peter Straus returned to the station in 1958 from a stint with the International Labour Organization and set out to give WMCA a respectability that no other Top 40 station had won. To the charts and deejays (labeled the "WMCA Good Guys"), Straus added two regularly scheduled news broadcasts an hour, editorials on major issues, documentaries, and a nightly interview show with Barry Gray. Teens flocked to the station to hear the hits, while what Straus called the "egghead material" sanitized the station's image. WMCA improved its ratings, made money, and tied advertisers and rock even more closely together.

WABC solidified rock 'n' roll's stronghold in New York. What was most important about the WABC success story was that it marked the first network involvement in Top 40; WABC was the flagship of the ABC Radio Network.

Ironically, ABC turned to Top 40 out of desperation, for its owned-and-operated stations were doing so poorly that there was a widespread speculation in the industry that ABC would sell them off. Aside from its O&Os, the ABC Network also was in dire straits. In 1958, even with 315 affiliates, ABC was losing nearly $4 million a year. Its problems were compounded by a foolish programming decision the previous year. Entirely out of sync with the times and trends, ABC Radio renamed itself the American Broadcasting Network (ABN) and decided to offer live programming, including lots of live music. Its day was built around "personalities," each backed by live bands. The network continued with "Don McNeill's Breakfast Club," and added Jim Reeves at midday, Jim Backus in the afternoon and Merv Griffin at night. The approach failed miserably: neither existing affiliates nor independent stations found the live programming desirable. ABN was changed back to ABC Radio.

So the ABC high command decided to concentrate on making the O&O stations the leaders in their markets. The key move was sending Hal Neal, general manager of WXYZ, Detroit, to take over WABC, New York. Neal signed up programming consultant Mike Joseph, and together they converted WABC to an aggressive Top 40 station. It was no easy decision, for on the WABC staff were middle-of-the-road legends like Martin Block (of "Make Believe Ballroom" fame). But WABC boldly bought up their contracts and brought in a team of proven Top 40 deejays. The new format made its debut on December 7, 1960. Six months later Neal hired Dan Ingram, arguably the best Top 40 deejay ever, and installed him in the afternoon prime time, 2:00 to 6:00 PM. In 1962 Rick Sklar was named program director and began fine-tuning the machine: he tightened the play list, switched deejay assignments, and introduced elaborate promotions. In his first year WABC conducted "principal of the year" balloting among local students. More than six million votes were received. (Students were permitted to vote as often as they wished.) The following year more than 174 million ballots were received, which took an entire month to count and required the hiring of 60 office temporaries who worked in a large Manhattan arena. Another successful Sklar promotion in 1963 was the Mona Lisa contest. Seeking to capitalize on the publicity attendant to the visit of Da Vinci's masterpiece to the Metropolitan Museum of Art, WABC offered to give prizes for the largest, smallest, and "best" paintings of the Mona Lisa. The station received more than 30,000 paintings. The smallest was painted on a microdot, while the largest would have covered a baseball infield. Salvador Dali was asked to select the best, and chose a small painting that showed Mona Lisa smiling from the window of a Mercury space capsule. Such promotions reaped dividends. In 1962 WABC soared into first place in New York City's ratings—and thus became the most widely listened to station in the country—and stayed there for 16 years, until deposed by the disco format of WKTU-FM in late 1978.

Part of WABC's success undoubtedly came from strong leadership; Neal eventually rose to become president of ABC Radio (he stepped down in 1979 and died in February 1980). The station also benefited from the financial resources of the network; and it was blessed with a magnificent 50,000-watt, clear-channel, nondirectional signal that blanketed a wide part of the East. WABC also profited from some confusion among its competitors. WINS, where Alan Freed had reigned, was in turmoil from the payola probe. It also had many old-line announcers on its staff, and unlike WABC, was not willing to buy them out. In March 1962 WINS decided to abandon its rock format, starting with a nonstop marathon of Frank Sinatra music. It generated favorable publicity for the station, and lots of complimentary newspaper coverage, but it also chased away the teen listeners who had hung on after Freed was gone. WINS failed to build a middle-of-the-road audience and switched back to Top 40. It had some moments of glory, particularly when its star deejay, Murray "the K" Kaufman, managed to ingratiate himself with the Beatles, get exclusive interviews from inside their hotel and even to promote himself as the "fifth Beatle." This was no small coup at the height of Beatlemania, but too many teens had found other stations, and finally, in 1965, WINS went to an all-news format. WMGM was playing Top 40 music, but its mood and especially its anouncers were aimed at an older audience. They simply were not compatible and in 1962, the station threw in the towel, changed its call letters to WHN and went to a beautiful music format. WMCA held out the longest. But with the proliferation of FM rock stations in the late 1960s, WMCA's fate was sealed and the station switched to an all-talk format in 1970.

WABC became the most widely copied station in the United States. The ABC network, of course, followed the formula at its other O&O stations, and started cutting its deficit. Whatever they thought of rock 'n' roll, no advertisers could turn their backs on such large audiences. In markets large and small, Top 40 radio became entrenched and profitable. The debate ended over who was listening to Top 40; so did the derogation of the format as a teens-only sound.

Into this thriving, well-oiled machinery, onto as grand a stage as they could possibly desire, came the Beatles. They brought to popular music more excitement—and enjoyed greater commercial success— than anyone since the heyday of Elvis Presley. They penetrated the radio audience from preteens to grandparents as no one had since the advent of television.

4

FORMATS

The new general manager was ranting and raving about the station's low ratings. He called in his program director and said he wanted the station to rank No. 1 among 18- to 34-year-olds by the end of the next ratings period.

The p.d., who had been with the station nine years, asked: "Do you think we can maintain our reputation for quality programming and still pull in a much larger audience?"

The general manager leaned back in his armchair, thumped his sales reports, and said, "My definition of quality radio is whatever the No. 1 station is doing!"

RADIO's search for listeners, and for blocks of them that could be isolated as audiences, had led to specialization and localization in the 1950s and 1960s. The black audience and then the youth audience were identified and programmed for. Eventually as many as a dozen formats, each with a particular target audience in mind, were developed.

These formats are not sought by radio stations to provide diversity for its own sake. They are not mandated by the Federal Communications Commission (although a federal court has ordered the FCC to pay attention to preserving unique formats). Nor are they provided in order to satisfy listeners' demands. The purpose of these formats is to enable radio stations to deliver to advertisers a measured and defined group of consumers, known as a segment. To a certain extent, then, the history of radio formats is linked loosely to the history of marketing research. As research grew more sophisticated, formats grew more specialized. A station that once sought "blacks," for instance, might now seek blacks between the ages of 18 and 34, especially men, with salaries above $12,000. A competing black station in the same market might seek black women between 24 and 55 years old. Each will be able to find advertisers who want to reach those specific audiences.

The earliest radio research was a good deal less scientific and precise. The first ratings were begun in 1930 by the Cooperative Analysis of Broadcasting, a service organized by Archibald Crossley for the Association of National Advertisers. The findings, known as "Crossley ratings," were based on telephone interviews—the numbers selected at random from directories—and the method of "telephone recall," where listeners were asked to recall what they had listened to for the past several hours. In 1934, C. E. Hooper introduced "Hooperatings," developing the "telephone coincidental" method, where persons called—again selected from phone directories—and were asked what they were listening to at the time of the call. The first Hooper ratings were monthly national reports. In 1940 he offered city reports in 16 markets for the first time and in 1942 his national surveys became semimonthly. The Hooper Ratings became a dominant force in the 1940s; in 1946 the Cooperative Analysis of Broadcasting and its Crossley ratings folded, and sold Hooper its subscribers.

The Pulse, Inc., founded in 1941 by Sydney Roslow and his wife Irma, provided competition for Hooper. Roslow, who had a Ph.D. in psychology, did research for the Psychological Corporation for a decade before setting up his own firm. The key to The Pulse system was its original method: home interviews, in person, with all members of the household available. The Pulse's start was modest; for the first three years it surveyed only New York City, with four local stations as clients. Then N. W. Ayer, the massive ad agency, signed on. In 1944 The Pulse added a second market, Philadelphia, and in 1946 Boston, Chicago, and Cincinnati. Hooper continued to survey more markets, while The Pulse did a deeper study within its markets. "We're not researching broadcasting," Roslow was fond of saying. "We're researching people...audience composition, the number of listening families with babies, how many of them own stocks and bonds, their reactions to TV and radio commercials, audience analysis in relation to ownership of autos and air conditioning, how many cigarette smokers in a listening family."

The radio industry and advertisers debated the merits of personal interviews versus phone interviews—personal interviews generally reported a higher rate of listenership; personal interviews were also a good deal more expensive than phone surveys. Both ratings were used by stations and advertising agencies and grew rapidly during the 1950s: In 1958 The Pulse covered more than 200 radio markets and Hooper about 175. In 1952 Hooper began offering the first surveys of car radio usage—almost laughable in their simplicity and lack of scientific method. In San Francisco, Hooper had college students and off-duty cops quiz drivers stopped at red lights about their listening habits.

But even as the industry grew dependent on The Pulse and Hooper, the complaints and questions about methodology and accuracy began. Telephone surveys that relied on phone books failed to measure accurately both the poor, many of whom did not have phones, and those with unlisted numbers. As many as 30 percent of America's phones may be unlisted. One radio consulting service, McGavren Guild of New York City, advised clients in 1979 that 47 percent of Los Angeles home telephones had unlisted numbers. Since most unlisted phones are in homes on the upper end of the demographic scale, surveys that rely on listings are not demographically balanced. The Pulse, which did not use phones, had other problems. Some critics complained that the responses of persons "trapped" in their living rooms by interviewers might be colored by impatience or a desire to please.

Another complaint against both services was that they failed to register accurately listening habits of minority groups. A disproportionate number of minority families had no phones, or lived in areas interviewers were inclined to avoid. Spanish-speaking homes were sometimes interviewed by people who spoke only English. The ratings services conceded the problems but still kept issuing ratings.

In 1964, Roslow spoke to radio executives in Los Angeles and admitted that he selected households on the basis that the Spanish-speaking population was 7 percent in Los Angeles, even though the 1960 census showed nearly 11 percent. The Pulse in its sampling also failed to distinguish between Spanish-speaking households, which are major consumers of Spanish-language radio, and households with Hispanic surnames where English is spoken, a common situation in Los Angeles.

Although the methodology and accuracy of the ratings services were increasingly criticized, agencies relied almost entirely on the ratings to make their time buys, and stations used them to sell advertising.

In March 1963 the government intervened: For two years a House

Special Subcommittee on Investigations, led by Owen Harris of Arkansas, who had chaired the payola hearings, heard witnesses from advertising agencies, radio stations, the networks, the rating services, and statistical experts both from the private sector and the Bureau of the Census. Most criticized the ratings. In 1965 the committee issued a report called *Broadcast Ratings: The Methodology, Accuracy and Use of Ratings in Broadcasting*. It was critical on all three counts. The committee found that in some instances ratings services were inept, with ill-designed, sloppily executed research. In other cases the services were accused of misrepresenting their findings. The committee found one case where a service estimated the nationwide audience for a show carried by 179 stations at 99,000, yet at the same time reported that 118,000 homes in a five-station area had tuned in that same show.

Even as the probe was going on, the broadcast industry began to police itself, forming the Broadcasting Rating Council, on January 8, 1964, to set minimum standards and to accredit ratings services. The National Advertising Bureau invested more than $300,000 in the All-Radio Methodology Study, which weighed the strengths and weaknesses of various methods and standardized terms and measures.

But if all this public airing and standardization was useful, it did not solve the problems. The hearings dramatized how much more difficult radio is to rate than television, for two reasons. In every market, there are far more radio stations available than television, and a good deal of radio listening is done out of the home. Tackling these problems with in-depth and accurate research takes an enormous amount of money. Ideal research would cost so much that stations would not support it.

During the mid-1960s another ratings firm began to share the spotlight: the American Research Bureau. ARB, founded in 1949 but overshadowed by Hooper and The Pulse for nearly 15 years, discovered a method that considerably reduced the cost of surveys: it provided listeners with diaries to fill out and mail back, eliminating interviews and phone bills. By the late 1960s Hooper's prominence was greatly reduced, and the firm merged with the Daniel Starch research organization, which specialized in print media research. In 1970 ARB was taken over by the Control Data Corporation, a computer firm, and soared to dominate radio ratings as thoroughly as Nielsens dominate television. The firm changed its name from American Research Bureau to Arbitron in 1973, claiming that too many people mistook it for a government agency. In 1970, ARB had 475 clients; by 1980 it had 1,400. The Pulse continued to be run by the Roslow family until it went out of business in 1978.

Arbitron, using its parent firm's computers, pioneered the use of sophisticated demographic data. It also understood well a lesson of the business: Although its costs were picked up mainly by the stations, the audience it had to please was the advertising agencies. Arbitron's findings came in neat, colorful printed books, and they arrived on time. The Pulse report was cranked out on mimeograph machines and often arrived late.

As Arbitron became dominant in the 1970s, it too received its share of complaints. The chief criticisms have been that Arbitron uses phone directories to pick homes to send diaries to, and that it does not measure accurately blacks, Hispanics, and also the key 18- to 24-year-old group. In response to the first complaint, Arbitron developed what they call the Expanded Sample Frame, or ESF, which uses computers to pick random phone numbers. Those numbers are checked against directories, and the listed ones are dropped, leaving a sampling of unlisted numbers. Arbitron offers ESF only in some markets and charges extra for the service.

The other problems are more controversial. Black and minority groups have often been critical of all ratings services, for radio and television. They argue that segments of the population are excluded from proportional representation by the services. Arbitron agrees there's a problem; it also knows its clients want the numbers. A major problem with these groups is that their rates-of-return of the diaries are lower than others. Arbitron has tried several alternatives. It pays a fee in these groups to keepers of diaries (ranging from 50¢ to $2 a week). It phones people and fills out the diary for them over the phone. Spanish-language diaries and bilingual interviewers have been added. Thus Arbitron uses a different methodology with these groups, but compares the findings anyway. The 18- to 24-year-old group is similarly underrepresented for the same reason: its members seem reluctant to fill out the diaries. Unlike minority groups, however, they're not complaining to Arbitron. They neither speak as a group nor do they seem to care whether their listening habits are accurately measured. But the stations that seek them do care. Station managers with progressive or album-oriented rock (AOR) formats say they suffer at Arbitron's hands.

Arbitron critics contend that its ratings hurt the different rock and ethnic formats, while aiding the middle-of-the-road, news, and talk formats, whose audiences are both older and more responsive to the diaries. The most common fear about Arbitron is that there's no major service to compare it with. But competition has emerged in recent years from other services:

—RAM Research uses a one-day, 24-hour diary. It is available in the Top 50 markets and 14 others, and offers weekly reports—but no weekly cumulative audiences.

—Media Statistics Inc., which publishes *Mediatrends,* a monthly report, and special reports called *Mediastats.* The service won some acclaim when its monthly reports were the first ratings service to take note of the phenomenal rise of the disco station WKTU, New York City, in 1978.

Stations and advertising agencies would probably be happiest if one of the emerging services challenged Arbitron's dominance. But the mortality rate is high. Two other services tried to enter the field in the late 1970s and failed: Burke Broadcast Research, founded in 1977, went out of business in 1980; Trac-7, set up in 1978 by Audits & Surveys, Inc., at the request of the Radio Advertising Bureau, folded the following year.

Market research and ratings may not seem glamorous, but make no mistake: they are at the heart of the radio industry. It is important to understand the measures these firms use. There are four basic ones:

—*average quarter hour:* the average number of persons listening to a station during a given 15 minutes.

—*"cume":* the cumulative audience; the estimated number of

persons who listen to a station for a minimum of five minutes within any given time period.

—*rating:* the average quarter-hour audience as a percentage of the market population for any given demographic, or, the percentage of the population a station is reaching.

—*share:* the average quarter-hour audience as a percentage of the market listening for any given demographic; or the percentage of the people listening to radio that a station is reaching.

That is only the beginning of radio research. It grows more and more sophisticated. Advertisers love, seek, and demand tight demographics, and radio has scampered to comply. Out of this market pressure new formats evolve, each seeking to deliver an audience that is easily definable. Once a station adopts a particular format, music, patter, advertising, and news will be tailored to fit together neatly.

Current formats include:

MOR (Middle-of-the-Road)

One of the paradoxes of the middle-of-the-road, or MOR, format is that although it's one of the most widely employed formats in radio, it's also one of the hardest to describe. The result is that the clearest explanations of what MOR *is* are descriptions of what it *is not*. It is "not too soft, not too loud, not too fast, not too slow, not too hard, not too lush, not too old, not too new," said *Broadcasting* magazine in 1972. Various station managers trying to describe it in positive terms sound either evasive, pompous, or foolish. To wit:

—"A modified top popular sound, supplemented with standards and sprinkled with humor."

—"Middle-of-the-road conservatism in music. . .and in general, just plain folksy talk to 'em instead of over their heads."

—"Directed to satisfy the intelligence of the listener, entertain and inform at as high a level as possible. . .I feel hollering, screaming and continuous raunchy music is tiring and nerve-wracking and an infringement upon one's intelligence."

—"The music is pop standard plus contemporary current releases in good taste with a lyrical beat."

An MOR format aims to please adults who don't like a steady diet of teenage music, classical music, or jazz, and who want to hear a blend of old favorites and current releases by favorite performers. But the music has changed in the last decade. As the rock audience of the 1950s and 1960s grew up, and became the over-30 crowd, it brought to adult formats a different taste in music. The MOR of the late 1950s and 1960s was laden with ballad singers and crooners like Sinatra, Andy Williams, Tony Bennett, Patti Page, and Peggy Lee. The Beatles were once synonomous with rock 'n' roll, but their ballads, like "Yesterday" and "And I Love Her," are often heard on MOR stations these days. The trick, most programmers agree, is to keep the music growing so that it catches up with the adults in their 30s and 40s. Some stations reject this approach, and will never add Lennon and McCartney to Bennett and Sinatra. But the majority constantly mix in contemporary music. This trend among radio stations has been accelerated as more performers record music that fits many formats. The Supremes, for example, were at first a hard-core "soul" group played only on Top 40 and rhythm 'n' blues stations. Now they sing in nightclubs and their ballads are MOR material. Carly Simon, James Taylor, Neil Diamond, and John Denver can be heard on Top 40 stations, and to some extent on progressive or AOR stations—but also on MOR stations.

The MOR format has developed a diversity that has led to a number of new terms for formats best listed under its umbrella. One is "adult contemporary." Adult contemporary stations are basically MOR, but slant their musical selections by stealing from Top 40 stations the less strident hits. Their prime demographic audience is the 25- to 35-year-olds and tired of the intensity of contemporary stations geared to teenagers. Another MOR spinoff is "soft rock," where again the key is seeking listeners weaned on rock 'n' roll, but tired of stridency and abrasive promotions. What sets adult contemporary and soft rock stations apart from conventional MOR is that they emphasize their music and seek audiences that want heavy doses of it. Traditional MOR has relied, always, on the personalities of its on-air staff. The most important of these is the morning deejay.

Most station managers agree that "as the morning goes, so goes the station." So the traditional MOR station has a pleasant morning deejay who plays pleasant music, keeps weather and traffic reports up to date, tells anecdotes, and delivers a fair amount of news as well. With variations, the pattern continues throughout the day.

If this sounds not so different from the Arthur Godfrey show or Martin Block show of the 1940s, it's because MOR radio is the best remnant on the air of the Golden Age. But by learning to adapt and update its musical selections (even if new names have to be invented for the format) MOR has ensured that it will remain not just on the air but among the most popular formats.

Black and other Ethnic Formats

Unlike many other formats, which target a specific age-and-income group—Top 40 going after teens; talk shows after adults—black radio is targeted by race alone. For 20 years, with few exceptions, it acted as though all blacks were the same, which is perhaps not surprising since most stations were white-owned. Black radio was thus a generalized format, offering music that appealed to different tastes, usually a mix of rhythm 'n' blues (later called "soul" music), gospel and jazz; news oriented toward blacks; ads that were thought to appeal to blacks, and announcers with exaggerated black accents or predilections for dialect.

The first all-black-programming station was WDIA, Memphis, which went on the air in early 1947. The same year WVON, Chicago (the call letters stood for "*V*oice *o*f the *N*egro") became the first black-owned station on the air. While black formats proliferated, black ownership did not. By 1958 it was estimated that between 50 and 60 radio stations offered black programming exclusively. By 1966 more than 100 stations had all-black formats and by 1978 approximately 250 stations. But as of 1979 only 76 stations were owned by blacks. (See Chapter 7.)

Black radio also was in the forefront of community service, providing announcements for social clubs, churches, charities, government programs for minorities, and so on. The late 1950s and

1960s produced little experimentation; black stations continued their general interest programming and worked aggressively at trying to attract more national advertising. By the early 1960s, some black listeners were drifting away from black stations to competing media. Some may have been bored with a predictable, unchanging sound. More blacks owned televisions. And more black music was played on white stations. With the civil rights movement and then the "black pride" movement, the stations flourished again. Market research was improving as well, and more retailers were seeking the expanding black market. Radio was by far the dominant black medium, and research showed that the average black listened to more radio than the average white, and was more brand conscious as well.

As black radio became less parochial and more filled with national advertisements, programmers sought to present their listeners with a more sophisticated, less stereotyped sound. Jive-talking deejays, commercials for jewelry and cars with "easy credit terms," and skin lighteners grew scarcer, although they did not disappear. Zenas Sears, who had been one of the first white deejays to play black music and later became vice president of WAOK, a black-oriented Atlanta station, captured the new spirit nicely when he told *The New York Times* in 1968, "Our men have to speak well. It's been clean up the language or get off the air in this city. No more y'all or other jive talk. Racial pride is a very important part of the business."

The new, sophisticated sound ("racial pride is good business") accurately reflected the times and the concerns of many blacks, and in the late 1960s black radio steadily made money. In 1968, FCC Commissioner Nicholas Johnson, never one to duck controversy, spoke to the National Association of Television and Radio Announcers, an organization of black professionals, and demanded more improvement in black radio. "Soul music is not enough," Johnson told the group, calling for black history through radio drama, more information, investigative pieces, editorials, and programming involving listeners.

More and more public service and community programming appeared. WWRL, New York City, introduced a talk show, "Tell It

Like It Is," with topics like "The Negro and the Draft," and "The Ghetto School Crisis." WLIB, New York, won a Peabody Award for its "Hot Line" show. WCHB, Detroit, helped find food and shelter for riot victims; KXLW, St. Louis, provided free spot advertisements to black merchants starting businesses.

In 1973 the first break came in black radio's tradition of aiming for a general audience. WBLS, New York, programmed by deejay Frankie Crocker, took to calling itself a "progressive black" station. It played no gospel, no traditional jazz, no old ballads. Instead it offered album selections of soul music, disco, and uptempo jazz by black artists. WBLS enjoyed phenomenal success, and at one point was the most widely listened to FM station in the country. As a result, its format was widely copied. KDAY, Los Angeles, which had been stumbling from format to format with no success, switched to a progressive black sound in 1974 and challenged the traditional black station, KGFJ, which had been doing well for nearly two decades. KDAY prospered. In many major markets, black stations began competing with different formats, aiming for different black audiences. One advertising executive exaggerated only slightly when he told clients, "There are Negro gourmets, Negro surfers, Negro garden lovers. These are the special markets within a general Negro market." By the late 1970s more and more black stations were turning away from tradition to modern demographic research; unfortunately they also carried less community service material to "tighten up" the format.

Formats similar in shape and problems to black radio are geared to other specific ethnic groups. Of the many groups in this pluralistic society, only Hispanics find radio stations programmed entirely in their native language. Other groups must settle for programming only during certain hours, and in many major markets (where immigrants tend to settle), some stations have historically carved out modest profits by dividing their operations into different language programs.

WGES, Chicago, offered 32 hours a week of programs in German, Italian, Polish, and other tongues until Gorden McLendon converted it to a rhythm 'n' blues station in 1962. WEVD, New York, offers programming in Yiddish, Hebrew, Italian, Greek, Portuguese, and German. The use of different languages—each of which is aimed at and attracts an entirely different audience—undoubtedly cuts into WEVD's ratings. But the station, whose call letters are the initials of the socialist activist Eugene V. Debs, is owned by *The Jewish Daily Forward,* a Yiddish newspaper, and has a commitment to community service that goes beyond profit. In 1979 the *Forward* sold its AM station to a group specializing in religious programming; the FM operation continues. Most foreign-language programming, unable to compete effectively for profits, is now found on noncommercial radio.

Spanish-language radio is the magnificent exception, drawing huge audiences and in some cases stunning profits in markets with heavy Hispanic populations. These include New York City, whose large Latin population is about 70 percent Puerto Rican; Miami and its massive Cuban community; and the Southwest and California communities where Chicanos represent a large segment of the population. The first all-Spanish radio station in the United States was KCOR, San Antonio, which went on the air in 1947. In Miami, Spanish-language stations have consistently been ranked number one or number two overall in the market, and English-language stations have sought ratings that cover the Miami-Fort Lauderdale area, rather than just Miami, in order to be able to pull a larger share.

Miami currently has five Spanish-language stations. (WFAB, the first in Miami, lost its license in 1975 for fraudulent billing practices.) The stations attempt to give Cubans living in the area a sense of identity and pride and a feeling of belonging. The stations flaunt their Cubanism: WQBA, the most successful, and the top-rated station overall in Miami, is pronounced—without the W, of course—CUBA. WRHC takes its call letters from *R*adio *H*avana *C*uba. WQBA, like WFAB before it, and two current competitors, WOCN and WRHC, have a general format for Cubans, like the traditional black station. They provide a mix of music, news, soap operas, community service, and advertising aimed at all Cubans. Two newer stations, WCMQ and WCMQ-FM, aim for a younger audience, especially in their music—again following the pattern of black stations.

In New York City, WADO has emerged as the leading Spanish station through an aggressive promotion and research campaign. Nelson Lavergne decided not to settle for local retailers, but to prove to national advertisers that his station could help them. He commissioned research at five supermarket chains, and extensively canvassed the small bodegas (groceries). He can demonstrate to national firms how many cases of a given product were sold at supermarkets and how many in bodegas. The bodegas, he proved, were doing more than $1 billion a year in retail sales. (There are more than 6,000 in New York City.) Lavergne's work helped the station up its sales from $1.7 million in 1972 to $2.8 million in 1977. But of course he has had to make an enormous investment in research costs to produce his own figures, instead of relying on the ratings services. And how many stations of any format are capable, or willing, to do that?

Top 40

The birth of Top 40 was told in Chapter 3, and it is fair to say that in structure and content it remains much the same as it was 20 years ago. Its success spawned imitators in other areas: rhythm 'n' blues stations copied Top 40, using a different list of hits, and many country and western stations did the same. (The trade papers provide charts of best-selling records in these areas.) Over the years Top 40 picked up a new name, "contemporary," that is used interchangeably. Other changes have involved little more than tinkering.

The most important came in 1965, when Bill Drake was hired to boost the ratings of KHJ, Los Angeles. Drake was extremely successful—KHJ rose to number one in the market—and he was hired as a consultant for all the RKO-owned stations. He eventually became a vice president of RKO, then quit to form a consulting and programming firm. Bill Drake has come to be known as "the man who cleaned up Top 40."

His ideas were refinements of the tight play list and frequent rotations, pushing for a complete elimination of clutter by limiting the number of station identifications and shortening them. He cut back on deejay chatter, and was a proponent of holding commercials to well below the 18-minute per hour maximum of the FCC: Ads on Drake-consulted stations never exceeded 14 minutes per hour. The net result was a Top 40 format the motto of which was "much more music."

Probably Drake's most notable reform was the concept of running two songs together, or having the song begin under the deejay's introduction, or as the news ended. This eliminated the problem of dead air. Drake's formats served as a model for many stations. But he was criticized for "depersonalizing radio," "turning it into a juke box," and "sterilizing rock 'n' roll." That was because he insisted that each station was more important than its deejays. Drake demanded that his air staff closely follow his rules, and he ran a tight ship.

That year also brought the first all-oldies format, at KWIZ, in Santa Ana, California. Oldies, which are top hits from previous years, had been played regularly on Top 40 stations since 1959 to spice up current hits. (Chuck Blore, a McLendon aide in Texas, claims to have introduced hourly oldies at KFWB, Los Angeles.) A keystone of Top 40 radio is that the music must sound familiar to listeners, and oldies fit right in. Programmers noticed that whenever they had call-in request shows, most listeners asked for old, not current, hits.

In the late 1960s, Top 40 started to lose listeners in a key demographic area: the 18- to 24-year-old males who were defecting to progressive rock stations to hear their favorite albums. (See Chapters 6 and 7 for an extensive discussion of progressive FM radio.) Top 40 stations panicked. The whole premise of Top 40—repeating the best-selling singles—seemed in danger, for album sales were beginning to dominate the recording industry. (By 1972, album sales were more than 86 percent of the retail record volume.) Many Top 40 programmers—including Drake—dabbled with the format and started to play album selections as well as hit singles; as a result, the stations started losing both younger *and* older listeners. By 1972 Top 40 stations had returned to basics and found their ratings on the rise. They showed new strength in an equally desirable demographic group, the 24- to 35-year-olds, and they began to add, increasingly, a variety of oldies to their playlists. The radio industry found that people who grew up on Top 40 in the 1950s and 1960s would stay with it and oldies helped them find the station familiar.

By the end of 1972, Top 40 had regained its hold. The format was top-ranked in six of the fifteen largest markets—New York, Dallas, Houston, Philadelphia, Seattle, and San Francisco—and second-ranked in seven of the others. But in the last few years Top 40 has been slipping slightly. New formats like adult contemporary, easy listening, and soft rock, all of which play some Top 40 material, have drained listeners in the 24-to-45 age groups. The disco boom has also put a crimp in Top 40.

Nowhere is this more apparent than in New York City, where WABC was tumbled from first place by FM disco rivals. It remains weak in the 18-to-24 listening group, which seems to prefer progressive and album oriented rock stations.) But Top 40 will undoubtedly remain a potent format, even if not the dominant one. Because it is so trendy, it will adapt to new musical taste. If disco remains popular, Top 40 will perhaps become predominantly disco. The foundation laid in place more than 25 years ago is still sound.

Disco

The question about this newest of radio formats is not whether disco has done well, but whether it will last. Some predict that the disco sound is a mere fad, like calypso, or more recently, Jamaican reggae. But a larger number of radio and music industry executives see disco as the second coming of rock 'n' roll, with all the attendant impact and durability.

In 1975 a number of stations, including KSFX, San Francisco, WKYS, Washington, WBLS, New York, and WGCI, Chicago—all FM stations—started to mix disco music into their programming and found their listeners liked it; ratings improved. But the detonator of the disco explosion came in 1978 with the release of the film *Saturday Night Fever*. The success of the film—and the enormous record sales of its soundtrack, well over 20 million copies—signaled a wide audience for disco music. Disco palaces flourished, more than 18,000 across the nation. One survey showed that nearly 45 million

Americans had been to a disco, and that more than 17 million attend regularly. Disco developed subsidiary industries: fashion, cosmetics, roller-skating gear. It became enthroned in our culture: some department stores began to substitute disco for Muzak in their elevators, and television stations and networks began to use disco music to get in and out of commercials during ballgames. One radio executive decided it was time to have more than a toe in the water.

Edward L. Cossman runs the nine radio stations that are owned by SJR Communications, a subsidiary of the San Juan Racing Association in Puerto Rico. In 1976 SJR bought two New York City stations, WHOM and WHOM-FM. The all-Spanish format at the AM station was retained, but the ethnic programming on FM (Greek, Hispanic, and East European blocks of music) was discarded for a soft rock format, and the call letters were changed to WKTU. By 1978 the station was showing a very modest profit. The staff was pleased with its progress; Cossman was not. Station employees said Cossman visited a disco one Wednesday night and was impressed by the upper middle class ambience and clientele. That Friday he ordered the station to switch to all-disco by Monday. One worker was sent to a record store to buy 100 albums, and on July 24, 1978, WKTU became the first all-disco station in the country.

The first tangible measure of the change was that nearly 80 percent of the advertisers canceled their spots, because they sensed that the new format would attract a dramatically different audience. (Soft rock is strongest among 18- to 35-year-old white women, while disco seems to draw a mix that is one-third black and one-fifth Hispanic.) But the format rolled along, picking up listeners. Some scoffed at the idea of a "disco station for whites." But the Fall 1978 ratings offered proof that Cossman was right. In the July/August ratings WKTU had earned a 1.4 share of the audience. In the October/November ratings by Arbitron WKTU earned an 11.3 share. It was one of the largest increases ever registered by a station in a rating period. It put WKTU, in just three months, into the number one spot in New York—and thereby, in the country.

There were several startling ramifications to this rise. First, it proved that FM was competitive with AM—some said it proved that AM was dying as a music medium. Second, it truly marked the end of a historic era in radio, because it knocked out of first place WABC, which had been the top-rated station in the country for 16 years. WKTU's rates rose from $60 for a 30-second spot to $300; the station had no trouble finding advertisers. The industry gaped; some questioned the ratings. Programmers everywhere waited to see what subsequent rating books showed.

More than a year later, WKTU and WBLS, the progressive black FM station that played a lot of disco, sat atop the rest of the New York stations. WABC had fallen out of the top five, and was dropping.

By the end of 1978, the ABC network had switched two of its owned stations, KSFX, San Francisco, and WDAI, Chicago, to all-disco. In Fort Lauderdale, WCKO-FM went all-disco; and WBOS, Boston, WCAU, Philadelphia, and WTWR, Detroit, (all FM) were nearly all-disco.

Disco radio has an unusual demographic reach. WKTU drew heavily among young blacks and Hispanics as well as among middle-class and upper-class whites. Among its most faithful fans were the black middle class and the emerging gay community.

There has been some question as to how long disco will last. Some radio analysts say three to five years. Others, including Cossman, note that rock 'n' roll was expected to be a fad as well, and predict long-range success.

Beautiful Music

Beautiful Music (sometimes called "Good Music") is a vague term that reveals little of the format's actual content. What "Beautiful Music" is, however, is not a matter of taste or debate, but a highly automated format that is quite successful in holding listeners for extremely long periods of time. Its content is lush, highly orches-trated, "sweet" arrangements of old standards, popular hits, show tunes, and semiclassical pieces. Beautiful Music is also called "wall-to-wall" music, and "musical wallpaper": It is intended to fill the environment unobtrusively. A variation of it is Muzak, the instrumentals often heard in elevators, supermarkets, and department stores.

The modern Beautiful Music format goes back to the 1940s, when several independent local stations programmed nothing but music, lush and tasteful, as an alternative to the news-drama-features-and-music mix on the networks. The best-known pioneers were WPAT, in Paterson, New Jersey, and KIXL, in Dallas. KIXL, owned and programmed by Lee Segall, emphasized charm and grace. Segall insisted that advertisements be low-key, and sought out soothing, charming male announcers, generally with deep voices. "It was the first station I'd ever run across that had snob appeal," said a competitor.

Gordon McLendon started the first "modern" Beautiful Music station in San Francisco, in 1959, changing the call letters from KROW to KABL, pronounced "cable," to conjure up the romanticism of the city's cable cars. To further set the mood in between beautiful musical selections, an announcer would say, "As the fog rolls in under the Golden Gate Bridge..." or "As sunlight shimmers across the bay...." Reflecting the low-key announcing and musical selections, McLendon wisely eschewed cash giveaways and other aggressive promotions; contests offered snob appeal, like winning one of the world's rare jewels to wear for a week. KABL rapidly soared in the ratings, and remains, 20 years later, one of San Francisco's top-ranked stations and a model for other Beautiful Music stations.

An amusing footnote to KABL's success was McLendon's attempt to copy it in Buffalo, New York. The call letters, WYSL, were pronounced "whistle." McLendon and his staff aimed for the same romantic effect: "The sunlight glinting off the Delaware Building..." and so on. But residents knew they didn't live in a romantic San Francisco East. McLendon soon dropped that element. But he remained committed to Beautiful Music, and when he abandoned all-news at XETRA, Tijuana, and WNUS, Chicago, (see Chapter 5), they played Beautiful Music, as did KOST, Los Angeles.

A big milestone in Beautiful Music came in 1965, with the blossoming of FM programming. FM's superior fidelity was a better conduit for Beautiful Music, and many stations turned to it. The true modernization of the format began about 1968, at the hands of Jim Schulke and his staff. Schulke, who had a background in television, started working in radio to capitalize on the FM boom he anticipated. In 1968 he founded Stereo Radio Productions, to provide tapes and advice to Beautiful Music stations. By 1970 he had made two stations number one in their markets—the first FM stations of any type to be rated number one—with WOOD, Grand Rapids, Michigan, and WEAT, West Palm Beach, Florida. Schulke's SRP has set the standard of excellence for this type of automated programming services.

Schulke and his peers provided the answer to a problem of Beautiful Music: how to keep down the cost. Studies have shown that people who turn to Beautiful Music stations use them as background music, unlike listeners to all-news or to radio call-in shows. They want the music on, but unobtrusively. This required as few commercial interruptions as possible. While many music and news stations ran up to 18 minutes of commercials an hour, Beautiful Music stations found they lost listeners if they ran more than ten minutes, and some ran as few as four-and-a-half. Automated programming provided the cost-cutting solution. No on-air personnel. No engineers to operate the turntable. With these costs eliminated, stations could run only four minutes an hour of ads and still make money.

Schulke and a leading competitor, Bonneville Broadcast Consultants—part of the Mormon Church's media empire—took the Beautiful Music programming to a more sophisticated level. They provided slightly more uptempo music during morning and afternoon rush hours, light and fluffy music for housewives during midday, and romantic music at night. Schulke emphasized uptempo music in the spring and summer, and romantic music in the fall and winter. He also polished McLendon's idea of long blocks of music, with commercials bunched together. Schulke is given credit for introducing the 15-minute block of music—though he says he copied it from WDBN, Cleveland—and the 55-minute hour of music. The methods worked: in 1975 Schulke had 60 station clients. Fifteen were rated first in their markets, 19 were second, 10 third, and 10 fourth. In 1979 Schulke sold 90 percent of SRP to Cox Communications for nearly $5 million.

In the last decade Beautiful Music stations pioneered an occasional "commercial-free hour." These promotions brought complaints from advertising industry groups, who suggested that commercial-free hours might make listeners think that something was wrong with commercials. Beautiful Music also has had other problems. Because the music is in the background, it might be inferred that listeners don't pay attention to commercials. The format has had particular trouble generating local advertising. It is also weak—often extremely weak—during the 6:00 to 9:00 AM slot, when listeners want more services. And precisely because the format is so effective as background, Beautiful Music stations have found they must press their call letters home through other means: billboards, print media ads, and advertisements on television.

Nevertheless, Beautiful Music can provide vigorous competition for MOR stations. It is extremely strong among women listeners in the 18- to-45 age group.

Country

Country music predates radio, of course, and has been a fixture on radio almost from the beginning. The "Grand Ole Opry" became a staple on WSM, Nashville, in 1925 and is still broadcast live each weekend—radio's longest running show. But the modern country format, playing hit country and western records and nothing else, did not emerge until the 1960s.

It came about in reaction to rock 'n' roll Top 40. As rock began to dominate the charts, stations that played Top 40 hits no longer played country music. Less country music was on the air in the late 1950s than in the previous 25 years. Country music had gained national exposure through the powerful all-night stations in the 1920s, and through the popularity of the singing cowboy movies of Ken

Maynard, Gene Autry, and Roy Rogers in the 1930s and 1940s. During the mobilization for World War II, many Northerners were trained in the South and heard country music for the first time. By the late 1940s, varieties of country music—sometimes folk music with a country accent, sometimes ballads with a country and western or cowboy flavor, like Vaughn Monroe's "Riders in the Sky" became popular. Then, during the 1950s, the music took a back seat to rock 'n' roll.

By the early 1960s many stations were casting about for an alternative to Top 40 rock or MOR ballads. They turned to Nashville, capital of the country music recording industry. These stations found that what made Top 40 work—snappy deejays, repetition of hit songs, and high-powered promotions—gave country music stations a competitive sound. Local advertising jumped right in, seeking adult audiences that Top 40 wasn't reaching. National advertising took a bit longer because the advertising agencies seemingly stereotyped country music fans as people who didn't wear shoes, had no bank accounts or credit ratings, and operated illegal distilleries. It took several years of diligent promotion and sales work by stations to change the agencies' minds. Country stations pulled substantial audiences, and eventually the national advertisers came around because country radio was not only drawing fans in rural audiences but in major markets as well.

In the 1970s the line between country music and pop music blurred. Many performers seemed to "cross over" and record music suitable for Top 40 *or* country stations. In 1974 the Country Music Association named Olivia Newton-John, the Australian pop singer, Country Entertainer of the Year. Many old-time country artists— who were not producing hit singles, and hence not getting air play— lobbied against the tight play lists of country stations and against the Country Music Association. But the CMA ignored them, and the stations, with their improved ratings, kept to the tight play lists.

Country formats added to the music straightforward news report- ing and a heavy emphasis on weather reports, presumably to aid the farmers and truckers among their listeners. Country stations put together a solid demographic audience of 25- to 45-year-old men and women, and have laid aside the barefoot-in-overalls image. By the mid-1970s more than a thousand stations described their format as country.

Talk

Talk radio comes in many forms. The oldest type involves talk *in the studio,* among one or more hosts, sometimes with guests. They tell stories, read poetry, bait one another, laugh at each other's jokes, and add personal commentary to stories in the news. This programming is usually strongest in the morning: many stations have found it an effective way to provide several hours of service—news, weather, traffic—in a conversational, pleasant, low-key manner. Few stations do this around the clock; the notable exception being WOR, New York, which decade after decade sticks with an almost pure talk format and stays near the top of the ratings.

During the 1950s a variety of other talk programming emerged, each using the telephone. These fell into three broad categories: interviews with notable guests, where callers were often able to join in the questioning; advice shows, with experts answering listeners' questions; and wide-ranging call-in shows where listeners could talk about whatever was on their minds.

All of this is talk *programming;* the talk *format* means a radio station is devoting the vast majority of its programming to different types of talk shows. A station typically might have a midnight-to-dawn call-up-and-chat show, followed by a 6:00 to 9:00 AM news-and-information block, followed by a 10:00 AM to 1:00 PM housewives' corner, interviews with public officials from 1:00 to 3:00 PM, another advice-show from 3:00 to 4:00, a news block from 4:00 to 6:00, and then an evening call-in show of lively discussion and debate on issues in the news.

Telephone call-in shows (also dubbed telephone radio, open-mike radio, open-forum radio, dialogue radio, talk-in radio, talk-out radio, and back-talk radio) became popular in the 1950s, as the sound quality of telephone lines improved. As early as the 1930s, deejay

John J. Anthoney invited listeners to call in, but instead of going live with the call he paraphrased their comments. In the mid-1950s Todd Storz added a call-in show to WHB, Kansas City, while KDKA, Pittsburgh, featured Ed and Wendy King on "Party Line" in the late evening. More talk shows came on the air in the early 1960s, seeking adult audiences.

In 1966 KABC, Los Angeles, went to a 24-hour talk format, then KLAC, Los Angeles, switched to a 24-hour call-in format. When the stations' advertising took a jump, a few stations were inspired to switch to all-talk, and many more added additional talk shows. In 1973 *Broadcasting* estimated that "no more than 20 stations have scrapped their record libraries" for all-talk.

From a programming point of view, talk formats offer several advantages:

—They build strong and immediate links to the community by providing a forum for local issues. Talk-show hosts are popular guests at civic functions. . . and are often considered more respectable than disc jockeys.

—It is easy for talk-show stations to demonstrate their public service commitment, because they often allow the listeners to set the agenda for discussion.

—The format generally attracts adults; its target audience is 35 and up (a problem with talk audiences, from sponsors' point of view, is that they can be "too old," with little disposable income).

—The format stands out dramatically among music formats in crowded markets.

—Well-done shows with professional hosts attract loyal listening audiences (but another major problem of call-in shows is repeat callers—who do nothing day after day except sit around and call the host).

—It delivers a *foreground* audience: that is, an audience that definitely wants to listen, to concentrate on the radio rather than keep it in the background. CBS, which heavily committed its AM stations to talk programming in the 1960s, contended that radio advertisers would be justified in spending up to twice as much, on a cost-per-thousand basis, for a talk station's audience as for some music stations' audiences. The network later decided that all-news would be even more profitable, and converted six of its stations to that format. (See Chapter 5 for a discussion of all-news radio.)

—Some broadcasters insist that talk-format advertising has more credibility with listeners.

Talk formats also have disadvantages. In addition to audiences that are "too old" and repeat callers, the leading problems are:

—It is an expensive format, far more so than music. Talk formats require a large staff (often with a producer for each host) and incur enormous costs in phone lines and tape equipment.

—On-air controversy helps build audiences, but many advertisers are reluctant to sponsor controversial shows.

—The format relies on untrained participants—its listeners—who can be boring.

—Legal and ethical problems can arise despite the use of a delay device that tapes calls and broadcasts them 7 to 30 seconds later, thus giving the host a chance to bleep out or erase obscenities, slander, or matters of poor taste.

During the late 1960s, call-in shows of all types generated a lot of excitement in the industry. They were heralded frequently as "the best thing to happen to radio since records." Controversy erupted in the early 1970s over what was called "sex radio" or "topless radio." The pioneer in this field was Bill Ballance of KGBS, Los Angeles, a station owned by Storer Broadcasting. In early 1971 he began a 10:00 AM to 3:00 PM show called "Feminine Forum," the goal of which, he said, was to discuss with callers "the male/female relationship." Ballance admitted to being a flirt, a provocateur, and a sexist. He titillated listeners with comments like: "Meet me in the rose garden, my dear, and I'll pluck the aphids off your buds." And his listeners turned one another on with their "true confessions" and sexual problems.

Controversial incidents included a mother-in-law who described how, after her daughter complained of her new husband's clumsy technique, she took the young man into her bed to teach him the tricks. The next day the daughter called to tell Ballance she was upset, and so was her father, who'd heard the broadcast at work. But the station rose from number 16 to number one during his time slot. The show spawned imitators left and right, and sex radio took off. Ballance's "Feminine Forum" was syndicated into 30 markets, but complaints of obscenity and suggestiveness continued to grow.

At first, the FCC seemed reluctant to get involved since it had no power over program content. But finally, on March 28, 1973, FCC Chairman Dean Burch, addressing the NAB, denounced "topless radio" as prurient trash and described it as a "new breed of air pollution...with the suggestive, coaxing, pear-shaped tones of the smut-hustling host." As a consequence, he said, the FCC was opening an inquiry into prurience and obscenity on the airwaves.

Stations got the message rather quickly. The next day "Feminine Forum" was renamed "The Bill Ballance Show," the host stopped flirting and using terms of endearment with callers and the announced topic for the day was "How are you living with the meat boycott?" Other sex talk shows followed the leader, and within weeks sex talk on the radio was rare. Just to keep the heat on, less than two weeks after Burch's speech, the FCC fined an Illinois radio station, WGLD, Oak Park, $2,000 for broadcasting indecent material.

An interesting footnote to the sex talk programs: Burch said the FCC had received more than 3,000 complaints against such programming but attorneys for the Storer Broadcasting Company, in searching FCC files, found only 20 complaints about Ballance.

But talk radio, and call-in radio, survived without sex. The advantages and the problems of the format remain. So does the excitement: When the CBS network hosted President Carter's first call-in show on March 5, 1977, more than nine million people tried to call (although only 42 got through). And in polls, an overwhelming majority said they liked the show.

Classical/Jazz
For all their inspiration and brilliance as musical forms, classical music and jazz have fallen on hard times in radio: At last count there

were just over a dozen full-time classical stations in the country and perhaps half as many all-jazz. Many others, especially noncommercial stations, offer substantial programming of each or both, but the figures are nonetheless depressing.

Classical music has a long, dramatic history on radio. Early demonstrations of radio's potential—more than a decade before commercial braodcasting began—featured classical music or operatic singing, such as Enrico Caruso from the Metropolitan Opera House in New York City in 1910. Live symphony concerts were common fare on the networks in the 1930s, and in 1937 NBC formed its own symphony, led by Arturo Toscanini. When Columbia Records developed the long-playing, 33-1/3 rpm record in 1948, radio's ability to play recorded classical music was greatly enhanced. Classical stations were a chief beneficiary of the development of FM radio, with its superior sound.

But the classical format has been a victim of the increasing competitiveness of radio stations vying for the advertising dollar. By its very nature classical music is hard to mesh with advertising. Since there are no "singles," and few short pieces, stations have a choice of interrupting longer pieces for ads—unthinkable to music lovers—or running long blocks of commercials between pieces.

Perhaps the most interesting characteristic of classical formats is the fervor they arouse in fans when a station attempts to change away from them. In Atlanta, Syracuse, Washington, New York, Hartford, and other cities, irate listeners have gone to the stations, the FCC, and the courts to fight a change in format. Sometimes they have won remarkable victories.

In Chicago in 1977, General Cinema Corporation, which owned WEFM and sought to change its programming from classical to popular music, negotiated an agreement with a listeners' group. It would pay WBEZ, a noncommercial station in town, $40,000 a year to help provide classical music in the Chicago area. General Cinema also agreed to give WBEZ $100,000 for a new transmitter and a record library, and donated its own classical record library to WNIB-FM, another local station.

In New York in 1975, the Starr Broadcasting Group bought WNCN, a classical station, and converted it to rock 'n' roll. More than 105,000 listeners petitioned the FCC, which declined to hold a hearing. But the protest caught the ear of the GAF Corp., which bought the station from Starr for $2.2 million, invested $1 million in improved facilities and restored the classical format, which remains today. Star contended it had been losing $300,000 a year, but GAF put WNCN modestly into the black in two years.

Meanwhile, the FCC had been taken to court over its refusal to hold a hearing on the possible loss of a classical format. Among the complainants were the WNCN Listeners Guild, a group called Classical Radio for Connecticut, and the Office of Communication of the United Church of Christ; they won. In June 1979, the U.S. Court of Appeals ordered the FCC to hold full hearings when a "unique" format was threatened and if listeners complained. The FCC was unhappy with the decision and contended it would need to open an "office of music appreciation" against its will. It filed an appeal with the U.S. Supreme Court that as of this writing has not been resolved.

Jazz formats face many similar problems in attracting and holding a large enough audience to remain profitable. Jazz programming—rather than formats—has a long history on radio. During the 1930s and 1940s, live concerts were standard fare on networks and on some large local stations. During the 1950s and 1960s, many stations continued to play some jazz. A 1964 survey showed that jazz received a fair amount of air play, especially in the 50 largest markets, where about one-third of all stations played jazz about 15 percent of the time. About the same time, KNOB-FM, in Long Beach, California, proclaimed itself "the world's first all-jazz station."

With the flowering of frequency modulation in 1965, most jazz shifted to FM, which was much more compatible with its sophisticated sound. As play lists grew tighter, jazz seemed to disappear from MOR stations. It remains a vital force in American music and enjoys a reasonable amount of radio air play. Its home now is generally the noncommercial stations that do not have to worry about interrupting long compositions for commercial breaks.

It is unlikely that the number of all-jazz stations will increase beyond the handful in larger markets.

Religious

Religious broadcasting dates back to the 1920s. But in the last decade it has been perhaps the fastest growing format. Current estimates are that *each week* another radio station switches over to a religious format. (About one television station a month is converting to religious broadcasting.) This revolution has been called the Electronic Church. But it is important to distinguish among the different types of religious broadcasting.

Since the 1920s, some churches have owned radio stations. These are nonprofit and noncommercial and are funded by the religious bodies that own them, often aided by listener contributions. Other stations carry religious programming provided by churches. This programming includes sermons, talk shows, advice-to-the-troubled, and so forth. Additional religious programming comes from entrepreneurial evangelists, some of whom make millions of dollars through contributions and sales of religious articles like Bibles, "holy water," and prayer cloths. What has been most notable about religious broadcasting in the last decade is the rise of commercial stations that have switched to the religious format as a way to make money. Religion has proved to be good business, as well as God's business.

Among the earliest religious stations were KFSG, in Los Angeles, founded by the evangelist Aimee Semple McPherson in February 1924; KFUO, in Clayton, Missouri, which went on the air December 14, 1924, owned and operated by the Lutheran Church-Missouri Synod; and KPPC, Pasadena, California, which began broadcasting on Christmas Day 1924 under the direction of Dr. Robert Freeman of the Pasadena Presbyterian Church. Another pioneer was the Moody Bible Institute of Chicago, which put WMBI on the air in 1926. These early stations carried sermons and services, but little else.

This religious programming showed that it could learn the lessons that all of radio was learning in those days: to acquire other functions. By the end of the decade WMBI was offering a "Radio School of the

Bible," and as radio dramas became popular on commercial stations, religious stations began to offer religious dramas, usually stories from the Bible. But religious programming ran into a hurdle in the late 1930s when the FCC decided that stations serving "special interest groups"—and it lumped churches in with labor unions and others— were not in the public interest. The FCC said it would no longer license church stations; churches interested in broadcasting turned their attention to getting religious material on the networks. The Federal Council of Churches sought network time for its members and the National Religious Broadcasters was organized in 1944. The networks were agreeable and Sunday sermons by distinguished preachers became standard fare.

After World War II the FCC agreed to license religious groups within the newly available noncommercial FM band. These organizations also began to provide more program material to the networks and to local stations, seeking to escape from the Sunday-for-sermons pigeonhole. The Lutheran Church of America offered news and interview programs to talk stations. The Baptist Radio and Television Commission provided a blend of music and interviews to MOR stations. The programs were well received by broadcasters, who were happy to have free programming that satisfied public service requirements. Ultimately religious programming was tailored to every format; perhaps the most radical example was the God Squad, a rapid-fire blend of moral messages and rock 'n' roll for Top 40 stations.

Two developments in the 1960s paved the way for the proliferation of religious stations. One was the enormous increase in stations on the air that followed the opening of the FM spectrum. The other was the veritable explosion of religious music that burst out of Nashville. Songwriters and musicians began to set religious lyrics to a wide variety of popular music, including folk, country and western, MOR, and rock 'n' roll. The music proved popular and record sales were substantial. It became clear that radio stations could flourish by playing this new music. The religion format established a firm commercial base.

There are different types with different music; they include contemporary Christian, Jesus rock, Southern gospel, spiritual, and MOR religious. Stations generally stick with one type of music, based on the demographic audience it attracts. A typical conversion took place in Los Angeles, where KBRT went from a conventional MOR format to "contemporary/inspirational," trying not to save lives or sell religion, but to reach a section of the community. Many other stations followed suit, particularly in markets crowded with more than a dozen music stations. Religion broke through as a successful format: In 1974 there were 118 stations with a religious format; by 1977 there were 415; In 1979 there were more than 1,100. Most of the stations provided news, weather, and sports in addition to religious programming. Some of them provided straightforward news; others introduced the news by saying: "Here's the news of today, and the promise of tomorrow," or followed it with, "the news that never changes, the Word of God." There were religion-oriented promotions and giveaways. Listeners seemed to like it and the format became entrenched.

Radio station owners obviously have many programming options to choose from. Successful stations rarely change formats, but unsuccessful operations will change and change and change again, hunting for that segment of the audience they can effectively deliver to the advertiser. These changes can have a wrenching impact on tens of thousands of listeners and a sharper impact still on station employees. It's certainly no fun to get up in the morning and turn on your favorite station and find unfamiliar programming, different personalities, and an ambience you may not care for; most listeners will twirl the dial and not come back. It's less fun to pick up your paycheck at a station and find a pink slip inside.

While automated stations need to change only their tapes to get a new format, the majority of stations, in making a switch, will seek new on-air personnel whose personalities better suit the new format. Just how jarring this can be may be seen in this report one radio consultant filed with a station on how well its old personnel fit its new format. (The names are omitted because the report was confidential.):

—" _____ too hip, needs to communicate with common man. Very talented. Needs direction, discipline. Keep."

—" _____ unexciting, bland. Only for weekend and utility."

—" _____ old school, much talent, mature. Likes old sounds. If he'll learn, will be an asset. If desirous, needs chance."

—" _____ bright, happy, young, appealing. Great potential. Needs training."

—" _____ happy, cornball, old audience gone, will never come back. Meaningless today. Terminate."

5

RADIO NEWS

An announcer was getting ready to go on the air with the 1:00 o'clock news one weekday afternoon in 1954 when his secretary rushed into the office. As she was returning from lunch a truck had crashed into a crowd of window shoppers outside the studio. The announcer suggested to the news director that he go outside and do a firsthand report on the air.

"What for?" said his boss. "We'll get it from the wire services."

FOR all the prominence Walter Cronkite and his colleagues in television news have achieved, radio remains the medium by which most Americans first hear the news. Radio's role in delivering information in crises—blackouts, storm alerts, rioting—is well-known. Surveys and studies have measured its speed and penetration in delivering urgent news:

—During the nuclear-reactor incident at Three Mile Island in Pennsylvania in March 1979, 56 percent of the local residents said they first learned the news by radio. Twenty-three percent said they heard about it from friends or family, and 14 percent from television.

—When Senator Robert F. Kennedy was shot on June 4, 1968, 56.5 percent of Americans learned of it from the radio; 20 percent from television; 6 percent from newspapers.

—When George Wallace was shot on May 16, 1972, radio beat TV as a news source by a four-to-one margin.

—During the great Northeast Blackout of 1965, radio was the sole news source in the affected areas for many hours. Outside the Northeast, a majority of Americans also heard the news first on their radios, among them President Lyndon B. Johnson, in a car on his Texas ranch.

Even on the calmest day, radio is the first news source for most Americans. As people get out of bed to the radio and eat breakfast with it on, they hear news of the world, the nation, the state, and the region. . . as well as the weather and traffic conditions that await them ouside their front doors. All day long, especially during commuting hours, radio remains the primary news source. Only in the evening does radio take a back seat, as people turn to television newscasts and newspapers: recent studies have found that Americans say they *rely* more on television news.

Radio news is nearly as old as radio itself, but only in the last 20 years have technology and a commitment to local reporting made it imaginative and substantial. In radio's infancy, when voice transmission was still experimental and signals were exchanged in Morse code, the first news of the Titanic disaster to reach the United States came by a radio signal from a ship at sea. Another milestone was when KDKA, Pittsburgh, inaugurated its service on November 2, 1920, by broadcasting the presidential election results. It was the first of a fledgling industry's many memorable newscasts. By the 1930s radio correspondents were filing live reports from the field. A breakthrough came on May 6, 1937, when Herbert Morrison, an announcer for WLS, Chicago, was in Lakehurst, New Jersey, to record the arrival of the German dirigible *Hindenburg*. Morrison was not equipped to broadcast live; he was on assignment to gather an item for his station's library of recordings, and he was hoping to demonstrate the practicality of making recordings in the field. When the *Hindenburg* burst into flames while docking, the blast actually jarred the needle off the record, momentarily interrupting the recording. His engineer put the needle back on the disc, and Morrison resumed his report. Hours later it was broadcast on the NBC Blue network, the first time a radio network used recorded material.

Radio news was weakened during the 1930s by a long, drawn-out battle with newspaper owners, "The Press-Radio War," as papers sought to impede broadcast news coverage. But two dramatic developments at the beginning of World War II established the preeminence of radio news. One was the on-the-spot coverage of the war in Europe, broadcast live to the U.S. networks by short-wave radio. The most famous were Edward R. Murrow's reports from London, including:

> I'm standing on a rooftop looking out over London... off to my left, far away in the distance, I can see just that faint red, angry snap of anti-aircraft bursts against the steel blue sky, but the guns are so far away that it's impossible to hear them from this

location...I think probably in a minute we shall have the sound
of the guns in the immediate vicinity....You'll hear two
explosions. There they are!

That was in September 1940. The other came 15 months later: the
Japanese struck at Pearl Harbor. Radio not only was first with the
news, it had the only news. It was midday on the West Coast and late
afternoon on the East Coast. There were no Sunday afternoon
newspapers, so from the time the bulletin went on the air until
Monday morning, the only source of news was radio. Americans
stayed with the broadcast throughout the evening and tuned in the
next day to hear President Roosevelt ask Congress to declare war in
his famous "day of infamy" speech.

Radio's impressive track record in *delivering* the news was marred
by its skills at *reporting* the news. Telephone technology did not yet
produce sound quality suitable for broadcast. The networks
experimented with field correspondents using short-wave radio.
Some carried transmitters strapped to their backs, in a square pack
similar to a World War I infantryman's. During the 1937 Easter
Parade on New York's Fifth Avenue, CBS sent Robert Trout out to
report in top hat and tails, with a transmitter in his hat! But short-
wave presented problems: It was full of static and could not penetrate
buildings. Radio news had a greater problem still: until after World
War II, tape recorders were nonexistent.

The first recording device was the wire recorder, developed in 1898
by Valdemar Poulsen, a Dane. It recorded telephone conversations
on a piece of stainless steel wire—like piano wire—with a magnetic
coating. Its capacity was about one minute of speech. The system
was refined, but not dramatically, over the next 45 years. Only when
the Allies liberated Berlin did they discover that scientists working for
the Nazi government had perfected a tape recorder, a machine that
substituted a tape of paper, coated with a magnetic layer, for the wire.
Its sound quality was better, it was easier to handle, and it could
record a far greater amount of information.

In 1947 the first American tape recorders, modeled on the
Germans' magnetophones, were introduced by Ampex. The 3M

Manufacturing Corp. soon developed the magnetic ribbon, a forerunner of today's tape. One of the earliest uses of the tape recorder in American radio was at ABC, where Bing Crosby convinced the network to purchase twelve from Ampex to record and play back his programs. But these tape recorders were massive machines, larger than most home refrigerators. They did little for in-the-field reporting. The breakthrough, as with the portable radio, came with the development of the transistor. By the mid-1950s much smaller recorders were available: they weighed between 12 and 20 pounds and could be carried over the shoulder on a sturdy strap.

With these recorders, stations could now equip newsmen who interviewed newsmakers and taped reports on the scene for later use. To the networks, which were trying to cover the whole world for their affiliates, the recorder was a boon they were quick to capitalize on. International events or interviews with European leaders, for instance, rarely came at a time when they might be easily broadcast live.

Local stations were reluctant to send out reporters. Instead, they simply used announcers to read stories prepared by staff writers. Some stories came from the news services; others were stolen from local newspapers. Still another device that both supplemented a station's coverage and served as an effective promotion was paying listeners for "news tips." WCKY, Cincinnati, was one of the stations to use news tips. Starting in 1947, Todd Storz picked it up at KOWH, Omaha, in 1949, but the ploy was still sufficiently new in 1957 for *Broadcasting* magazine to devote a large story to the use of news tips by WWDC, in Washington, D.C.

An early pioneer in local news coverage was Gordon McLendon. He put newsmen in the field, and with his usual promotional flair, equipped them with bright-red trucks containing short-wave radios. The KLIF, Dallas, truck gave the station a visible presence around town. Since many stations watched and imitated McLendon, news trucks, news vans, and news cruisers became the rage, especially in the Midwest. But McLendon's innovations were slow to catch on in the big cities. One reason was union contracts, which, in some major markets, required that any time a reporter went out with a tape recorder, he had to be accompanied by a recording engineer. The expense precluded most field reporting. Big cities also had problems with short-wave reception. But mostly, stations did little local reporting simply because they didn't think it necessary.

News operations were fleshed out in 1954 when United Press International began to offer an audio service. UPI began with regional feeds, and by 1958 offered a national service, useful for independent stations uninterested in network affiliation. UPI got into the field early, beating its archrival, the Associated Press, by nearly two decades. In time UPI signed up more than 1,000 stations. It currently charges from $65 to $500 weekly, depending on the size of the market, and now provides 22 daily newscasts of four-and-one-half minutes each, plus six extended sports reports. UPI Audio also provides about 100 news and feature stories a week on feeds local stations can record. The Associated Press operation, known as APRadio, began in October 1974, with about 230 subscribers; it now has more than 500. APR's rates are similar to UPI's, and so are its services.

In the late 1950s, some big city stations took a cue from smaller stations and began to do extensive field reporting. New York City, oddly enough, was one of the last holdouts. It was nearly the end of the decade before radio news reporters hit the streets regularly. But if it had been a long time coming, local news reporting blossomed in the 1960s. It was abetted by improved equipment: superior telephone lines over which news reporters could play back tapes to the station, and cassette recorders that were easier to handle and cheaper to buy. Stations stocked up on equipment and began to compete in news coverage. But not all stations. Some insisted—and still do today— that they can adequately cover their area with one news reporter, working by telephone with a tape recorder.

To an industry convinced that music, whether live or recorded, was a vital part of radio, the notion of a station that presented listeners nothing but news seemed ludicrous. But many newsmen thought it was an idea waiting to happen. All it would take, they said, was a bold station manager and some good reporters.

A forerunner of such radical programming was WAVZ, New Haven, Connecticut, which two former newspapermen, Victor Knauth and Daniel Kops, bought in 1949. Their plan was to turn the music format into a "newspaper of the air." Their competition came from two New Haven newspapers recently acquired by a single owner. WAVZ, a 1000-watt, daytime-only station, hired eight reporters and a city editor. The reporters used wire recorders to bring listeners on-the-scene reports. Knauth and Kops divided the programming into segments of hard news, society, drama reviews, book news, and editorials. They did, however, retain some disc jockey shows. WAVZ won a DuPont award and a Sigma Delta Chi award in 1951 for its local reporting, and ten years later a second DuPont award for its editorials. It helped pave the way for all-news radio.

In 1960 L. Ray Rhodes and J. Gil Paltridge converted KFAX, San Francisco, to what they called "America's first all-news station." KFAX based its programming on the hour, which began with a 25-minute newscast. On the half-hour a 15-minute newscast reviewed the day's top stories and looked at one story in depth. The gaps between newscasts were filled with commentary and news analysis, business and financial reports, sports, and newsfeatures that included science, cooking, religion, and brief panel discussions.

KFAX attracted listeners and local sponsors, but not national advertisers. Madison Avenue agencies refused to buy time on KFAX until it was one of the top five stations in the Bay Area. They were interested in reaching mass audiences, not in subsidizing experimental formats. KFAX never made the top five, and after seven months, with a loss of the owners put at $250,000, KFAX switched to a music format. (In 1959 KLIQ, Portland, Oregon, announced it would become "the world's first all-news radio station," according to a report at the time in *Sponsor* magazine. But a search of the KLIQ file at the Federal Communications Commission indicated the station never fulfilled the promise of its press release.)

The first commercially successful all-news operation went on the air on May 6, 1961. Its call letters were XETRA (pronounced "X-

TRA") and it was based in Tijuana, Mexico, although it did not seek a Tijuana audience. XETRA, a powerful 50,000-watter, aimed at the large audiences of Southern California, and particularly at greater Los Angeles. It was operated by Gordon McLendon.

Before XETRA went on the air, the station was known as XEAK and played rock 'n' roll, but McLendon changed it when he signed a contract to sell air time for the station, and was asked by the owners to recommend programming that would be competitive in the Southern California market. Since there was a glut of various formats he decided to try a station to which one could tune 24 hours a day and get nothing but the latest news.

McLendon's XETRA presented only hard news, and skipped the various features and editorials that KFAX had tried (and which are common on current all-news stations). What he had in mind was more of a headline service than in-depth coverage. XETRA began a new newscast every seven and one-half minutes. McLendon constantly tinkered with his format, and eventually stretched the rotation to 15 minutes, and then to a half-hour, as he discovered that most greater Los Angeles residents spent more than a half-hour commuting to work.

McLendon went to great lengths to disguise XETRA's Tijuana base of operations and to pass it off as a local Los Angeles station. On the air XETRA's jingles would say, "The world's first and only all-news radio station. In the air everywhere over Los Angeles." or "at 690 on your Los Angeles radio dial." The only address ever announced was the Los Angeles sales office. The station was required by law to give its call letters and location every hour. McLendon handled this by having them done in Spanish in a soft, feminine voice, backed by Mexican music and followed by a description in English of Mexico's tourist attractions. It was all too easy for listeners to assume that they were hearing an ad for Mexico rather than the call letters of a Mexican station.

Competitors for the Los Angeles audience fired off complaints to the FCC, calling McLendon's operation "camouflage" and contending that it was certainly unethical, if not illegal. If McLendon weren't stopped, they feared, other Mexican stations would jump in and divert more advertising dollars away from American broadcasters. The FCC took no action, and McLendon simply ignored his critics. He had the zeal, and the patience to take a loss until the format caught on; many advertisers held off in the first year until ratings proved XETRA was drawing a substantial audience. But McLendon had a national reputation and promotional skills: Madison Avenue knew his track record. Even in XETRA's first months on the air it received advertising from national sponsors like L&M and Alpine cigarettes, Western Airlines, and several breweries.

By its second year XETRA was turning a profit, helped by the fact that it employed no reporters. XETRA relied for its news on AP and UPI wires, and on a clipping bureau from which it borrowed the news stories of major American newspapers. Shortly after it went on the air, XETRA subscribed to the Los Angeles City News Service, a local wire service that reported on city affairs in depth. The short newscasts and limited number of stories covered meant McLendon could get by without reporters. The station used twelve announcers, who rewrote the wires and read them. For variety, they rotated every 15 minutes. Always audible in the background was the tick-tick-tick of wire-service teletype machines; whatever its shortcomings, XETRA sounded like a news operation.

XETRA's success provided a solution to McLendon's problem with his Chicago station. He had acquired WGES in 1962 and promised, in his application to the FCC, to retain its 32 hours a week of programming in German, Italian, Polish, and other foreign languages. Five days after his license was approved, McLendon changed the call letters to WYNR and switched to rhythm 'n' blues music. Once again the FCC was deluged with complaints, and this time the commissioners paid heed. One of the critics was Chicago Congressman Roman Pucinski, part of the powerful Daley machine, who demanded that McLendon's license be revoked. (Pucinski's mother was one of the canceled Polish broadcasters.) The FCC inquiry lasted nearly two years and was still under way when in 1964 McLendon announced the transformation of the station to WNUS (pronounced "W-news"). It became the first successful all-news operation based in the United States.

With an eye on the FCC, McLendon told the press, "Scores of prominent civic leaders indicated a desire for more news broadcasts. When asked whether they felt an all-news radio station would serve the community well, they were overwhelmingly enthusiastic." The FCC decided not to open a formal hearing, and McLendon retained his license.

WNUS was modeled on XETRA. It started with a 15-minute rotating newscast, eventually shifting to 20 minutes, then a half-hour. McLendon continued to insist on hard news only, and he continued to rely on wire services rather than reporters for his news. From his Dallas operation he copied the "news van"; he had three, each with a "telesign" that displayed news on the roof in lights as the vans drove around town. They were intended as much for promotion as for reporting.

Other innovations at WNUS demonstrated McLendon's knack for mixing business and promotion. To give New York agencies and corporations a feel for his product, McLendon opened a New York telephone line where dialers could hear three minutes of WNUS. And while he found it harder to come up with stunts suitable for all-news radio than for Top 40, McLendon did hire Dr. Richard Kinney, associate director of a school for the blind in a Chicago suburb, to go around the world and record his observations of foreign capitals for WNUS listeners. Kinney was deaf and blind.

WNUS went into the black just short of its second anniversary. But it never gained a dominant share of the market. In 1968, with competition in their markets from other all-news stations that relied heavily on local reporting, XETRA and WNUS switched to music formats.

McLendon broke new ground in all-news radio in several ways. He established its credibility with advertisers; he showed that it could be promoted aggressively. Through his charisma and his energy, he gave it standing in the marketplace. But his insistence on only hard news may have precluded long-range success. As audiences became more familiar with all-news radio, their taste became more sophisticated. They wanted more than headlines, and they seemed to want aggressive, on-the-spot local reporting.

The next breakthrough came in New York City, when Group W converted WINS to all-news programming, bringing the format into the nation's largest media market and home of the advertising industry. Group W had a different vision of all-news than Gordon McLendon, and was determined to avoid the "rip-and-read" headline approach, presenting both longer stories and some feature material. Ironically, it turned to all-news as a second choice. When it bought WINS in 1960 for $10 million, the station played rock 'n' roll and was among the top-rated stations in the city. But WABC switched to Top 40, and cut the WINS audience dramatically. There were more than 40 stations heard in New York at the time (by 1979 there were more than 70), and Group W cast about for an unusual format. Its leaders were familiar with McLendon's experiments at XETRA and WNUS and decided to convert WINS to an all-news operation. WINS donated its massive record library to Fordham University and unveiled its new format on April 19, 1965. (Five months later Group W converted KYW, Philadelphia, into its second all-news station.) The new all-news format was very different from McLendon's.

WINS and KYW did not rely solely on wire-service copy and offered more than hard news. Each station hired reporters and sent them out with tape recorders. Group W's other stations provided news bureaus in major cities (Chicago, San Francisco, Boston, Pittsburgh), and they all shared a Washington bureau and correspondents overseas. (In 1966 Group W acquired KFWB, Los Angeles, and converted it to all-news in 1968.) As a result they were able to provide on-the-scene reports that were more interesting than wire-service copy. In between news stories, WINS and KYW offered in-depth reports, features, shopping hints, theater reviews, and editorials. McLendon had argued that the worst thing that could happen to an all-news sation would be for listeners seeking headlines to tune in and hear a book review in progress. Group W demonstrated that an audience would stick around for news features as well as hard news.

In November 1965 the great Northeast blackout gave WINS an opportunity to show its potential. It performed with distinction, and a study showed that 22.6 percent of the radio audience listened to its coverage. Its ratings were up substantially thereafter.

By 1967 seven all-news stations were on the air. When WCBS, New York, became the eighth on August 28, 1967, it represented another milestone. WCBS was the first network O&O to try all-news, using the vast resources of a major news-gathering organization.

What WCBS had to do was find out if a major market could support two all-news stations; it also had to establish its own identity among listeners. It decided on a format that offered even more features than WINS: legal advice; advice from Dr. Rose Franzblau, the late psychologist who also wrote a syndicated newspaper column, and two traffic-spotting helicopters for up-to-the-minute reports on road conditions in the greater New York area. It also instituted "Report on Medicine," which brought the station more mail than any other feature, and horse racing results with live calls of the races.

WCBS designed its format with the goal of holding its listeners longer. WINS and its predecessors had sought instead the largest possible quarter-hour audience. When Lou Adler became news director in 1971, he added another refinement, a double anchor. It lent a more conversational tone to the news, as the anchors talked to one another as well as to the audience. In effect, Adler had married the personality of an MOR deejay to the concept of all-news. Ironically, Adler's refinements left WINS, a pioneer in feature reporting, sounding like a hard-news station next to WCBS's twin anchors. Over the years, each station built up a strong local following, with little overlap. Between them the two all-news stations share about 10 percent of the greater New York area's listening audience; it has been estimated that as much as 35 percent of the area's population tunes into all-news at some time during the week. In January 1980, WINS joined the ABC Radio Network as an affiliate, combining its own local news department with the international newsgathering organization.

The next landmark in all-news radio came in 1975, when NBC decided to offer an all-news service on a network basis to stations around the country. Until that time all-news had succeeded in only the largest markets. NBC set a goal of converting 75 stations in the top 100 markets into all-news operations. The project was a dismal failure. NBC lost about $16 million in a year and a half.

The NBC News and Information Service (NIS, as it was known), went on the air June 1, 1975, with about two dozen affiliates. Of those, three-quarters were AM stations, the remainder FM. NIS provided 46 minutes of news and feature stories an hour, including two ten-minute hard-news reports. Participating stations were required to carry the two major news reports, where the network sold six minutes of commercial time. Beyond those reports they could take any or all of the remaining service, and sell up to twelve minutes of local advertising.

A unique feature of NIS was that it required member stations to pay for the service, rather than—as in traditional network practice—compensating them for carrying the network. Fees ranged from $750 to $15,000 monthly, depending on market size. NBC officials had concluded that they could not afford to run NIS without fees, because of its high operating costs. But salesmen pushing the service had the task of going to stations that were either independent or receiving compensation from a network, and convincing them not only that an all-news operation could flourish in their market, but that it was worth investing in. The cost to the local station would be high: service fees to the network, substantial promotion to educate listeners about the new service, providing more local news, and a loss of revenue while potential advertisers waited to see if the format worked.

"What we had to do was to go to radio stations and tell them, 'Everything you've done to this point in your career is wrong, and you're gonna do something you never even dreamed of,'" said Alan Walden, who was executive producer of NIS. " 'You're gonna get rid of all your disc jockeys, all your records, no dues to ASCAP or BMI, you're gonna do news!' That's a hard sell to station owners. And it takes time. We didn't have a whole lot of time. We were told in January of 1975 that this thing might happen. We were given our official go in April, and given 60 days to put in on the air. And we did it. The service worked. What we had going out of here was in good shape. But it wasn't going into enough places. We were a very hard sell in the major markets; we were frozen out of a lot of major markets. Perhaps we should have been in them before we even went on the air. . . . We shouldn't have gone on the air with as few stations as we did."

The consensus among radio executives and broadcast journalists was that NIS was a fine news operation. The problems were not in the news end but in management. NBC made several major errors:

—*It planned poorly.* The network didn't do enough research and didn't talk to enough broadcasters. Bob Mounty, who was general manager of NIS, said NBC feared that CBS would learn of its plan and do it first; six of CBS's seven O&O stations were all-news.

—*It didn't allow enough time and money.* Many observers inside and outside NBC felt that NIS would need at least five years to turn a profit. When NBC lost $16 million in a year and a half, it discontinued the service. In a similar situation, ABC looked the red ink in the eye and committed $25 million to a new network service.

—*It didn't put NIS on the network's AM O&Os.* WNBC, New York, is a 50,000-watt station and the flagship of the network. By not converting it to NIS, the network lost credibility and created an impression, which was widely reported in the press, that NIS was an "FM news service." Walden, NIS's executive producer, faulted his superiors. With WNBC, New York, and WMAQ, Chicago, Walden said NIS "could have driven Westinghouse out of the news business."

Jack Thayer, who was president of NBC Radio during the NIS fiasco, blamed bad luck as well for the news service's failure. He said he had approved plans based on 1973 budget figures, which showed many radio stations losing money. By 1975, he said, the economy had turned around, radio was catching a lot of spillover advertising from television, and many marginal stations had turned profitable.

Despite its failure NIS had a significant impact on all-news radio. It greatly increased the number of all-news stations and brought the format to markets that had never had it before. At its peak NIS had 72 stations; about 40 stayed all-news after its demise. There had been 16 before NIS went into operation.

In the last few years two trends have developed that are, in effect, retreats from the all-news format and further illustrate how journalists and business leaders differ in their view of all-news. The first is that many all-news stations now carry live broadcasts of ball games. Some of the staff newsmen are unhappy, but executives point out that ball games build audiences at times when all-news draws fewer listeners: evenings and weekends. (Baseball games would not work for a West Coast all-news station because, with the three-hour time difference, East Coast road games on weekdays would fall during the afternoon drive time.) Stations have found that many sports, especially baseball, have enough built-in intermissions to provide adequate space for news reports during the game.

The second retreat is more drastic: some stations have maintained all-news only during morning and evening drive time. For the rest of the day, they offer a variety of sports, information and talk, which is less expensive programming. Of all the formats, the pressure to maintain peak audiences is perhaps keenest at all-news stations because operating costs are so enormous. A music station must pay its deejays, a talk station its hosts; each will maintain a small news staff, sometimes just one person. But an all-news station must maintain the staff to come up with more than 40 minutes of news each hour. A survey of news directors by *Broadcasting* in 1974 produced estimates of how much all-news costs compared to music programming that ranged from 60 percent to 6,000 percent more. With the increase in automated music stations, the cost of all-news looms as a formidable obstacle to broadcast executives. The added costs include a large staff, subscriptions to more wire services, news cars, tape recorders, and helicopters. Except in times of crisis, all-news stations generally draw (or, if there's more than one, share) no more than 15 to 20 percent of an audience. So it's usually only in large cities that all-news radio is profitable.

But wherever they can turn a profit, all-news stations will endure: the format is the most important development in radio news in the past quarter-century, although it affects relatively few stations. The tailoring of news to match other formats, on the other hand, has affected thousands of radio stations. Many Top 40 stations try for an uptempo newscast, full of punch and colorful phrases; Beautiful Music formats look for low-key announcers; classical stations seek an intellectual, thoughtful-sounding newscast; progressive or album-oriented rockers encourage the "laid-back" approach, and some religious stations punctuate their news with "hallelujahs!" and "praise the Lords!"

This tailoring is done on the theory that news is a small part of the station's overall offering, and not the primary reason the listener tunes to the station. Program directors feel that unless the news blends in, listeners will be jarred into attentiveness, dislike the change of pace, and switch stations: the dreaded tune-out. Studies of radio listening have shown that listeners to music stations do indeed tune to a station for its sound. But the same studies show that most listeners want to hear some news on their station and would not tune out. In a recent APRadio study only 10 percent of listeners polled said they didn't care about hearing the news. Nonetheless tune-out remains the fear of program directors and station managers.

One of the problems with changing the *tone* of a newscast to match a format is that it puts the emphasis on entertainment rather than information. Far worse, however, is shaping the *content* of news to a format. Some stations analyze the demographics of their audience and tell them what they think listeners want to hear, as Mitchell Stephens of New York University found in his recent study of radio news:

—"On this hot and muggy TGIF morning," said a newscaster on a Top 40 station in Richmond, Virginia, "I've got some tips on this heat wave...the wonders of cow dung...the dangers of skateboards... the clean air bill...and the Q94 beach patrol."

—At an MOR station in New York state, the news director said news was geared to "an older, often retired audience."

—A religious station in California conceded it left "gore and smut" to other stations.

—At a progressive rock station in California, the news director said news reports covered "drugs, sex, liberation movements, government bungling, and corruption."

The danger is clear: Stations that are responsible in their news programming will draw on network or wire services for national and world news to complement their choice of local items and features. Many, unfortunately, are irresponsible. If listeners depend on these stations as a source for news, they are being short-changed.

But if this is the bad side of local news, the good side is that many stations have come up with inventive news programming to supplement whatever hourly newscasts they offer. One of the most dramatic is the use of "minidocumentaries." For example, KMOX, St. Louis, ran an 18-part series on heart disease, and a four-part series on ghetto crime; WBZ, Boston, ran an 18-part report on rape; WCCO, Minneapolis, carried "Anatomy of Food Prices: Who Gets What?" every day for a month. These reports usually are aired several times a day, with a new segment each day.

Network news changed as well. At first, network leadership was paralyzed. After all, their thinking went, they had made their mark before the new kid on the block—television—came along. But eventually it became apparent that it was their news—and precious little else—that made them valuable to affiliate stations. So they began expanding news services. Tape recording, better phone lines, and satellites have strengthened reporting from around the world. Currently more than 80 percent of the material sent out by the networks is news and news features—on ABC more than 90 percent. News shows can be their biggest moneymakers, for they get the best "clearances" (the industry term for how many affiliates carry a network show). The noon news, for example, might be carried by every affiliate, a 100 percent clearance. By assembling the largest possible audience, the network can justify charging advertisers its highest rate.

From the affiliates' point of view, network news gives them in-depth coverage around the world and around the nation—often by well-known names from television like Walter Cronkite, John Chancellor, David Brinkley—and spares them the impossible expense of maintaining their own correspondents. A 1977 Gallup study found that people prefer to hear their national and international news from a network news team, rather than hearing that same news from a familiar local announcer.

As the affiliates' needs became clear, competing news services evolved to provide supplementary coverage to affiliates and complete news programs to independent stations. UPI and AP both offer audio news services. They were joined in 1968 by the Mutual Black Network; its five-minute hourly newscast stresses issues affecting minority groups and the Third World. In 1973, the National Black Network was formed to provide similar service. Other specialty networks offer sports and weather coverage and regional news. National Public Radio also provides news services to affiliate stations. (See Chapter 8.)

With this increased competition and the increase in news supply, network headquarters had to start paying more attention to affiliate needs and demands. This led to news and feature feeds at different times within the hour and shorter, more upbeat newscasts. Once again the networks followed the lead of local stations in shaping news to formats.

ABC was the pioneer in this area. It startled the broadcast industry with the announcement in 1967 that on the following January 1 it would offer four different network services. Just as all-news was the most significant development in local radio news, ABC's implementation of four networks was far and away the key innovation in radio network news in the television age.

The four networks were named Contemporary, Entertainment, FM, and Information. Contemporary news was geared to Top 40 stations, and delivered to advertisers the massive audiences of the ABC-owned Top 40 stations. Entertainment news was geared for MOR and country stations; FM was aimed primarily at FM rock stations; and Information News targeted other adult formats. Information News most closely replicated the traditional network news.

The four-network strategem was the brainchild of Ralph Beaudin, a corporate vice president, who thought that ABC lawyers could convince the FCC to approve the system. The FCC, to encourage competition, had issued in 1941 "chain broadcasting regulations" that barred networks from providing more than one service to two affiliates in the same market at the same time. (Ironically, ABC's roots lay in the FCC's order to NBC to divest itself of either its Red Network or its Blue Network. In 1943 NBC sold the Blue system to the American Broadcasting System, Inc., which soon renamed itself the American Broadcasting Company.) Beaudin convinced the corporate directors to try the four-network plan, and Elmer Lower, president of ABC News, was asked to put the system together. Lower brought in Tom O'Brien, the director of radio news. Bob Pauley, the president of ABC Radio, was excluded from the planning. When he learned of the network's commitment to the project, he resigned, and soon became head of Mutual Broadcasting System, where he was a fierce critic—and complainant to the FCC—of ABC's set-up.

The Beaudin plan was a brilliant solution to a costly problem that plagued all four networks: coast-to-coast telephone lines had to be rented by the hour but were being used only a small fraction of that time. Network officials estimated they were wasting millions of dollars.

ABC tried to fill the 60 minutes this way: On the hour the Information Network carried a five-minute newscast, with additional ten-minute and three-and-one-half-minute blocks during the hour. At :15, the FM Network carried a five-minute newscast. At :30, the Entertainment Network ran five minutes of news, and at :55, the Contemporary Network did the same. The Entertainment Network also carried, once a day, the 50-minute Breakfast Club with Don McNeill. Paul Harvey's 15-minute and five-minute commentaries, ABC's most popular shows, were carried on the Entertainment Network and made available to other ABC affiliates.

"The major problem," O'Brien said, "was setting a style and knowing what audience you had for each one of the networks. . . . A lot of stations dropped us, especially those little 250-watters around the country. They couldn't see sharing the compensation, which we cut. . . . It got better after about a year, when we got to know some of the stations and what they needed." ABC might ask a correspondent to file four stories, differing in tone and style, one for each network. Another problem, O'Brien said, was "The fellow who ran WMAL in Washington didn't want WWDC to promote ABC, because he was the ABC station in town. WMCA, in New York, didn't want its listeners to remember that they heard an ABC news service; they were in a ratings race with WABC. Same thing in Los Angeles, with the KABC competition." But ABC stood firm.

In early 1968, as the operation began, reaction at CBS and NBC was skeptical. "I was surprised when I heard of it," said Sam Cooke Digges, president of CBS Radio. "We saw it as a natural disaster for network radio, a fragmentation of the network image." NBC's Bob Wogan recalled: "I can't remember anyone at NBC who really thought the concept could work. The idea was to run one network, not splinter it, scattering it into different areas."

ABC needed to back its daring with a firm, long-range commitment; no one expected that the four-network plan would succeed quickly. "We went on the air on January 1, 1968, with only one commercial sponsor, Wrigley," O'Brien said. "We had so many Smokey the Bear and public-service spots it was very slow going." By any measure—and each observer has a different one—ABC lost a lot of money. O'Brien placed the figure at about $12 million, while CBS officials think ABC lost more than $25 million. But the investment paid off. ABC had about 600 affiliates when it switched to the four-network system. By 1969 it had 1,013. By 1980 it had more than 1,600.

While CBS and NBC were interested observers, the Mutual Broadcasting System went on the attack before the FCC. (Mutual Broadcasting has traditionally been known as the weak sibling of the four networks. Historians Erik Barnouw and Sydney Head contend it has never held a truly competitive position among them. Even when it moved out of last place in number of affiliates, it had too many small stations and too few large ones. Mutual has occasionally been first with an innovation: It provided the first news feed geared to black stations; it contracted with Reuters, the British news agency, for overseas coverage, which for a time gave it correspondents in some Communist capitals when the other networks had none; and it carried the David Frost interviews with Richard Nixon. But it never has been a leader, or even a serious competitor, of the other three networks. In the last few years MBS has enjoyed a financial resurgence, purchased its first owned stations—WCFL, Chicago, and WHN, New York— and hired Tom O'Brien away from ABC.)

Mutual's attack on ABC was led by Pauley, the former ABC executive. The Mutual complaint contended that ABC was engaged in monopolistic practices intended to drive Mutual out of business and with illegal competitive practices involving network time sales. The FCC stood by ABC and dismissed the Mutual claims. So Mutual started additional network services of its own. It created the Mutual Black Network and offered three different newscasts an hour: five minutes at the hour and at the half-hour and a service for Top 40 stations at five minutes to the hour.

As the additional services paid off, it was only natural for NBC and CBS to consider additional operations. CBS added sports and drama, but no additional network news, and tied its seven AM O&Os together in a private network that operates independently of CBS News. Founded in 1969, it was called PLNX (for "private-lines-news-connection"). Now known as the CBS Radio Stations News Service, based in Washington, it provides a number of services to the seven stations. Its reporters serve as a Washington bureau and also as national correspondents, traveling to major stories. They also file live reports to the stations on items with a local angle: What the local congressman is doing or the progress of bills of particular regional interest. The service also puts together each weekend a newsfeature "magazine," and, most interestingly, provides for the live exchange of news reports among the stations. If there is a major air crash in Chicago, for instance, WBBM will notify its fellow stations that a live report is coming up and when. Stations can elect to carry it live, to tape it—or to ignore it. The unusual hookup in 1979 carried more than 3,000 news stories among the seven stations.

In 1973, CBS became the first network to extend its news feed to affiliates to 24 hours a day. NBC and Mutual followed in 1974 and ABC in 1976. NBC, we have already seen, then tried the NIS, and lost a good deal of cash and credibility. In mid-1979, NBC began experimenting with a second network, aimed at album-playing rock stations that reach the 18- to 34-year-old demographic. The news service, called "The Source," offered conversational two-minute newscasts each hour and extensive features, including concerts and interviews with rock musicians. NBC said it would start signing up affiliates and selling time in 1980.

The networks have also been experimenting with new equipment. The technological revolution in radio continues. New developments that should improve radio news in the next decade include:

—*transceivers:* These are improved two-way radio systems that permit news people in the field to feed directly onto the air, live; to talk to other reporters in the field, or with an anchor person or editor in the studio; and to listen to the show as they get ready to file reports. Transceivers are expected to improve field quality enormously.

—*low-frequency extenders for telephone reports:* Coupled to a telephone by the reporter, this device boosts the quality of the phone transmission so that the studio gets a clearer, stronger signal. Executives predict that reporters will be able to file clear reports from any telephone, anywhere.

—*satellites:* Already in use, the satellites will be more heavily relied on for transmission. Satellites spare the networks a reliance on telephone lines of varying quality. They will increase the speed and penetration of network news reports.

—*computer-run video display systems:* News writers work on a keyboard hooked into a computer. Whatever they write is stored in the computer's memory and can be read from a TV-like screen. Wire service stories can be fed directly into the computer. A list of stories, or any single story, can be called on screen. The system will be invaluable both for its neatness and efficiency in retrieval of stories by writers, editors, and announcers and for archives. CBS has been the pioneer in radio VDT (for "video display terminal") systems, experimenting at KCBS in San Francisco. The other networks also are studying their use. At the present time, VDT systems cost too much for most local news operations to consider.

One element of radio news is indisputably clear: There is a good deal more of it available than ever before. More in-depth reporting, more commentary, more features, and more hard news are being broadcast. Despite the increased availability of material, many stations are seeking shorter or fewer newscasts. But the next time a crisis arises, people will reach for their radios to hear the latest bulletins. No refinement in television or newspaper technology is ever likely to change that.

6

FM

The bulk of popular music radio programming in this country today is devoted to absurd jingles...babbling hysterical disc jockeys...The tempo is Go! Go! Go! The air is replete with such blather as "here comes another twin spin sound sandwich" and "here's a blast from the past, a moldy oldy that'll always last." Top 40 radio, as we know it today and have known it for the last ten years, is dead, and its rotting corpse is stinking up the airways.

—**Tom Donahue** of KMPX-FM,
San Francisco, *Rolling Stone,* 1967.

THE Federal Communications Commission ordered "the opening of the FM spectrum" in July 1964, which led to a steady climb in both the quantity and quality of FM operations, and eventual parity with the older system of program transmission, AM.

FM stands for *f*requency *m*odulation, AM for *a*mplitude *m*odulation. Modulation means the process of changing some characteristic of the radio wave. (Consider why change is important: if a siren howls constantly, it carries no meaning to those hearing it. It is only when a siren interrupts a silence that its message—to be alert—is clear.) In the earliest form of electric transmission, the telegraph, modulation involved interrupting the signal. In Morse code, the variables were the length of the signal (dots and dashes) and the intervals between the signals. Roughly speaking, amplitude modulation means a change is effected in the volume of the signal: the distance between the height of the radio wave and its trough is increased. Frequency modulation involves a change in the pitch of the signal: the height of the wave is constant, but the distance between each crest changes. In its earliest days, radio had one predominant problem: spotty reception. Static from both atmospheric conditions and other broadcasts made clear, continuous reception of a single signal very much an uncertain situation.

Edwin H. Armstrong, an inventor and the holder of several patents for early AM radio devices, resolved to tackle the static problem. In 1922 he sold RCA a patent for the superheterodyne circuit, which greatly enhanced a receiver's ability to separate signals, and became a millionaire. In a basement at Columbia University in New York City, he sought at his own expense to develop a means of broadcasting without static. RCA, in purchasing the earlier patent, also bought

119

first refusal on Armstrong's subsequent work, and he labored long and hard under the impression that RCA was most interested in his work. But what started out as a partnership ended in years of controversy and legal struggle.

Armstrong's work went well, if slowly. In 1933 he took out four patents and notified RCA that his work was ready for inspection. When David Sarnoff and his aides arrived at Columbia University, Armstrong unveiled "frequency modulation." RCA asked him to install an FM transmitter at the Empire State Building for tests. The receiver was placed 70 miles away, in Westhampton Beach on Long Island's south shore. The tests were a complete success: the range of sound and the clarity and the freedom from static were a revelation to those familiar with broadcasting problems. Armstrong expected RCA to exercise its option and put the FM system into production. But RCA stalled. After a year with no word from corporate headquarters, Armstrong was asked in April 1935 to remove his equipment from the Empire State Building.

Armstrong, bitter at RCA, decided on a public demonstration of FM. Scheduled to read a paper at the convention of the Institute of Radio Engineers in November 1935, Armstrong presented an FM broadcast as well. He rigged a transmitter in Yonkers, just north of New York City. The surprise demonstration stunned the engineers, who, as their astonishment passed, burst into applause. Gathering strength from their plaudits, Armstrong headed for the FCC, seeking spectrum space for FM broadcasts. In Washington he began Round One in a series of head-to-head confrontations with Sarnoff and RCA.

Armstrong thought he brought the FCC—and thereby the public—a better form of radio. RCA did not contest the merits of FM, a tactic that certainly would have failed, but instead offered the FCC a shinier apple: It applied for spectrum space for television. The issue before the FCC was how much room remained in the spectrum and what to do with it. After due consideration the FCC turned down Armstrong's request for an experimental station. (One of RCA's witnesses at the FCC hearings was C. B. Jolliffe, only weeks before the commission's chief engineer, but now in RCA's employ.) But Armstrong lobbied on, offering as proof his successful field experiments, and the FCC granted him a license. In 1937 he built a 50,000-watt FM station in Alpine, New Jersey. W2XMN went on the air in 1939, and its performance became Armstrong's most convincing argument for FM development. CBS decided to throw its weight behind FM and encouraged manufacturers to produce receivers. The FCC received 150 applications for FM stations. In Round Two before the FCC, Armstrong and his new (and mighty) allies, turned back the RCA challenge. The FCC removed Channel 1 from television and assigned it to FM. The FCC also ruled that all televisions must employ FM sound for broadcasting. Armstrong seemed to have won. Then World War II began. In 1942 the FCC froze all station allocations for the duration of the war, with 30 FM stations on the air. FM was widely used in military radio, but domestically it was virtually in the closet, making little dent in the public consciousness against 909 AM stations.

With the war's end, the tide turned in Washington, and Armstrong lost Round Three. The FCC decided to move FM radio to a different range of frequencies: from 42–50 MHz up to the 88–108 it occupies today. The immediate effect was that the half-million sets sold before the war were rendered obsolete. Fans and set owners were alienated, perceiving FM as an unstable industry.

Embittered, Armstrong turned his attention to legal clashes. At the FCC's direction, television was using FM sound. Westinghouse, Zenith, and General Electric were paying Armstrong royalties for his FM patents. RCA and some smaller companies refused. RCA offered instead a million-dollar settlement, far less than Armstrong would have been entitled to in royalties. Armstrong sued in 1948. The fight dragged on. In 1953, fatigued, frail, and bitter, Armstrong suffered a stroke. He became isolated from his family and friends. On February 1, 1954, Armstrong committed suicide by jumping from the 13th-floor window of his Manhattan apartment. RCA settled with his estate for $1 million. But his widow pressed suits against the smaller companies, and over 13 years she won each case.

Despite the shift in frequencies and the problems it caused, many broadcasters were optimistic about FM immediately after the war. The sound was so superior, they thought, that FM was bound to dominate radio. By 1947 more than 900 licenses had been issued for FM operations. But operators faced a double bind, caught between AM and television. AM had benefited from technical progress during the war and made substantial reductions in static. Most Americans owned only AM radios. Weighing what new products to buy, people looked at FM, about which they did not know much, and television, a heavily-advertised glamour product whose differences from and advantages over AM radio were obvious. To build an FM audience, broadcasters had to convince the public to buy FM sets. Without a substantial audience, FM radio could not attract advertisers. Without advertisers FM license holders did not have the revenue either to mount promotional campaigns or to develop unusual or distinguished programming to attract new audiences. These problems were compounded by the mediocre quality of some of the FM radios on the market—receivers that were not well made enough to demonstrate the superiority of FM sound.

In an effort to promote FM and acquaint a wide radio audience with its potential, the FCC proposed simulcasting—broadcasting identical material simultaneously on AM and FM—to free FM radio from the need for advertisers and the costs of program development. Of course simulcasting was not in the best interests of independent FM stations: They were scratching for survival and could hardly compete for advertising when their competition's rates were subsidized by AM operations. (Years later, in the order that opened the spectrum, the FCC noted, indirectly, the sacrifices these independent stations had had to make; the FCC acknowledged that in 1964 most independents were still not making a profit and suggested that their prospects for profits would be improved when they no longer had to compete with simulcasting competitors.) Despite the independents' problems, the FCC decided that the long-range interest of radio would best be served by simulcasting. FCC critics suggested that the commission was preoccupied with television and not thinking clearly about what radio needed. In any case, a majority of the applicants for FM licenses were AM broadcasters. Some thought an FM license would eventually prove lucrative; others wanted to cover their tracks with an inexpensive backup system.

By 1948 the optimism of the previous year was gone. Only three of the 114 FM-only stations showed a profit. More than 100 applicants who had received licenses and construction permits returned them to the FCC. It grew worse. In 1949 AM and FM reeled under a nationwide recession, and radio revenues had their smallest annual increase since 1938. In all, 212 commercial FM stations went off the air. But amid this stumbling, trial-and-error handling of FM, the FCC set aside a slice of the revised FM band, from 88-92 MHz, for noncommercial educational stations, which in 1947 began to proliferate. (See Chapter 8.) Slowly, steadily, they built modest audiences, proving to listeners that FM *was* technically superior, establishing that there was an audience for alternative programming and raising, albeit in small quarters, some public consciousness about FM.

But commercial FM broadcasting stations were still doing poorly and the public wasn't buying:

	FM Stations on Air	FM Receivers Sold
1950	676	2,200,000
1952	626	670,000
1954	554	233,000
1956	534	229,000
1958	577	375,000
1960	813	1,600,000
1962	1,078	2,600,000

The popularity of FM started to grow, in the late 1950s, for precisely the reason for which FM was first hailed: its superior sound.

Through the early- and mid-1950s the idea of FM was kept alive by independents willing to take a loss in the expectation of better days to come, by a growing number of college radio stations, and by AM-FM simulcasting. Listeners who switched to the FM band couldn't help but note the clarity. These developments provided the tinder. High fidelity recording equipment, and later, stererophonic sound, provided the spark. Quite simply what happened was that a substantial number of Americans were developing more sophisticated ears for music, and demanding higher standards. Improvements in phonographs, including cartridges, styli, and speaker systems, had demonstrated amply how well music could be reproduced. The market for this high fidelity equipment grew by leaps and bounds in the late 1950s. And many consumers began to seek the same fidelity from their radios that they got from their phonograph systems. As early as 1957 stereo albums were on the market, offering the richest sound yet available for home use. Even before FM offered stereo broadcasting, its clarity and richness did more justice to stereo albums than AM radio could.

Stereo, as a recording process, divides the music being performed into two "tracks," one along each side of the groove on the record. Each track is then fed into a separate speaker, and listeners hear a sound more diverse and complex, as it has two distinct sources rather than one. For instance, with a jazz quartet, the drums and piano might be assigned the left track, the bass and trumpet the right track. The result is a richer, denser sound than one speaker could possibly provide.

In 1961 the FCC authorized stereo broadcasting of FM and 57 stations tried it. The FM signal is broader than AM, and on any assigned frequency—for instance, 98.7 on the dial—a station could broadcast two closely related but different signals. This technique of putting more than one signal into a frequency is known as multiplexing. Stereo broadcasting proved popular: By 1970 668 FM stereo stations were on the air and the number continued to grow. (The narrow AM signal did not lend itself to stereo broadcasting for many years. See Chapter 9.)

The superior sound of stereo created a ripple effect in the marketplace. Equipment manufacturers began developing increasingly sophisticated stereo equipment, which in turn created a demand for more stereo broadcasting. This "FM sound" had two other facets: fewer commercials and longer periods of uninterrupted music. Noncommercial FM stations accepted no advertising; commercial stations found few sponsors, and they had little money for promotional stunts. Because there were so few interruptions, the medium was ideally suited to run longer compositions.

The modest FM growth from 1957 to 1964 provided a solid foundation and a growing audience (the first FM car radios were introduced in 1963). Then the FCC intervened with an order aimed at AM and FM stations owned by the same company (the dual holding was called duopoly) that were simulcasting. In its historic order, the FCC noted:

> Our proposals were based upon the view that the time had come to move significantly toward the day when AM and FM stations should be regarded as component parts of a total "aural" service for assignment purpose...eventually, there must be an elimination of FM stations which are no more than adjuncts to AM facilities in the same community.

The FCC ordered AM-FM license holders in cities with a population of more than 100,000 to broadcast original programming on FM at least half the time they were on the air. The FCC estimated that about 100 stations were affected; other observers placed the number nearer to 200.

There were several aspects to the FCC order. On the one hand the commissioners were fulfilling their oft-stated and occasionally followed doctrine of serving the public interest by increasing program diversity. On the other hand, their motivation came from an AM problem: The spectrum was full, especially in major markets. In May 1962 the FCC had ordered a freeze on AM license applications while it pondered what to do with the congestion. There were nearly 4,000 AM stations on the air (and almost 1,000 FM stations). Still the clamor continued for more licenses. With nowhere left to turn on AM, the FCC took a new look at FM, about which it had been unable to make up its mind since World War II. The commissioners decided that the time was right to let FM stand, free from AM, on its own legs.

But even as FM's new day dawned, many people in the radio industry saw clouds. This included some FCC commissioners; the vote for the nonduplicating rule was 5–2. Among the critics was Commissioner Robert T. Bartley, who although he eventually voted *for* the rule, complained: "People should not have to switch to AM to get program material they desire. FM should be all-inclusive...." Some broadcasters complained that their experiments in original FM programming had led to listener complaints: the public asked them to resume simulcasting. Other broadcasters and trade organizations argued that the FCC had no business regulating programming. Decisions on what to put on the air, they contended, should rest with individual stations. More than 100 of them filed applications for waivers with the FCC, asking exemption from the nonduplication rule. The FCC, while generally unsympathetic, extended the deadline for compliance from July 1, 1965, to January 1, 1967.

As the FCC attempted to lead, many station operators elected not to follow. In addition to filing waiver applications and lobbying in Washington for reconsideration of the rule, some broadcasters turned to fascinating schemes to comply with the nonduplication policies. The FCC had defined simultaneous broadcasting as that being "within 24 hours before or after the identical program is broadcast over the AM station." Some stations decided they could comply by taping AM broadcasts and using them after 25 hours. This is hardly what the FCC had in mind, but some station managers consulted with their legal departments and decided they could get away with it. Other stations cut back the hours of AM programming, reducing the number of FM programs they would need to equal half their AM load. But the major of those affected complied without deceit, and were dragged screaming and kicking into newfound profits. "I made a mistake," recalled Gordon

McLendon, the Texas broadcaster. "AM broadcasters by and large, and I was among them, fought the FCC tooth and nail. Todd Storz made a terrible mistake, terrible: he never did get into FM. None of the Storz stations to this day are FM. I did get into FM, but like many AM operators I had to be dragged in. The FCC wanted the good AM operators, who could best afford to do so, to develop this fine new medium, and we did. But it was largely because of the push of the FCC and some of their very alert staff members. Almost singlehandedly, the FCC forced the development of the FM spectrum. If not for the FCC, FM might not have come along for another 10 or 15 years."

However cantankerous the broadcasters, by the mid-1960s FM radio could no longer be denied. Several social and cultural developments found in FM their perfect medium.

Eventually the availability of FM changed the very face of rock 'n' roll, which until the mid-1960s was consigned to the Top 40 stations alone. From rock's beginnings well into the 1960s, most rock songs were written and recorded in lengths of two and one-half to three minutes—precisely because the writers and artists sought AM radio exposure. These stations emphasized short songs, many breaks, promotional jingles, and so on. One study found a typical AM Top 40 station might in one hour play 22 commercials, 73 weather/time/contest announcements, repeat the station's call letters 58 times, throw in a three-and-one-half-minute newscast and play about a dozen songs. But as FM grew (and not so coincidentally, album sales grew), more and more rock musicians turned their hands to more complex and longer compositions. The three-chord simplistic rock of the 1950s remained a staple of AM radio; the more complex popular music found an outlet on FM. Musicians felt free to experiment with longer songs, because they knew albums containing those songs had a chance to get FM air play. So as a genre, popular music (particularly rock 'n' roll) was rejuvenated. Among the early pioneers on this frontier were Bob Dylan, who in 1965 recorded "Desolation Row," eleven minutes long, and the Rolling Stones, whose "Going Home" the following year was also eleven minutes long. In 1967, the

Doors had a seven-minute-long hit, "Light My Fire" (although they offered AM radio an edited three-minute version), and Arlo Guthrie achieved prominence with "Alice's Restaurant," which was 18 minutes long.

But the emerging music, as important as it was, pales beside the explosive force that made FM socially significant: the political and cultural movements of the 1960s. The adolescent rebellion of the 1950s, even when it addressed social problems, was essentially inarticulate ("rebels without a cause"). A decade later this discontent ripened into an informed, sophisticated, and highly articulate political activism. It began with the civil rights movement, starting with the Freedom Rides in the early 1960s. It had deeper roots in the labor movement. But it spread through the nation after 1963, honed by the assassinations of John F. Kennedy, and, to a lesser extent, Malcolm X. Its cause became the antiwar movement. As early as 1963 there were protests against American involvement in Vietnam. By 1965 massive, coordinated demonstrations occurred regularly as the war was escalated by the Johnson administration. What was significant from radio's point of view was that the activists took (as labor organizers and civil rights protesters had before them) certain songs as their anthems. And certain songwriters—Dylan, Phil Ochs, Tom Paxton—and singers—Joan Baez and Judy Collins, most prominently—became willing instruments of the movement.

The strength of the youth market had been ably demonstrated by rock 'n' roll in the 1950s; record companies had learned to cater to young taste. Whatever their corporate investments, regardless of whom their executives might support for office, companies moved to record and market the protest music of the 1960s. This was nothing new; RCA Records was busy signing Elvis Presley even as its corporate president, Robert Sarnoff, was denouncing rock 'n' roll. Columbia Records signed Dylan and Pete Seeger; Elektra Records signed Ochs, Paxton and Collins. But even as record companies signed protest singers and the public bought their albums, these performers had little access to the mass media, including radio.

Television steered clear of controversy, and would not broadcast the protest music. Seeger, a social activist with leftist connections, was blacklisted for 17 years, until a 1967 appearance on the Smothers Brothers television show. Dylan, after a successful New York City concert in April 1963, was invited to appear on the Ed Sullivan Show, provided he agreed not to sing "Talking John Birch Society Blues." Dylan refused. (It wasn't only political controversy that television steered clear of. When the Rolling Stones were invited on the Sullivan show in 1967 to sing their hit "Let's Spend the Night Together," Sullivan insisted they change the lyric to "Let's spend some time together," and the Stones, a good deal more eager than Dylan for exposure, agreed.) Television was not alone in avoiding the protest music of the 1960s. AM radio stuck to its hits-based formats, and thus excluded the protest singers. An exception was Peter, Paul, and Mary's version of Dylan's "Blowing in the Wind," a low-key antiwar song that they turned into a hit single in 1963. Newspapers, in their music criticism and in news and feature stories, had little to say about the new poets of protest. It was FM radio that gave this music of the 1960s—whether it was rock, folk, or jazz—exposure in the mass media. (The "underground press" discussed the music but never achieved true mass impact.)

From the mid-1960s on, this music and its media arm, FM radio, took on a new dimension. Social protests continued and indeed escalated, and many people opted for what came to be called the counterculture: "alternative lifestyles" that acted out protest on several levels. Widespread dabbling in drugs was commonplace, casual or offbeat attire standard. These lifestyles had their music as well—and that music was played on FM radio. The stations that played the recordings of bands like Big Brother and the Holding Company, Jefferson Airplane, Country Joe and the Fish, and Moby Grape became known as "underground radio." But they weren't underground at all. They were easily accessible with a flip of the FM dial. Significantly, this underground radio became prime-time entertainment for many young Americans. Television had not changed its programming to draw in this substantial audience, and viewership in the young adult market plummeted in the late 1960s.

Some films tried to fill the void, notably "Easy Rider" and "The Graduate." But most evenings this audience just "did its thing," whatever it was—even if it were something terribly conventional like studying—in front of FM radios, instead of television.

Underground radio soon came out of the pigeonhole the other media had placed it in, and after a while was dubbed "progressive FM radio." Its influence on culture and society far outweighed its revenue; even in its heyday it did not dominate FM radio programming. But it was an important part of the FM story in the 1960s.

Jack Gould of *The New York Times* offered some easily recognizable characteristics of this new mode of broadcasting in a slightly-after-the-fact acknowledgement of the impact of "progressive radio" on May 20, 1970 (ironically, a month after *Rolling Stone* had analyzed the "death" of progressive radio):

—"The technique of picking 'cuts' or segments from long-playing rock albums, which often do not make the list of the top 40 rock tunes offered on single 45 rpm disks."

—"The lyrics of hard rock virtually constitute an arcane language, difficult to comprehend because of the blurred diction of so many rock artists."

—"Stereophonic FM, which surrounds the listener with sound, is purposely raised in volume by the young so that they can physically sense the vibrations of the audio waves and emphasize what one college graduate characterized as the social schism between generations." (Indeed, some albums contained on the jacket a note to consumers: "We suggest that you play this record at the highest possible volume in order to fully appreciate the sound....")

—"Unlike the rapid-fire delivery of earlier rock disk jockeys, their new FM counterparts talk in low and seductive voices."

Perhaps the most readily identifiable element of the progressive FM sound was its use of "sets" of music, where the disc jockey grouped songs using several criteria: songs on the same theme, several songs by the same performer, different interpretations of the same song or songwriter, or similarity of musical sound.

This progressive FM radio had muddled roots. There are three versions of how and where it began:

—The East Coast, WOR-FM story
—The West Coast, Tom Donahue story
—The "young turks" of college radio story

Any habitual listener to WOR-FM must have been startled at 6:00 AM on July 30, 1966. Instead of the usual simulcast of WOR-AM's talk show "Rambling with Gambling," a particularly raucous rock song, "Wild Thing" by the Troggs, came blaring across the airwaves. Thus WOR-FM chose to herald the end of its simulcasting and to introduce new FM programming. The station, owned by RKO, was getting a five-month jump on the FCC deadline.

The new WOR-FM seemed designed for the counterculture audience. The station commissioned graphic designer Milton Glaser to create posters featuring long-haired musicians and plastered them all over town. The changeover in format at WOR-FM came during (though not because of) a strike by on-the-air personnel: There were no disc jockeys at the station until October. The programming ran song-to-song, interrupted only by pretaped promotions and occasional advertisements. Word about WOR-FM spread through the tri-state area (New York, New Jersey, and Connecticut) and the station began to build a sizable audience of young adults. By the time the deejays went on the air on October 8, 1966 (they included "Murray the K" Kaufman, Scott Muni, and Rosko [Bill Mercer]), WOR-FM was quite a visible tree in the city's media forest, heralded by *The Village Voice* as "the only place to hear vital new music and hear it well."

WOR-FM's glory was not to last, however. A year later, a clash of personalities, and in-house politics, brought the format down. The struggle—which led to the dismissal or resignation of the deejays— served to obscure WOR-FM's seminal role in radio programming, and perhaps explains why so many chroniclers have found the roots of progressive radio in San Francisco. But the evidence clearly shows that Tom Donahue, the so-called "father of progressive radio," did not take his first steps until March 1967.

Like Murray the K, Donahue was a veteran of the East Coast Top 40 wars of the late 1950s and early 1960s. He worked on the air as "Big Daddy" (he weighed nearly 400 pounds) and was a star at Philadelphia's WIBG-AM. During the 1960 payola probes Donahue (though never charged or implicated) resigned from WIBG and left for San Francisco, where he joined KYA-AM, a Top 40 station that billed itself as "the boss of the bay." He quit in 1965, during a broadcast from a glass booth at a teenage fair, according to his widow Rachael. They sat at home and listened to records for more than a year, she said, until one day Tom had a vision. He realized the records they listened to were never on the radio.

"The next day, Tom got on the horn and started calling FM stations until he found one whose phone was disconnected," Rachael told *Radio & Records* magazine in 1978. "That was KMPX...the station was in a lot of trouble. Its format was varied foreign languages. It was losing money." Deejay Larry Miller already was doing an all-night show on KMPX of the type Donahue envisioned. Full-time progressive programming was implemented on April 7, 1967, with the Donahues in charge, using their own records. Listener support was rapid and rabid: Fans decorated the studio with bells, tapestries, incense, candles, and a Viet Cong banner. The Donahues set a few simple rules, Rachael said: "No jingles, no talkovers, no time-and-temp (Tom took the clock out of the studio), no pop singles."

Donahue, who died April 28, 1975, at age 46, described the KMPX experiment in a 1967 *Rolling Stone* article as "a format that embraces the best of today's rock 'n' roll, folk, traditional and city blues, raga, electronic music and some jazzy and classical selections. I believe this music should not be treated as a group of objects to be sorted out like eggs with each category kept rigidly apart from the others." At the same time that he was revamping KMPX, Donahue began a similar overhaul of KPPC in Pasadena. Within a year, the Donahues and their staffs were embroiled in a heated labor dispute. They struck in March 1968 and whimsically named their union the Amalgamated Federation of International FM Workers of the World. Many musicians supported the strike and entrepreneur Bill Graham provided food for the pickets. The dispute was never settled, and Donahue moved his operations and staff to KSAN, San Francisco, in May 1968.

Because of his size, his zeal, his links to the Haight-Ashbury community in San Francisco and his alliances with other public figures like Graham, Jefferson Airplane, and the Grateful Dead, the legend began that Donahue fathered progressive radio. But he was months behind WOR-FM.

There was a third, more diffuse source of progressive FM programming. While WOR-FM in the East and Donahue in the West were making waves in the commercial marketplace, a similar movement had begun on many campuses. It attracted less attention because it was spread out, unreported, its stations of low power, and after all, its leaders just kids. But these kids had descended on college radio stations and tried to make a case for playing the new music. The most persistent were permitted to air their material a few hours a week. These shows went on the air, in some cases, before the WOR-FM experiment.

One of the best-known of the college shows was run by Tom Gamache, at WTBS, owned by the Massachusetts Institute of Technology in Cambridge, Massachusetts. The station had a modest 30-watt signal but was capable of reaching Boston's large university population. Gamache started in 1966 with a show called "Tee Time." Now a record company executive, Gamache said he designed the show as "a travesty of commercial radio." He brought in his own records to play and did phony commercials, most of them related to marijuana. Gamache, whose on-the-air name was Uncle Tom, developed a wide following and switched to Boston University's WBUR, which had a 20,000-watt signal. Eventually he joined WBCN, and ran Boston's first commercial progressive rock show.

In New York City, Fordham University's WFUV offered a Saturday show, starting in late 1964, called "Campus Caravan," anchored by one of this book's authors, Peter Fornatale. He offered album material, thematic groupings of songs, interviews with musicians, and topical comments underscored by appropriate musical selections.

This generation of college broadcasters produced two ripples: they encouraged more people to enter college radio's ranks, which in turn led more college stations to switch to progressive FM. And they graduated or dropped out and went into commercial radio, like Gamache and Fornatale. These young turks received some due—the critic Richard Goldstein, in his formidable "Pop Eye" commentaries in *The Village Voice*, often took note of them—but they did not attract enough of a mass audience or enough media attention to become a prominent force in American broadcasting. Only commercial success would certify the new programming.

And that became the crux of progressive FM's problem: could it survive commercially? Could it pull in advertising revenue? In 1967, 1968, and 1969 progressive FM was put to the test. And it passed...if station owners weren't greedy. Initially the stations drew ads from concert promoters, motorcycle shops, "head shops," and sandal makers; its only national advertising came from record companies. But as the audiences grew, and as sales of FM receivers flourished, more advertisers came on board: manufacturers of musical instruments and stereo equipment. Eventually airlines and beer companies joined. By the 1970s suburban home developers and auto makers had watched the children of the 1960s grow up and become affluent and had followed them through their medium, FM radio.

The late 1960s found strange bedfellows in FM radio: social critics and activists, drug users, and corporate giants. The on-the-air personnel at progressive stations often treated their medium as a personal political platform, a tool in a social movement—and only secondarily a business. The stockholders, of course, did not agree. Eventually the different points of view clashed.

As FM progressive radio demonstrated its commercial potential, the ABC network decided to take the plunge. Its first attempt was called the "LOVE" format: a Lutheran minister, Brother John Rydgren, was the deejay. The music was generally mild counterculture, built around the theme of love. It more or less flopped, and ABC switched to a straightforward progressive format that also was unsuccessful. After a while ABC switched to a more structured format, playing recognizable FM hits—popular songs from popular albums—and grew successful with it.

Progressive radio, for all its impact, was but a small piece of the radio revenue pie. To mix a metaphor, it was a trail-blazing piece of pie. It was left to another format, Beautiful Music, to demonstrate just how profitable FM could be. Jim Schulke's Stereo Radio Productions started racking up impressive ratings performances in 1969 and 1970. Schulke said the turning point was the Arbitron ratings of April/May 1972: 29 FM stations were rated among the top four in their markets. Twenty-eight of them were Beautiful Music stations, and all but three were programmed by Schulke. The MOR format also did well on FM, though never as well as Beautiful Music. Just as progressive FMs demonstrated that they could deliver the much-sought-after 18- to 24-year-olds to advertisers, Beautiful Music and MOR delivered—and indeed, with far greater profitability— substantial older audiences.

These early successes paved the way for intensive demographic research into FM audiences. They demonstrated to Madison Avenue that FM could draw. And they helped sell more FM sets, as listeners came to appreciate the original programming. Progressive FM even helped prove that radio could attract listeners away from prime-time television.

As the 1960s ended, as the age of assassinations seemed mercifully to pass, FM radio, rock 'n' roll, and the young adult market were all feeling their oats. They had been vindicated by time. For some they were art, for some big business, to everyone they were successful. But the pendulum already had begun to swing: the tides of conservatism were washing over progressive FM, brushing away some of the sand castles that had been built.

=7=

THE 70s

After nearly five decades of operation, the broadcast industry does not seem to have grasped the simple fact that a broadcast license is a public trust subject to termination for breach of duty.
—Chief Justice Warren Burger,
at the time a judge on the U.S. Court of Appeals, 1969

137

THE 1970s were a decade of enormous growth and profit for radio on nearly every front: formats were refined and polished; the networks enjoyed a resurgence; FM grew and grew and grew some more, eventually passing AM radio in total audience (although not yet in profitability). Public radio flourished as well. It was a decade without the flux in radio of the 1950s and 1960s. No untapped audiences were discovered. No new modes of broadcasting were unveiled. It was a time of consolidation, as radio's profitability was established beyond dispute and licenses came to be more highly valued than ever. Prices soared, and more and more stations passed into the hands of multiple-license holders. As with other mass media, the concentration of ownership increased.

At the same time, radio again came to be perceived as a massive industry to be reckoned with. A variety of probes and challenges arose: of its ownership by conglomerates, of its cross-ownership with other media, of how well it served the public interest, and of its opportunities for minority groups. Increasingly complex regulations and license challenges by citizens' groups stirred broadcasters to talk of deregulation of radio and to lobby for it at the Federal Communications Commission and on Capitol Hill. The debate continues.

On a different level, programming, radio changed in several ways. As techniques and equipment became more sophisticated—with the proliferation of computerized, automated stations—programming became more conservative. For a variety of reasons, decisions on what to play came to be made by fewer and fewer people. In the end, the public heard less diverse music, especially on progressive FM radio stations.

139

Progressive FM was killed by its own success: As it drew more and more advertising accounts it had to make changes in the format to retain them. As FM rockers demonstrated their hold on the 18- to 34-year-old market, advertisers fell all over themselves trying to get on the air. FM ad revenues, which had totaled about $40 million in 1967, climbed to $260 million by 1975. With their increased revenue, many stations hired bigger staffs, especially for their sales departments, bought better equipment, and moved to more comfortable quarters. Boston's premier progressive FM station, WBCN, for example, moved to the penthouse of the Prudential Tower. These changes led to higher overhead and made the stations more dependent on advertising revenue. Like AM stations before them, they learned to play the ratings game. These developments struck at the very heart of what progressive FM had been in the 1960s. Socially and culturally many stations had stood as media rallying points of the politically active and the counterculture. In their music policies and in their business operations, stations changed. Initially, decisions at many stations had been made collectively by personnel. At staff meetings in the late 1960s, some stations had decided not to accept advertising for products whose merits they questioned, such as "junk foods." Others refused to advertise products made by firms that provided the American government with material for weapons. Still others drew guidelines based on "the sound" of the commercial. KSAN, San Francisco, which had been at the focal point of the progressive movement, was among the stations that bent. A turning point came at a staff meeting to discuss whether to carry an advertisement for Standard Oil's additive F-310. One KSAN employee insisted that independent testing had shown that it did not improve automobile performance. KSAN's Tom Donahue responded with one of his most famous dictums: "Radical community stations are supported by advertisers with money. If you get in bed with the devil, you better be prepared to [bleep]." KSAN carried the ad. Donahue's prophesy proved a truth that all but noncommercial stations had to live with. Owners came to expect profits and sought to maximize them.

Personnel who at first worked for survival wages (or less) came to earn respectable salaries. Those who would have it another way changed jobs or dropped out of commercial radio.

As salaries of station personnel rose, to some extent their values changed as well. Some progressive radio people kept the faith; others had their heads turned. "There's too much money and status and dope for them to change and fight now," one progressive deejay complained. Another sneered, "The only time an FM staff would hold a struggle meeting these days is if there was a pound of cocaine that needed dividing."

As advertising policies began to change, so did station rules on news coverage. Station managers and owners were aware that national advertisers were listening now, and they cracked down hard on news and feature coverage that was one-sided and argumentative. Often their news people made it easy: At KSAN, Roland Young read over the air a speech a Black Panther leader had made in which he said, "We will kill President Nixon." Young urged listeners to send similar messages to the White House. He was fired. At Boston's WBCN, disc jockey Charles Laquidara was suspended after he followed an advertisement for cameras by telling his listeners that they were made by a company that helped "kill all those Cambodian babies."

Musically, the stations changed as well. The trademark of progressive FM was that each deejay decided what songs to play, using only his or her taste and judgment. These deejays had been free from Top 40 charts, free from best-selling albums. But no more. What had been progressive radio in the 1960s was rapidly soaked up into a new umbrella format, known as album-oriented rock, or AOR.

Some stations sought a new image, and wanted a term to replace progressive, which they thought stigmatized them as underground, with an audience of hippies stoned on LSD. Where once they had wanted to cater to the counterculture to build audiences, now they wanted to let banks and automobile makers know that their audiences were respectable people. Some of their listeners *had* changed as they grew up, left school, and took jobs. Even if their musical taste was the same, they no longer wanted "head trips" from their deejays.

Probably AOR's most successful practitioners were Lee Abrams and Kent Burkhardt of Atlanta. They developed a format, "FM Superstars," that was widely imitated. The key was familiarity. On Top 40 radio the songs, which were so frequently repeated, were familiar to the audience. Abrams and Burkhardt tried to make *the performers* familiar. They would base their recommended play lists around groups of recognizable songs from popular artists. Dozens of stations signed with Abrams and Burkhardt; others developed their own formulas to switch from progressive to AOR. "People don't like to be surprised" was a common explanation. Stations began to mirror audience taste by closely monitoring album sales. AOR proponents were vocal in their criticism of progressive FM operations. They opposed "too much deejay freedom," "too many choices, not enough familiarity," "total freedom for incompetents."

A sign in one station that was converted to AOR summed it up nicely: "The Age of Aquarius is over—and now it's time to kick ass."

In the early 1970s consultants toured the land, visiting stations, speaking at industry groups, and writing articles. Since stations were not owned by members of the counterculture, owners and managers were receptive to the idea of increasing profits by limiting disc jockey freedom. The progressive FM movement, which at its peak had more than 300 stations, ground to a halt. By the mid-1970s, there were only about two dozen progressive stations. By 1980 there were but a few.

Many stations undoubtedly improved in quality when they used consultants and took decisions out of the hands of disc jockeys who might be less than the best. But as more and more stations signed up with consultants who tied them into informal networks of research and programming techniques, there was a drastic reduction in the number of people who decide what goes on the air, the gatekeepers. In communications theory, "gatekeeper" is a term denoting the person who decides what gets through the gate and into the communications channel. It can be a network official who decides which commercials are in good taste and which are unacceptable, or the editor who decides what story to put in the paper, or the movie theater owner who decides what films to book. When radio stations are programmed independently, each program director makes his or her own decision: Each station has its own gatekeeper. A progressive station would have many gatekeepers; each disc jockey would decide what went on the air. But when stations go to a rigid format and retain a consultant to set their rotation and play list, that consultant becomes gatekeeper for many stations. Fewer people participate in deciding what goes on the air, and more power is concentrated in fewer hands. It also means, of course, that each year the American radio audience gets to hear fewer songs.

An even more efficient way of streamlining on-the-air decision-making at a radio station is through the use of automated equipment and program services. By the mid-1970s it was estimated that at least a seventh of all FM stations were substantially automated. Because it is cost-efficient, the number will undoubtedly continue to grow. With a computer and a package of sophisticated equipment, a station can remain on the air indefinitely without human participation. Automated stations can easily broadcast music, with a computer switching to recorded commercials at appropriate times. Prerecorded comments from disc jockeys can be interspersed and the computer can be programmed to give the correct time. It can pick up network news services and other "live" feeds. (A typical package at an automated station might include a computer with memory; four or more open-reel tape recorders for music; two or more tape-cartridge players for commercials—jingles and spot announcements—and an interface with other audio sources for news, network feeds, and so on.) Add to this a consultant who provides the tapes, and you have a local radio operation whose staff might consist of a general manager, sales personnel, an engineer, and a janitor.

"Do you want local programming that sounds terrible or national-type programming that sounds professional?" goes the sales pitch of firms marketing automated services. Some stations use the automated equipment to play music, then have the computer turn on the deejay's mike for 15 seconds so he or she can identify the songs. At these stations, news is usually done live. But others prefer to have the deejay prerecorded. A disc jockey can record all the material for a four-hour shift in about 15 minutes, and correcting mistakes is easy.

Although early experiments with automated equipment involved Top 40 formats, they have achieved their widest use at Beautiful Music stations, the very purpose of which is to provide "wall-to-wall" music with as little interruption as possible. But automation has been tried with virtually every format.

Automated radio may indeed be the wave of the future, if not the present. But it cuts to the very heart of the limited gatekeeper problem. Even as the number of stations on the air soars, the number of people determining what goes out over the air shrinks.

The Rev. Everett Parker, who heads the Office of Communication of the United Church of Christ, is a vigorous critic of the broadcasting industry and an activist for reform. He is pessimistic about the impact of automation. "Unique formats are going out the window," he said. "It's a lot cheaper to throw that tape in there and get rid of the people and make the maximum money. And what about the public interest; with an automated station you can't even have disaster warnings. How can you put out a warning when you're running an automatic tape?"

Proponents say automation is just a logical extension of subjugating disc jockeys to the station's identity. It guarantees a more professional, efficient sound and thus provides the listeners with better service. Opponents say it is dehumanizing—which is hard to dispute. It is one of the most striking developments of the 1970s and in some ways one of the most depressing.

Another form of centrally originated, widely distributed pro-gramming spread during the 1970s: "barter syndication." Robert Meyrowitz of D.I.R. Broadcasting in New York was one of its pioneers. D.I.R. provides selected stations around the country—about 250—with prerecorded concerts, interviews, and other fea-tures. The shows are provided free. In exchange, stations agree to clear the time for the shows and to promote them in at least 30 spot announcements a week. D.I.R. sells the bulk of advertising time within the show and keeps the revenue. Each station gets to sell a couple of minutes of local advertising, and gains quality programming it could not otherwise afford. The idea sounds simple, but it has made Meyrowitz wealthy and spawned many imitators.

D.I.R.'s first and most successful offering—and thus the most important barter syndication show in American radio—is the "King Biscuit Flower Hour," which provides recorded concerts by top-name bands. (It derives its name from "King Biscuit Time," a 1920s radio show sponsored by the King Biscuit Flour Company.)

The program is distributed on tape to one progressive or AOR station in a market. Meyrowitz claims that ratings have indicated that during "King Biscuit," every single station carrying the show at least doubles its normal audience, while some more than quadruple it. With a station in virtually every market, D.I.R. is then able to turn to sponsors and guarantee a sizable, national audience in the highly sought 18- to 24-year-old male segments.

The emphasis on FM profits in the early 1970s seemed to some advocates of progressive radio to be part of a larger design to thwart the counterculture. Surely in most cases stations decided their music, advertising, and news policies on the basis of what would make money, rather than because they were toeing a political line. But at least one controversial incident fueled the fires of those who saw the Establishment cracking down.

On March 5, 1971, the Federal Communications Commission issued a public notice to radio stations reminding them of their responsibility to screen all songs for lyrics that tended "to promote or glorify the use of illegal drugs." The concern in Washington over the "drug culture" was not new. For more than a year Vice President Agnew had been galumphing across the land, making speeches on that theme. In a typical one he said American youths were being "brainwashed" into a "drug culture" by rock music. Agnew singled out the Beatles' "With a Little Help From My Friends" and Jefferson Airplane's "White Rabbit." While Agnew's remarks touched off debates, radio stations paid little attention. The FCC order was something else, however. It threatened their licenses.

The FCC statement said in part, "Whether a particular record depicts the dangers of drug abuse, or, to the contrary, promotes such illegal drug usage is a question for the judgment of the licensee. The thrust of this notice is simply that the licensee must make that judgment and cannot properly follow a policy of playing such records without someone in a responsible position (i.e., a management-level executive at the station) knowing the content of the lyrics.... While this duty may be delegated by licensees to responsible employees, the licensee remains fully responsible for its fulfillment."

The commission's notice touched off a heated debate among musicians, fans, record-company executives, and deejays about which songs depicted the problems of drug use and which glorified it. The message to station owners was clear: Don't take a chance. Instead of listening to the lyrics and making sure of all the nuances, it was simpler not to play any songs about drugs. One of the first casualties was a Top 40 hit, "One Toke Over The Line," by Brewer and Shipley. Predictably, those stations—a majority—that elected to pull the song off the air issued statements about how "having had the nuances of the song explained to us we were distressed to learn..." Those that decided to keep it on the air said they interpreted the song as a warning about drug use. (Brewer and Shipley, for their part, denied the song was about drugs, although "toke" is common usage for a puff on a marijuana cigarette.)

The most vigorous and persistent critic of the FCC order was its own commissioner, Nicholas Johnson, who termed the notice "an unsuccessfully disguised effort...to censor song lyrics that the majority disapproves of; it is an attempt by a group of establish-mentarians to determine what you ought can say and hear...." Johnson urged broadcasters to resist but expressed fear that they wouldn't, given the power of the commission. For the most part, he was right.

One group that did speak up, if somewhat whimsically, was the Authors League, which asked the FCC to reconsider its order. The league's memo pointed out that stations would have to take a hard look at the "message" in such classic songs as "Tea for Two," "I Get a Kick Out of You" and "I've Got You Under My Skin." Others complained to the FCC that its order was having a "chilling effect" on free speech; that some stations were not just screening songs about drugs, but songs that advocated political positions, sex, and other "radical" views. Some stations told deejays that if they played a song with a political message, they would have to read a Fairness Doctrine statement. Few deejays wanted to follow a song with the announcement that "this station recognizes its obligation to present viewpoints other than our own. The views expressed in this song do not necessarily represent those of management." So deejays would generally skip the controversial songs, and the statement. A New Haven, Connecticut, station took the FCC to court over the legality of the drug-lyric warning. It lost.

Dean Burch, FCC chairman at the time, looked back at the public order eight years later and said that while he thought it had no chilling effect and was "very badly overblown," he wouldn't do it again. "As far as I'm concerned now [in 1979]," Burch said, "the public is a lot better off with a strong First Amendment than with a lot of horse [bleep] out of the FCC about drug lyrics and dirty words and all the rest."

Burch took a similar, though unofficial, action, in 1973 in a speech to the National Association of Broadcasters when he deplored radio talk shows that discussed sexual behavior. (See Chapter 4.) The shows quickly disappeared from the airwaves. "I have considerable concern about that now," he said. "That sort of thing really does trample on freedom of discussion." Burch's drift to First Amendment absolutism has come as he shifted from government regulator to communications attorney in Washington, fighting on behalf of industry clients who are pressing for deregulation. But he willingly conceded that both the notice on drug lyrics and the speech on "topless radio" were a product of the times.

"Those times"—the years of the Nixon administration—witnessed a widespread attack on the media, and especially the news media, that was organized and coordinated by the White House. It was not aimed at radio; its primary targets were the television networks and *The New York Times* and *The Washington Post*. The attack included caustic speeches by Agnew and Clay Whitehead, head of the White House

Office of Telecommunications Policy; visits by White House aide Charles Colson to the network presidents in New York; telephone calls from Herb Klein, White House director of communications, to network officials; FBI harassment of CBS reporter Daniel Schorr; a Justice Department antitrust suit against the television networks; and a good deal more. Nixon also instigated some Florida businessmen, including the finance chairman of his reelection committee there, to file license challenges against the Jacksonville and Miami television stations owned by *The Washington Post.* The challenges were eventually disallowed by the FCC, but station owners were learning: Watch out!

These actions, while not aimed at radio, caused ripples there as well. Any mechanism for license-challenging, any precedents that were established, would apply to radio stations. In addition, many multiple-license holders owned both television and radio stations. Finally, station owners were aware of two license revocations.

In 1970 the FCC refused to renew the license of WXUR-AM/FM in Media, Pennsylvania, a station that aired the right-wing views of fundamentalist preacher Carl McIntire. His programming had led to many complaints to the FCC about one-sided presentation of issues, personal attacks, and failure to ascertain community needs or to follow his programming promises. The station went to court, but the U.S. Court of Appeals upheld the FCC. This served to remind broadcasters that the license-renewal mechanism was in place and working.

The second class was entirely different in nature and impact. WHDH-TV was owned by *The Boston Herald Traveler,* and the decision to revoke its license was part of an ongoing investigation into cross-ownership among the media and its impact on diversity. What was so troubling to station owners when the FCC denied its license in 1969—the case dragged on until the Supreme Court upheld the FCC in 1971—was that a station owner lost its license without any demonstrated record of violations.

All of these actions—the license denials, the speeches, the threats, the public notice on drug lyrics—put broadcasters, including radio management, in a vulnerable position. Faced with economic opportunities for enormous profits and with a political climate that encouraged conservatism, it is no wonder that most radio stations were happy to go along and get along, making few waves in return for making many dollars. Ironically, the situation may not have been as bad as it seemed to station owners, because the FCC was not as active in the political wars as the White House had hoped and expected. To be sure, Burch, Barry Goldwater's 1964 campaign manager, did not get off to a good start at the FCC. Two days after he was sworn in, in November 1969, Nixon gave a televised speech on Vietnam, and Burch telephoned the presidents of all three networks to request transcripts of their news coverage and analysis of the speech. CBS President Frank Stanton later said he found the implications of Burch's call ominous.

After this initial gaffe, Burch kept the FCC aloof from administration pressure (with the exception of the drug lyrics episode). White House memos from presidential advisers including Klein, Colson, and speechwriter Patrick Buchanan are littered with suggestions that "we ask Burch to do this and that." For the most part, Burch didn't.

"I certainly had knowledge that the White House expected I would do something about what they considered a problem," Burch said in 1979, "but there was no direct pressure. I don't recall the White House ever making a filing as such with the commission, or requesting a ruling. We did get complaints from the right-wing groups." FCC Commissioner Tyrone Brown, an attorney for *The Washington Post* broadcast operations when Burch was chairman, said Burch and the FCC maintained their integrity and did not participate in the White House plotting.

If all the political maneuvering was causing broadcasters grief, it was only part of the story. Broadcast ownership was under scrutiny on other fronts.

In response to congressional concern about the role of conglomerates in broadcasting and also to appease two commissioners, Nicholas Johnson and Kenneth Cox, the FCC ordered an examination of broadcast ownership on February 6, 1969. The study put special emphasis on the ownership of broadcast stations by licensees with substantial nonbroadcast interests. It was not directed at the smaller station owners who happened to have other small business interests. The decision to open the probe was hardly unanimous—the vote was four to three—and observers expected the probe to die the following year when Cox's term expired. The FCC created a task force that picked six conglomerates to start with: Avco Corporation, with holdings in aircraft, space and missile systems, and financial and lending businesses; Chris-Craft Industries; Fuqua Industries; Travelers Insurance Company, and Cox Enterprises and the E.W. Scripps Company, both of which had substantial newspaper and cable television holdings.

"The probe was a waste of time," said Burch. "The conglomerates we were looking at, well, radio was really small potatoes for them, and it was almost idle to suggest that they were sitting around in their corporate headquarters thinking about how to screw the public."

But in 1970 the task force reported that two of the six firms, Avco and Scripps, had conducted questionable intracorporate dealings, and that none of the six had demonstrated any benefits the public derived from conglomerate ownership. The task force found that Avco tried to convince its subsidiaries to place all their advertising with Avco broadcast stations and to have its stations provide special news coverage of the subsidiaries. Scripps was found to have arranged reciprocal advertising deals between its broadcast stations and newpapers in Cleveland. The FCC commissioners were sufficiently impressed to vote, five to two, to broaden the probe. It proved to be a paper tiger.

The conglomerate task force filed its final report and recommendations with the FCC in December 1972. It reported one significant finding: Conglomerates enjoy an advantage over competitors in that they have quick, easy, and cheap access to advertising on subsidiary stations. The FCC mulled the report over for three years and then decided to close its probe. In a one-page notice (which in itself is remarkable among FCC notices) in June 1975, the commission said it had concluded that no separate rules were needed for conglomerates; they could be examined just like any other station owners. What was more remarkable than its conclusions was the FCC's refusal to make public the task force's report. Some citizens' groups, notably the National Citizens Committee for Broadcasting, pressed for the material and filed Freedom of Information Act requests. Eventually the FCC released some information and reported that it had lost some of the task force material. In all, it was one of the FCC's less distinguished performances.

The FCC's probe into cross-ownership started with an equal lack of enthusiasm. In 1968 the Justice Department filed a memorandum with the FCC pointing out "the existing concentration of media ownership in many of the major cities." The FCC was not unaware of the issue; in 1941 it had probed newspaper ownership of radio stations and decided no rules were needed. In 1970 the commission invited comments on a proposal to require separate ownership of daily newspapers and broadcast stations in the same city. The proposed rule-making was an attempt to get away from case-by-case scrutiny, which had led to the controversial decision—then under appeal—to deny *The Boston Herald Traveler* its television station. That case had let the newspaper and broadcasting industries know the FCC was serious about the cross-ownership/diversity issue, and what followed were years of filings, hearings, and polemics from interested parties. Finally, in 1975, the FCC issued its findings: Future cross-ownership within the same city was banned, but almost all existing cross-ownerships were left intact. In 16 cities, however, newspapers were ordered to divest themselves of television stations (seven) or radio stations (nine), where the FCC found there was no other source of news. The ruling left intact about 140 combinations, many of them in major cities.

The FCC was taken to court by the National Citizens Committee for Broadcasting (NCCB) and the Justice Department, which both thought the ruling did not go far enough—they sought complete divestiture—and by the broadcasting and newspaper industries, which thought it had gone too far. On March 1, 1977, the former prevailed: The Court of Appeals for the District of Columbia ordered an end to all ownership of broadcast facilities by newspapers (or newspaper ownership by broadcast companies) within the same city. A year later the Supreme Court overturned the appellate court, eight to zero, and upheld the FCC ruling. Future cross-ownership was banned, the 16 divestitures were ordered, and all other existing cross-ownership was preserved. Nicholas Johnson, who had become chairman of the NCCB after his FCC term expired, disgustedly announced that his group would return to "guerrilla warfare," that is, case-by-case presentations to the commission. The industries, while complaining on behalf of their 16 colleagues, were mightily relieved that they had escaped divestiture.

Johnson's promise of guerrilla warfare was no idle jest, though the battleground proved wider than cross-ownership. Led by a tiny, Washington-based public interest law firm, the Citizens Communications Center, many groups were turning legal and lobbying guns on broadcasters. It was the dawn of a broadcast reform movement.

The FCC had, for decades, been criticized as a regulatory agency in the hip pocket of the broadcast industry, which was just the way broadcasters thought it should be. When, in the 1940s, FCC Commissioner Clifford J. Durr suggested that the FCC pay closer attention to station performance at license renewal times, the industry and its trade magazines acted as though he had proposed nationalization. At Durr's prodding the FCC ordered some promise-and-performance research, and published a report in March 1946 called "Public Service Responsibility of Broadcast Licensees." It was known, popularly, as the Blue Book. Justin Miller, NAB president at the time, labeled the idea that the public owned the airwaves "hooey and nonsense." Proponents of Blue Book formulas were labeled socialists, and vitriolic phrasemakers charged that the commission wanted to substitute "Durrmocracy" for democracy. By the end of 1946 the Blue Book had been beaten back by the industry; it remained a statement of FCC principles but not of practice.

The FCC remained a bastion of unchallenged industry views well into the 1960s. But in 1966 two cracks appeared in the wall, produced by a most unlikely pair of allies. One was Chief Justice Warren Burger, at the time a judge of the U.S. Court of Appeals; the other was

Nicholas Johnson. Burger, an Establishment Republican, and Johnson, an avowed populist and Democrat, shared a deeply held belief that the airwaves did indeed belong to the public. In separate actions they put the industry on notice that it would be held accountable for its obligation to the public interest.

In 1966 the U.S. Court of Appeals reversed an FCC decision renewing the license of WLBT-TV in Jackson, Mississippi. Citizens' groups had sought to block the license, charging that the station's news coverage and programming were racist. The FCC renewed the license and tried to prevent the groups from participating in its hearings. Burger's decision granted citizens' groups full standing to challenge a station's license before the FCC. Still, the FCC dragged its feet, and three years later, the Court of Appeals intervened. In June 1969 the court withdrew the license of WLBT and sternly rebuked the FCC. Burger blasted the "scandalous delay," said the FCC was still treating the groups as "interlopers," and found a "curious neutrality-in-favor-of-the-licensee."

These actions opened the gates to citizen participation, and after Nicholas Johnson's appointment to the FCC, reformers found they had an ally in a position of influence.

Ironically, Johnson's appointment to the FCC came because the shipping industry *and* the maritime unions were unhappy with his work as a federal maritime administrator; he had labeled federal subsidies to the industry "a theft from taxpayers." On the FCC Johnson soon became a lightning rod for what he perceived to be the public interest and a persistent critic of the industry and his fellow commissioners.

In 1969, Albert Kramer, a Washington attorney, decided to establish a center for citizen participation in broadcast regulation. With support from the Midas International Foundation, the Robert F. Kennedy Memorial Foundation, and a volunteer staff, Kramer founded the Citizens Communications Center. He taught volunteers how to monitor stations and how to read through station files. Almost from the start, Kramer received numerous complaints from civil rights groups about discrimination in employment or programming at broadcast stations. Once the CCC had amassed an accurate listing of the station's programming through monitoring, it would help complainants petition the FCC to deny a station's bid for license renewal.

These petitions rarely succeeded; license renewal rates at the FCC all through the 1970s averaged nearly 99 percent. But petitions to deny forced broadcasters to show the FCC how they were serving the public interest and meeting the conditions of their license.

In 1969 two petitions were filed. In 1970 there were 15; in 1971 the total was 38. Between July 1972 and May 1977, 237 petitions were filed. Between June 1977 and August 1979, 110 more were received by the FCC, including 56 in California alone. In all, only a few dozen hearings were ordered, and as of 1979 only one petition had resulted in a loss of license. But the process served to remind broadcasters that people were out there listening to and watching them.

Citizens' groups began to move on other fronts as well. They requested meetings with the FCC and found chairman Burch and the other commissioners receptive. In January 1970 Action for Children's Television met with the commission; observers could not recall when—if ever—a public interest group had been there previously for a meeting. The next meetings did not take place until 1973. The first was on January 3, with the National Organization for Women (NOW).

NOW's president, Wilma Scott Heide, chose confrontation tactics for the meeting. Heide began by complaining about the time of the meeting and the seating arrangements, then read a statement that made extensive references to male and female genitalia and how they affected personalities. The commissioners did not find the rhetoric funny; by the time NOW put forward specific proposals for reform the commissioners were hostile. Nothing came of the confrontation. The NOW meeting had been arranged by the only woman on the FCC, Charlotte Reid (and only the second woman ever to serve as a commissioner). Two months later, the FCC's first black commissioner, Benjamin Hooks (appointed by President Nixon in 1972), arranged a meeting with Blacks for Soul in Television. Afterwards Hooks commented, "For the first time in its 30-year history the FCC talked to some black folks, and it will never be the same again."

Participants found the meeting constructive, and were promptly criticized by the broadcasting industry in general, and *Broadcasting* magazine in particular, for not giving broadcasters equal time. But the FCC ignored the criticism and in May met with the Latino Media Coalition, a Hispanic group, to hear its complaints.

Another controversial meeting came on November 12, with the National Black Media coalition, headed by James McCuller of Rochester, New York. Like the NOW meeting, it began with confronation. McCuller launched into a diatribe, one of the milder statements of which was "FCC and its silver-tongued writers must stop hiding behind the smoke screen of legal fornication." Burch and McCuller sparred verbally as the other commissioners sat frozen in their seats, some looking dismayed and others terrified, according to reporters. Near the end of the meeting. McCuller presented the FCC with the NBMC's petition for rule changes, but no one was in the mood to hear it. It went unanswered for several years.

But the wall had been breached, and citizens' groups ended the broadcasters' monopoly over conferences with the FCC. (Nonetheless, the FCC told a House subcommittee that its commissioners and high-ranking staff members had, from 1971 through 1975, made 781 trips to visit broadcast industry groups—and *seven* to visit consumer groups.)

"I think the citizen's movement has some value," Burch reflected in 1979, even though he labeled the meeting with NOW "the most bizarre meeting" he was ever at and the meeting with the NBMC "the tensest." "Those meetings did sensitize me a hell of a lot. My feeling is that the public hearing is a tool that the commission hasn't used enough. The commissioners tend to sit in their ivory towers and make great, cosmic decisions. But for my dough they'd be a hell of a lot better off—and there'd be a hell of a lot more rough justice dispensed—if they didn't have to wait for five or six years to get to the oral arguments and go through all this legalistic bull[bleep] that they do."

In 1974 Burch resigned, and Commissioner Richard Wiley, who had been appointed in 1972 (He had been the FCC's general counsel for two years.) was named chairman. Wiley also was committed to public involvement. He continued meetings with citizens' groups, and in an unusual action he opened his appointment calendar to the public, so they could see just which broadcasters he might be hobnobbing with. Most important, he pushed the FCC to establish a consumer affairs office. On March 18, 1976, the commissioners voted six to one to create the office, which, in Wiley's words would, "establish a point of contact within the commission for the average citizen who may phone or visit us—a means by which the public can cut through the bureaucratic maze to secure the right information from the right person. . . . " Without ever assuming the role of a public advocate, as some—notably Commissioner Hooks—had hoped, the consumer assistance office has worked well. Full-time staff are knowledgeable and their responses ready, and they have brought the commission a good deal closer to the public.

In addition to complaints about programming, blacks had begun to raise other problems they had with the media, including employment, programming, and discrimination by the ratings services. In the 1970s more and more minority organizations began to press the FCC to take steps to end the virtual economic blockade against minority ownership. Radio, a pioneer in programming for blacks, had received far fewer complaints in this area than television. But it came to be one of the prime targets of the drive for minority ownership for two reasons: There were so many more radio stations than television stations, and many of them were modestly priced. The drive for minority ownership was spurred by the addition of Benjamin Hooks to the commission.

In April 1977 the FCC, with Wiley still in the chair, convened a two-day conference on minority ownership. The FCC used the term minorities to include American Indians, blacks, American Eskimos, Hispanics, Aleuts, and Asian-Americans. The bulk of the discussion was on what might be done to deal with the two major obstacles to minority ownership: lack of financing and lack of information about what was for sale. Many speakers at the conference contended that however successful they were as business people, they could not get a hearing from any of the conventional sources of credit. Speakers also complained that broadcast sales were handled by an "old boy" network of brokers, meeting over cocktails in clubs where only white males were members. There was widespread agreement among all participants in the conference that financing help had to be arranged; there was disagreement about how to provide access to information.

As a result of the conference, Wiley and Hooks agreed to ask the Small Business Administration to revise its policies and make loans to investors in broadcast facilities. SBA policy had been not to loan money to media operations because of possible First Amendment conflicts. But in September 1977, the SBA announced that since the appropriate federal watchdog, the FCC, favored loans, it would permit borrowing of up to $500,000 for the purchase of radio stations. (It continued to refuse financing for print media operations, citing the lack of a federal overseer.) Industry observers estimate that $500,000 would buy most radio stations in markets of 500,000 or fewer people—about 80 percent of all radio stations in the United States.

Other financing projects began as well. The Ford Foundation put up $1 million to fund Syndicated Communications, Inc., which would work as a lead investor and syndicator seeking outside financing for minority ownership projects. The Storer Broadcasting Company announced in 1979 that it would make $1 million available to invest in a Minority Enterprise Small Business Investment Corporation (MESBIC), which would then be eligible to receive $4 million in SBA loans. And the National Association of Broadcasters, also in 1979, announced it had developed a $15 million minority broadcast investment fund. These projects were needed: in 1976, it was estimated, only between 40 and 50 radio stations (out of more than 8,000) were owned by minorities—about *one half of one percent.*

While an FCC Minority Ownership task force was doing its research, Hooks was lobbying vigorously for a rule-making that would require public notice, 45 days before, of all broadcast properties up for sale. Hooks and other proponents argued that such a rule was needed to break the "old boy" network, and to give minorities a chance at good investments as well as leftovers. Critics said that with broadcast properties so much in demand, public notice would only serve to drive up the price through bidding, making it even harder for minorities to assemble adequate financing.

On May 25, 1978, the FCC announced two major policies, based on its task force report, designed to increase minority ownership. One involved tax credits for sellers and the other permitted "distress sales" of stations whose licenses are in doubt. Each gives sellers strong economic incentive to seek out minority clients. The commission at the same time unanimously rejected Hooks's proposal for public notice; they thought they had found a better way. (Hooks had resigned in 1977 to become executive director of the National Association for the Advancement of Colored People. He was replaced by Tyrone Brown, who thus became the second black FCC commissioner.)

The tax credit plan allowed the FCC to issue certificates to station owners who sold to minorities that would defer capital gains taxes for two years. The distress sale plan was based on a proposal from the Congressional Black Caucus; it permitted license holders facing revocation hearings to sell, on an expedited basis, to minorities for "somewhat above rock-bottom prices but considerably below market prices," according to Martin Levy of the FCC. Previously, station owners who lost their licenses were lucky to recoup the cost of their equipment. FCC officials estimated that about 100 licenses a year were not renewed for various reasons.

Within five months early results were in and the task force reported that both programs were working, and that a number of sales to minority owners had been approved.

What made the problem of encouraging minority ownership even more difficult was that with the enormous number of stations already on the air, the spectrum, both AM and FM, was virtually full. Although long-range plans were being examined to increase the number of stations (See Chapter 9.), the problem was for the commission to find a way to help minorities acquire stations that were already on the air. Under Chairman Charles Ferris, who was named by Jimmy Carter in October 1977 to succeed Wiley, the FCC has taken other steps to increase minority ownership. In November 1978 it established a list of would-be minority buyers. And in early 1979 an Office of Minority Enterprise was opened. As of mid-1979, 76 stations were owned by blacks, 20 by Hispanics, and one by American Indians—the 1 percent barrier was broken.

In its landmark policy-making in 1978, the FCC noted, "While today's actions are limited to minority ownership because of the weight of evidence on this issue, other clearly definable groups, such as women, may be able to demonstrate that they are eligible for similar treatment." It is estimated by industry sources that there are fewer women station owners than minority owners. The end result of all this, reformers hope, is that minority ownership will in turn take the lead in providing superior programming for minority audiences and that it will open the gates to wider minority employment.

The FCC had taken steps to improve minority hiring a good deal earlier, though not without a kick in the pants. The Kerner Commission report on civil disorders in 1968 had criticized media opportunities for minorities. A year later, the FCC adopted rules that required licensees to be equal opportunity employers. In 1970 the commission added sex as an impermissible basis for discrimination, and required all licensees with six or more employees to file annual employment reports.

Civil rights groups saw this as a modest enough victory, but to many broadcasters it was simply yet another FCC requirement that created paperwork. They began lobbying against it. In 1976, the FCC, at Wiley's behest, amended the rules to exclude all stations with fewer than eleven employees. It was promptly taken into court by a coalition of groups that included the Urban League, the NAACP, the National Council of Churches, the National Organization for Women, and the United Church of Christ. The complainants argued that the new exemption would cover two-thirds of all radio stations in the United States, including precisely the ones with the best employment opportunities. The U.S. Court of Appeals in New York agreed unanimously, and in August 1977 rejected the FCC's rule change as "arbitrary and capricious."

It was an early skirmish in the long battle over whether to deregulate radio. Deregulation is a simple label for a complex and diverse series of proposals. "Deregulation is like Christianity," Ferris said in 1979. "There are as many versions as there are sects." At one extreme are proponents of total deregulation; they would rewrite the Communications Act of 1934 to remove the "public interest" provisions, eliminate the FCC, lift the limit on how many stations a licensee might own, eliminate equal opportunity regulations and allow stations to be bought and sold and to program as they wish, with no regulation of commercials, promotions, public affairs, or fairness. They would grant licenses permanently. These extremists believe market conditions alone would effectively regulate radio. At the other extreme are proponents of tight regulation. They would bring station licenses up for renewal every year, increase FCC monitoring of station promise versus performance, and apply strictly the public interest clauses now on the books. Various proposals have come from FCC commissioners, members of Congress, and other interested parties.

Radio has been in the forefront of deregulation talk because there are so many more stations: Proponents argue that the competition can effectively regulate performance. Others have said that if deregulating radio works, they would press to deregulate television as well.

When Burch was FCC chairman, broadcasters were encouraged to press for deregulation. "My view of the FCC," Burch said, "was that I didn't want to set a bunch of goals, that the industry would accomplish whatever it was going to and that our main job was to get out of the way. I don't think the government does anything very well. Radio is a classic example: Why the hell you renew radio stations is beyond anyone's comprehension; why we log [requiring stations to keep records of everything played on the air] is beyond comprehension." Others from the FCC also provided support. General counsel Ashton Hardy told a conference of broadcasters: "While some regulation to protect the public interest may be necessary, we must not forget that commercial broadcasting is a private enterprise. I cannot and do not accept the philosophy of some who would state that you should have no quarrel with undue government intrusion into your business affairs because you are 'public trustees.' To those who maintain that, I would say 'hogwash.' " The encouragement continued under Wiley.

Finally, Congress got involved. Representative Lionel Van Deerlin of California introduced bills in 1978 and again in 1979 to rewrite the Communications Act of 1934 from top to bottom. After extensive hearings and debates, neither bill was approved. Some legislators, however, continue to fight.

On all of these fronts, the case for and against deregulation has emerged:

Pro: Regulation has not worked well. It is uneven, illogical at times, and extremely time-consuming and expensive to the industry. "At what point can we say it's a zero benefit?" asked Burch. "Millions and millions and millions of dollars are spent every year on crappy regulations, just on the off-chance that some group may want to come in and file something."

Anti: The airwaves are a valuable national resource, just like public lands. Why should they be given to commercial broadcasters for private gain without ensuring public benefit?

Pro: The enormous variety of communications services available makes obsolete the 1934 law. More than 8,000 radio stations, National Public Radio, satellites, cable television, and home video recorders offer sufficient diversity to ensure all the public is served.

Anti: Despite the enormous growth in number of stations, there are would-be station holders who cannot get frequencies. Ownership is concentrated among wealthy white males.

Pro: FCC studies have shown that stations will provide more news-and-information programming than required, and fewer commercials than the maximum allowed, to stay competitive in their markets.

Anti: Some opponents say this is true, but that news coverage remains superficial. Others say the FCC's sampling was too limited and unscientific to be extended to the whole spectrum.

And so on and so on. It comes down to a basic decision about the use of airwaves. Should they be licensed to commercial broadcasters as profitable business, with public taste—by whatever means it is measured—determining what is acceptable programming? Or should the government, on behalf of its citizens, establish principles of a public interest to be served by demanding quality broadcasting?

In their extremes, these views of broadcasting are incompatible. The struggle involves how to resolve the two.

By the end of the 1970s the radio industry was basking under a bright blue sky. AM radio operations had maintained their profitability while many FM stations soared toward parity. More than half of all FM stations moved into the black, and the biggest and best rose steeply in revenue and value. An FM station began to lead the market in New York City and also in Washington, where eight of the top ten stations were FM. By mid-1979, FM was drawing 50.5 percent of the total radio audience.

And finally, even *network* radio operations again turned profitable in the 1970s. Between 1974 and 1977 the billings of the four major networks doubled from $60 million to $118 million. A major factor in their recovery was the spiraling cost of television advertising.

ABC remained the market leader, both in revenues and affiliates. Mutual came on strong. And CBS, which for nearly 20 years had been content to sit pat on the marginally profitable base, began innovative programming. First, in 1974, it offered the Mystery Theater, a return to the radio plays and dramas of the Golden Age. In 1979 it added the Sears Radio Theater, a nightly variety hour. (In January 1980, it dropped the program, which Mutual picked up and renamed the Mutual Radio Theater.) CBS also aggressively promoted sports— finding that even events also being telecast could be profitable. It scored big with football games—including Monday Night Football, which television had created—and with World Series coverage as well. And for the first time since the arrival of television, the networks began to beef up their programming departments.

Radio ended its first 30 years of coexistence with television in better shape than anyone had imagined in the dark days of the early 1950s. And the future looked bright: Unlike television, which was threatened by inroads from cable TV and home video centers, radio had not a cloud in its sky.

8

NONCOMMERCIAL RADIO

It is inconceivable that we should allow so great a possibility for service, for news, for entertainment, for education, and for vital commercial purposes to be drowned in advertising chatter.

—Herbert Hoover,
then Secretary of Commerce, 1922

Broadcasting as it exists now in the United States is a pitiful, unmitigated whore. At some stage in its history, there was a chance to turn it into a creative, artful, caring medium; but then all the toads came along, realizing the power of radio and television to hawk their awful wares.... Although most of this vital natural resource has gone into the hands of the speculator-ruinators, there is a portion of the FM band which has been set aside for commercial-free operations.

—Lorenzo Milam,
Sex and Broadcasting: A Handbook
for Starting a Community Radio Station, 1971.

THE public airways are like a great grazing land, upon which commercial radio stations, like sheep, graze at the public's pleasure, regulated by its shepherd, the FCC. But there's other life in the pasture, almost as hard to spot as field mice. These are the non-commercial radio stations.

Until about 15 years ago this image held up. Only since then have noncommercial broadcasters emerged as a readily identifiable breed, visible to the naked eye. If their impact is still small compared to that of commercial broadcasting, it is nonetheless growing. Stations have multiplied almost fourfold; nearly three-quarters of the 1,100 noncommercial operations have been in existence 15 years or less. During the same time, National Public Radio, the first noncommercial network, was born. But the numbers are not the whole story. Noncommercial radio, free of the commercial pressure to target audiences, has provided wide varieties of off-beat programming and educational services that have won small but loyal audiences. Although noncommercial radio seems to have turned the corner of public awareness, it has not yet overcome decades of disorganization and neglect and abuse by the federal government.

Since its inception, noncommercial radio has been called the "hidden medium" or the "forgotten medium." The appellations were apt: Only its listeners and participants knew of its existence. And the stations were a most diverse lot, for noncommercial radio includes a number of different categories.

More than 700 stations are licensed to colleges and universities. Some of these provide service to towns and surrounding areas; others are little more than campus media or training grounds for would-be

167

broadcasters. About a fifth of the stations are licensed to schools and local boards of education. About 70 are "community access" or "alternative radio" stations, that have gone on the air since 1962. Five are licensed to the Pacifica Foundation, a pioneer in listener-supported radio. Two are operated by New York City—the only noncommercial municipal stations in the country. (Dallas [WRR-FM] and Jacksonville, Florida [WJAZ-AM-FM] have municipally operated stations, but they are commercial, selling air time to advertisers and operating on a profit-and-loss basis.) And the balance are licensed to churches, religious organizations, and libraries.

Amid all this diversity—of audience, of motivation for broadcasting, of programming, and of personnel—it has always been impossible to find one voice that spoke clearly for what noncommercial radio needed. The stations have been clumped together under the banner of "not operated for profit" and ignored. They lacked an effective national organization to give them a unified voice, and they had no network to tie them together. That has changed. The postwar years—the television years—have been a time of birth and growth. But educational and other institutional stations are as old as radio itself.

The earliest educational radio station was 9XM at the University of Wisconsin at Madison (later licensed as WHA on January 13, 1922). The license for 9XM was held by Professor Earle M. Terry, who began sending out weather reports by Morse code in 1917 for nearby farmers. During the war, when radio operations were banned, 9XM had a special permit from the navy to conduct transmission experiments on the Great Lakes. When restrictions were removed in 1919, Terry resumed his Morse code broadcasts. He was eager to begin voice transmissions, but the necessary vacuum tubes were unavailable. Terry and his students built their own and began voice tests. By January 1921 the daily reports were voice transmissions. Other colleges clamored for broadcasting facilities. By the end of 1922, 74 had licenses; a notable exception was Columbia University, where the president, Nicholas Murray Butler, reportedly turned down a professor's proposal for a station: "Tyson, don't bother about that. There are gadgets turning up every week in this country."

Educators apparently envisioned the stations as a tool for teaching; by 1924 the University of Nebraska was charging fees for courses taught by radio. But even as campuses continued to sign up, commercial firms were getting licenses as well and waging a war with educational competitors. This was the period of the greatest confusion on the airwaves, with haphazard and overlapping transmissions. Many schools lacked the will or the funds to struggle for airwaves rights, and others were overwhelmed by industry.

Also in 1924, another type of station went on the air: the municipally owned and supported WNYC, New York. It was the brainchild of civic booster Grover A. Whalen, also credited with developing the ticker-tape parade. WNYC debuted in July of that year, with music, appearances by municipal officials, and live coverage of public hearings. In 1933 a reform candidate for mayor, Fiorello LaGuardia, denounced the station as an extravagance and pledged to abolish it. When he was elected he changed his tune and came to regard WNYC as a municipal treasure and, no doubt, a convenient electronic soapbox. In 1945 LaGuardia gave WNYC its grandest moment when he took to the air each Sunday during a citywide newspaper strike to read the comics.

In 1941 the city added WNYC-FM, chiefly a repository of classical music. Thirty-five years later, the city's fiscal crunch caught up with the station: Mayor Edward Koch decided to halt funding by 1980, urging the Municipal Broadcasting System to become self-sustaining through listener support and foundation grants. WNYC has tried energetically: It affiliated with National Public Radio; provided call-in shows with officials, consumer hints, municipal news, and live coverage of meetings on AM, and excellent classical music on FM.

At the fourth national radio conference in 1925, Commerce Secretary Herbert Hoover announced that the airwaves were full and that no additional licenses would be issued. The federal government's policy was to encourage the sale and barter of existing licenses, and many colleges and universities unloaded theirs for handsome payments. The situation grew worse still. As Hoover began sorting out the existing frequencies, many colleges received daytime-only licenses. Since a major incentive for them had been adult education—

at night—the licenses were not worth the expense of maintaining the operation. The Federal Radio Commission seemed, on almost every occasion, to show the back of its hand to educational institutions and to favor commercial broadcasters. And universities, particularly as the Depression began, had limited funds to fight on. By 1930 only a few dozen educational stations remained on the air. They closed ranks and counterattacked, forming the National Committee on Education in Radio, to lobby in Washington.

The NCER sought a modest goal: It wanted Congress to pass legislation that would reserve 15 percent of all available frequencies for educational radio. Bills introduced by Senator Simeon Fess of Ohio failed in 1931, 1932, and 1933. With the great congressional debate in 1934 over the Communications Act—which, when passed, would establish the FCC—educational radio got new sponsors, Senators Robert F. Wagner of New York and Henry D. Hatfield of West Virginia. They proposed a comprehensive three-part plan: that all current licenses be rescinded, that in the new allocation of frequencies and operating hours one-quarter of all channels be reserved for nonprofit use (They included not just colleges but religious, agricultural, labor, cooperative, and other nonprofit groups.), and that these stations be permitted to sell commercial time in order to meet costs. While the likelihood of passage was uncertain in any case, this last proposal doomed the bill. It divided the educators and blurred the line between commercial and noncommercial broadcasting. The Wagner-Hatfield Amendment was defeated 42 to 23. The final bill required that the FCC report to Congress on educators' access to the airwaves.

The FCC concluded in 1935 that commercial stations provided adequate educational programming and that no special frequencies were needed. Noncommercial radio ended the decade with barely 30 low-power stations, most of them daytime-only.

The first very small comeback came in 1940, when the FCC made its initial FM allocations: Five of the 40 channels were set aside for noncommercial use. Then came the wartime freeze and the decision in 1945 to move all of FM to new frequencies. In the new allocations, noncommercial radio received 20 of the 100 FM channels, from 88-92 MHz on the dial. It was the first major step on behalf of noncommercial radio.

In the public eye and ear, however, noncommercial radio was a nonentity. Only a handful of operations were successful. Two events in the late 1940s were seminal in the proliferation and the increased visibility and variety of this medium, though they had little in common.

The first came in 1946, when Lewis Kimball Hill, a radio newsman and pacifist who had served as a conscientious objector during the war, established the Pacifica Foundation. He applied for an AM license in San Francisco, where he was working as news director at KYA. Pacifica was turned down, but reapplied the next year for an FM license in Berkeley. On March 31, 1948, the FCC granted the Pacifica Foundation a construction permit for KPFA, a 1000-watt station. KPFA received the first noncommercial license that did not go to an educational or religious institution; it set a precedent for more noninstitutional stations to be licensed.

KPFA went on the air on April 15, 1949, with modest finances and a transmitter capable of producing only 550 watts of the 1000-watt authorization. In December the Internal Revenue Service approved the Pacifica Foundation for tax-exempt status, and the way was cleared for tax-deductible listener contributions. The station was briefly off the air in 1950 and 1951 for lack of funds, but returned on May 19, 1951. Listener support improved, and a Ford Foundation grant provided a new facility. KPFA has been on the air in the Bay Area ever since.

The second breakthrough came in 1948 when the FCC, seeking to encourage use of the reserved channels on the educational band, took a dramatic step that remains controversial. The FCC liberalized broadcasting rules to license 10-watt stations that could be operated on little more than pocket money. (The previous minimum had been 250 watts.) The FCC thought that by encouraging schools to get modest operations going, it would generate excitement and commitment and the stations would grow in power; their signals would reach beyond the campus and serve a wider public interest. It was not the first time the FCC guessed wrong: the overwhelming majority of 10-watters did not boost their power.

The first 10-watt station, WAER, was at Syracuse University, which had cooperated with General Electric in developing low-cost transmission facilities. It went on the air in October 1948. (WAER *did* increase its power eventually to 6,000 watts.) Dozens of others followed. The proliferation of 10-watters was useful. They helped promote the use of FM radio. They gave educational stations a national, if feeble, presence. Perhaps most important, they gave thousands of students and hundreds of faculty members the opportunity to use the equipment and go on the air. It was only when alternative forms of noncommercial radio evolved that the 10-watters became a nuisance. The FCC had failed to anticipate how crowded the FM spectrum would become. By the 1970s the 10-watters were cramping available spectrum space that was much in demand; a 10-watt station has an effective range of about seven miles, but its presence precludes a high-powered signal from coming into the area.

Critics of the 10-watters—usually would-be station operators—claim the FCC never monitors their performance. They point out that one Oklahoma station received a license after submitting a budget to the FCC that included $97 for construction costs and yearly operating costs of $130. Community-radio advocates are particularly unhappy with 10-watters that, they say, are nothing more than communications laboratories at universities or entertainment media for dormitories.

The 1950s and early 1960s, then, were quiet years for noncommercial radio. The 10-watters grew in number, but not spectacularly, and the Pacifica Foundation added KPFK, in Los Angeles in 1959. In 1960, a wealthy manufacturer, Louis Schweitzer, donated his commercial station, WBAI, New York, to Pacifica, giving the foundation a reach from coast to coast. (It added KPFT, Houston, in 1970 and WPFW, Washington, in 1977.) The Pacifica stations provided a wide variety of programming that was uncommon and sometimes controversial. Programming was extremely diverse and occasionally eccentric, mixing protest singers blacklisted from television (and not played on AM radio) with fine classical selections; panel discussions on political issues both national and local and international news from a pacifist, and sometimes left-wing, point of view. More important than the number of people they reached was the fact that they established a model for an alternative type of radio and demonstrated that listeners would support it.

The tumultuous early- and mid-1960s brought a growing awareness of the possibilities of noncommercial radio, though still on a modest level. The civil rights movement and the early antiwar movement received in-depth, often passionate, advocacy accounts on the Pacifica stations. There were only three at the time, but they were located in New York, Los Angeles, and Berkeley. As passions grew and more and more people took to the streets, they turned to the Pacifica stations for the most sympathetic coverage of their demonstrations and the most in-depth coverage of what was happening elsewhere. Listener contributions grew. The 1960s were the heyday of the Pacifica stations.

In the last decade they fell on hard times. The Berkeley operation remained strong, but WBAI grew divided and eventually crippled by internal political debates. Women, blacks, and Hispanics sought a greater voice in program control and were not easily accommodated. The station was knocked off the air by a strike for 50 days in 1977. WPFW, Washington, has had financial troubles. KPFT, Houston, has never attracted substantial support or awareness in the community.

In 1962, a new spice was added to the noncommercial stew; it was variously known as "community radio," "alternative radio," "public access radio," and "radio free radio." Its father was an eccentric named Lorenzo Milam, who was working at KPFA, the Berkeley Pacifica station. Milam had a vision of a medium he liked to call "free-form non-institutional radio," and he set out to build it.

"A radio station should be a live place," Milam wrote in the whimsically titled *Sex and Broadcasting: A Handbook for Starting a*

Radio Station for the Community, "for live people to talk their talk and walk their walk and know that they (and the rest of us) are not finally and irrevocably dead." If Pacifica had come to stand as a symbol of 1960s politics, Milam's view of radio mirrored the 1960s counterculture. The first station he organized was KRAB, in Seattle, which went on the air in 1962. It was followed by KBOO, in Portland, Oregon, a "repeater station" that simply picked up and carried KRAB's shows until it eventually developed its own programming. (Nothing better demonstrates Milam's eccentricity than the call letters of stations he was involved with. Aside from KRAB and KBOO there were KTAO, KUSP, KCHU, WORT, WAIF, and KDNA.)

In 1970 KDNA was established in St. Louis, the first community radio station in the Midwest. Tom Thomas, currently executive director of the National Federation of Community Broadcasters, was its manager. KDNA provided a base in the center of the country for community radio activity. Most of the organizing was done by word of mouth, through personal contact from political activities. One offshoot was a tape exchange that was dubbed "KRAB Nebulae." In 1971 Milam's book was published and attracted some national attention after it was listed in *The Whole Earth Catalogue.* Milam willingly became the resource center of this new radio. For several years he advised organizers and served as mail drop for this fledgling movement. In June 1975, the first attempt was made to organize community stations. More than 200 people gathered in Madison, Wisconsin, to exchange information, and to discuss how they might obtain part of the money the federal government was beginning to pump into radio.

The meeting ended with the birth of the National Federation of Community Broadcasters, with twelve member stations, only half of which were on the air. By 1979 it had 50 members, with 35 on the air. The goals and functions of the NFCB are to promote sharing of ideas and programs among member stations and to give those scattered stations a voice in Washington, not just at the Corporation for Public Broadcasting, but at the Federal Communications Commission, and the Departments of Education and of Health and Human Services, which provide grants for facilities.

The 13 years between the birth of KRAB and the founding of the NFCB straddle the conception and birth of the largest and most powerful voice in noncommercial radio, National Public Radio. If the NFCB came together on a grass roots level and has the limited clout that such organizing implies, NPR is quite the opposite. It is the prototype of a Washington-based, centrally run, quasi-government operation. The NFCB is based on the third floor of a rickety wooden house in Washington, and has a staff of three. NPR sits in glory on several floors of a modern office building down the block from the FCC and has a staff of 186. But precisely because it is a Washington institution it has a good deal of clout. It became both a service and a symbol: It gave to the 50-year-old idea of noncommercial broadcasting a highly visible umbrella. It offered the promise of a link among all the incredibly diverse types of noncommercial radio. That, at least, was the theory. In some ways the goals remain unrealized, but NPR marked a turning point in noncommercial radio.

Yet even NPR's creation was almost an afterthought. The first Carnegie Commission report on public broadcasting, in 1966, focused entirely on television. It led to the passage of the Public Broadcasting Act of 1967, which set up the Corporation for Public Broadcasting—and only at the insistence of Jerrold Sandler, head of National Educational Radio, were the words "or radio" included in the act. (National Educational Radio, part of the National Association of Educational Broadcasters, represented about 275 stations.)

NPR was designed both as a production center for programming and a network to link the member stations. The first step was to decide which stations would be eligible; CPB drew up minimum standards of eligibility:

—Stations had to broadcast at least 18 hours a day, 365 days a year (thus excluding all college stations that were closed during vacations or that held daytime-only licenses).

—Stations had to maintain a full-time professional staff of five and have an operating budget of at least $80,000 annually (thus excluding stations that had shoestring budgets and relied on volunteers).

—AM stations had to be at least 250 watts, FM at least 3,000.

—Stations had to have adequate facilities to provide for local program production and origination.

—Stations had to broadcast "programs of good quality serving demonstrated community needs of an educational, cultural, or informational nature intended for a general audience" (thereby excluding programming of religious or instructional nature, because it was not for a general audience).

The initial guidelines for eligibility excluded, right off the top, four-fifths of the stations that had been carrying the torch of noncommercial radio until NPR came along. Proponents of the guidelines, notably NPR officials, argued that a strong system of strong stations was needed to provide the first giant step toward "full-service public radio" and also to make the most effective use of limited funds. Opponents saw the heavy hand of Big Brother pushing for an American version of the BBC, at the expense of smaller stations.

The line was drawn, and the debate continues to this day. But it is not a battle line, for on many issues community broadcasters and NPR agree. The debate is often theoretical and always philosophical. Should public radio be decentralized, participatory, encouraging of access by all citizens, and run collectively; or should it be centralized, run by bureaucrats, and insulated from the people? It is like the difference between a town meeting and the House of Representatives: radio by the people or radio on behalf of the people.

When the CPB eligibility guidelines were issued in 1970, 73 stations qualified. By 1979, 199 were qualified. But NPR had affiliates in only two-thirds of the top 100 markets, and reached only about two-thirds of the country's population.

During its early years NPR seemed to suffer both from CPB's preoccupation with public television and from less-than-dynamic leadership. Some of the larger public stations decided that NPR wasn't enough, and that they needed more of a voice in Washington.

In 1973 they formed the Association of Public Radio Stations, with 108 members. This gave public radio two voices instead of one, but the impact seemed to be split rather than doubled. Each organization was frustrated. Only about 60 percent of the eligible stations had joined APRS, where dues were $1,300 a year, while NPR was bogged down in squabbling.

In informal talks, directors of both groups agreed that merger was probably the solution. Negotiations began in 1975 and stretched out for more than a year and a half. A key problem was that NPR wanted to absorb APRS, which wanted parity. Finally in the spring of 1977 details were hammered out: The groups would merge under the NPR name: station managers would elect half the directors, and a new leader would be sought. The stronger NPR had a good deal more clout in CPB. An extensive search for a new president followed, and to the surprise of almost everyone in the organization the search committee selected Frank Mankiewicz, who had served as press secretary to Robert F. Kennedy, and campaign manager for George S. McGovern. Mankiewicz's name originally came up on a White House patronage list; when he was approached by a member of the search committee and asked if he would be interested in heading NPR, he asked what it was! He had some credentials in broadcasting (as a radio commentator and television news anchor) but most of all he was the consummate Washington insider. He knew the ropes.

"I don't think they hired me for my management skills or for my nonexistent experience as a broadcast executive," Mankiewicz told *The Washington Post,* "but to get more money... mostly to get more recognition—increase general awareness of public radio. I think they wanted me to make waves." Mankiewicz's leadership on and access to Capitol Hill has capped a decade of growth for NPR:

—The budget grew from $3.2 million in 1973 to $12.5 million in 1979. Federal funding increased from $7.7 million in 1978 to $10.2 million in 1979. In NPR's early days, radio received only 9 percent of CPB's budgets, and television the rest. By 1979 it was 18.2 percent. (NPR's goal is 25 percent.)

—It provided live coverage for 37 days of Senate hearings on the

Panama Canal Treaties in February, March, and April 1978, attracting wide publicity and a 25 percent increase in its audience.

—It has increased its programming to include radio dramas, children's shows, and some Spanish-language programming.

—It won FCC approval to link its stations by satellite in 1980, greatly increasing its flexibility and the quality of its transmissions, currently sent on telephone lines. The satellite will feed programs to 192 receivers, called "dishes," scattered around the country; virtually every NPR station will have access to a dish. It will make possible at least four channels of programming. The plan also provides for 16 transmission stations—"uplinks"—around the country that will allow programming to originate somewhere other than Washington.

—It has won awards—the Peabody and Dupont—and public recognition for "All Things Considered," its 90-minute daily news show, which draws about three million listeners, making it the most widely heard noncommercial radio show ever. Each show generally includes news summaries, some stories explored in depth, foreign news from the BBC reporters, features and commentary, cultural reviews, and so on. So successful is "All Things Considered" that NPR hopes to add morning newscasts as well.

—Most important, it has increased awareness of public radio of all kinds. The gains have been extremely modest, to be sure, but they are at least a step in the right direction: a 1978 Roper survey of 2,000 people showed that 28 percent had heard of NPR, compared to 23 percent in 1977. Eighteen percent claimed to have listened to a public radio station, compared to 16 percent the previous year.

All this paints a rosy picture—and it certainly represents a more visible presence in the American mass media potpourri than noncommercial radio has ever had. But NPR also has its critics and its problems.

A key issue is how well, in leadership, participation, station diversity, and programming, National Public Radio reflects the diversity of American society.

The Carnegie Commission's second report on public broadcasting, in January 1979, known as Carnegie II, called for at least 250 more public radio stations. Its goals were comprehensive coverage and greater diversity. It seemed to side with the NFCB against a centralized NPR handing down programs from on high. The current setup, Carnegie II said, "does not reflect the pluralism that is such a highly valued characteristic of American society."

In policy statements, NPR seems to endorse diversity. Its pamphlet for member stations says, "A keystone of NPR philosophy and operating policy is the practice of seeking decentralized sources of program materials. National Public Radio acquires and distributes programs and reports supplied from every part of the country and the world by the staffs of member stations, independent producers and reporters, and foreign broadcasting agencies such as the British Broadcasting Corp., the Canadian Broadcasting Corp. and Radio Nederland. These are assembled with other materials produced by the NPR staff to make up the program service." Critics say it's just lip service.

National Public Radio does not accurately reflect American society. Its station standards favor the status quo, as does its board of directors: twelve members are station managers elected by station managers, and the other twelve are citizens elected by the board. Most of the station managers are men; even more are white. Asked how accurately the board of directors mirrored a pluralistic society, NPR Vice President Sam Holt snorted, "We have very few failures. We have no welfare recipients on the board." There are three blacks on the board, he added, but no Hispanics. Holt doesn't think it's a problem.

NPR's programming draws similar criticism. Studies of the NPR audience have shown that it is predominantly white, middle and upper class, with college-level educations. Because about 90 percent of NPR stations seek listener support and rely on it for 20 to 40 percent of their budgets, programming tends to focus on this demographic group—lots of classical music, jazz, and "All Things Considered." NPR officials concede that programming is targeted to "those likely to contribute." But they see a shift in the NPR audience; a 1978 Roper study indicated NPR was attracting slightly more minority and blue collar listeners. And in the last decade about a dozen stations that serve minority audiences have joined the network.

Community radio organizers, and leaders of the National Federation of Community Broadcasters, want NPR to do more. They view the satellite plans with mixed feelings: Will it be used to provide more mainstream service from headquarters, or will more community radio stations and independent producers be allowed access to the system's uplinks? Not everyone is optimistic. But if NPR is to grow steadily, it will have to diversify and also take advantage of the commitment to community radio of NFCB activists.

There are several areas of common ground on which the two public radio camps might gather. They are allies in the struggle against the 600-odd 10-watt stations that dot the landscape. NPR wants them out of the way in order to fill out its network and reach 100 percent of the population. The NFCB, even though some of its members are 10-watters, wants them out of the way, too. It feels the spectrum space could be better used. Both organizations were among the participants in FCC hearings on what to do.

The only group to speak up for the 10-watters was the Intercollegiate Broadcasting System. IBS was founded in 1940 at Brown University in Providence, Rhode Island, by a group of engineering students. Its first stations were carrier current: closed-circuit broadcasting to dormitories and other school buildings. After 1948, 10-watters began to join. By 1979 IBS claimed 260 10-watt members, 231 carrier current, and 120 higher-power FMs. But it is a small organization, based in Vails Gate, New York, with only two full-time employees. IBS organizes an annual convention, ties its members together with newsletters and a tape service, publishes the *Journal of College Radio,* and represents college radio before the FCC. IBS was overmatched in Washington on the 10-watt issue.

The FCC hearings were a turning point in the credibility of the NFCB. Its filing was well received at the FCC, and helped debunk its counterculture reputation. In fact, in its June 1978 findings, the FCC closely followed the NFCB's suggestions when it ordered these reforms:

—starting in 1980, stations of less than 100 watts, when they come up for license renewal, will be required to change channels to the commercial spectrum, if any room at all is available there. If not, they will be permitted to stay in the noncommercial band but only on the frequency that causes the least preclusion of other signals. And the responsibility for proving they are not interfering will be on the 10-watters, who will have to provide complete engineering justification for their placement on the band.

—10-watters will no longer be protected from interference. They will not be allowed to cause it, but will be allowed to receive it. In effect, they have lost their seniority rights to spectrum space.

—A five-year freeze on 10-watt licenses, until all existing stations have had their licenses renewed.

—All noncommercial stations must operate at least 36 hours a week, and at least five hours daily for six days weekly, except for school stations during official recess periods.

—Any station on the air less than twelve hours a day, every day, is subject to sharing its frequency, and the FCC will enforce sharing, rather than leaving it to interested parties to negotiate.

"I have no quarrel with NFCB and NPR as far as getting more stations on the air," said Jeff Tellis, president of IBS, in 1979. "I just find it difficult to swallow that it must be done at the expense of those that are already on and have made the investment. . . this message of 'Get out of the way, because the steamroller's coming through,' is very disconcerting when the policy all along had been one of encouragement to get on the air." The bottom line is that the 10-watters seem to have lost the war. Their numbers will decrease, and more powerful public radio stations will increase.

Among NPR, the NFCB, the 10-watt stations, the Pacifica Foundation, Carnegie II, and the FCC, there may be substantial disagreement over what the future of noncommercial radio should be—which would hardly be surprising given the past—but there is widespread certainty that it is a medium whose time has finally come.

It was noted earlier just how phenomenal the growth had been in the past 15 years. It seems rooted in three basic areas: the opening of the FM spectrum, the media awareness of young people, and a commitment by schools and colleges to provide courses in broadcasting.

The opening of the spectrum in 1965 did not directly affect noncommercial radio. But it led to a growing use of FM, an awareness of FM by radio users, and an increase in the number of all radio stations. Through the programming of "progressive rock," FM stations reaffirmed to teenagers the commitment that 1950s rock 'n' roll programming had made: that radio was the most responsive medium to adolescents.

These adolescents of the 1960s and 1970s grew up bathed in electronic media. They watched television every day, for hours at a time. They had radios to listen to in almost every room of their homes. When they went to college they found radio accessible—often more accessible than television.

Colleges and universities seemingly felt the same way. Some educators no doubt thought that the impact of the electronic media and how they were changing the world should be explored on campus. Others saw a student demand emerging and were delighted to sell credits to gratify it. The figures are revealing:

	1960-61	1965-66	1971-72	1974-75*
Number of colleges and universities offering a bachelor's degree in broadcasting	98	131	180	228
Number of enrolled undergraduate majors	2,600	4,000	12,000	17,250

*The last year for which figures in these surveys, compiled for the National Association of Broadcasters, are available.

Similar increases were found on the graduate level and in junior and community colleges. And many other campuses offered broadcasting courses but no degree programs. All of these classes sought to train students for positions in commercial broadcasting and also to improve communications skills that would be useful in any profession. These courses marked a dramatic change in broadcasting education. In radio's early days, schools that taught broadcasting at all generally sought to train announcers, and the courses were offered by speech departments. Only after the changes in local commercial radio in the 1950s and 1960s did educators perceive the need to train students as broadcast reporters, editors, and writers, and to acquaint them with broadcast management, broadcast law, and hands-on experience.

The tangled history of noncommercial radio makes clear how hard it is to answer the question, "What is public radio?" Truly, there is no simple answer.

But "Why is public radio?" is a good deal easier. For noncommercial radio in all its chaos and variety provides a number of valuable services that its commercial counterparts do not. For one thing, it trains personnel and has been the largest source of professional broadcasters since World War II.

Secondly, noncommercial broadcasters have often served the important function of consciously and consistently experimenting with programming. They are freer to challenge the limits of what is acceptable. These challenges have led to brilliant programming, and they have led to amateurish, self-indulgent disasters. They are on the cutting edge of permissiveness in a society where lines are not always clearly drawn. Through their efforts they help bring about definitions and discussions. A recent example was the WBAI broadcast that led to the "seven dirty words" case.

One afternoon in 1973, WBAI carried a George Carlin comedy routine in which he discussed seven dirty words he said could not be used on the air. A man complained to the FCC that he had been listening to the show with his young son; on the basis of that single complaint the FCC censured WBAI for airing the material at a time when children might be listening. Pacifica went to court, asserting that the FCC had no right to criticize the content of a show.

The U. S. Court of Appeals agreed, and found that the censure had breached WBAI's First Amendment rights. But the Supreme Court, in July 1978, upheld the FCC. The reprimand, Associate Justice John Paul Stevens wrote, was not based on obscenity, but on nuisance. A nuisance, he wrote, "may be merely a right thing in the wrong place— like a pig in the parlor... We simply hold that when the commission finds that a pig has entered a parlor, the exercise of the regulatory power does not depend on proof that the pig is obscene." The court said the FCC had the right to prohibit "patently offensive" material. (By judicial definition, obscene material appeals to prurient interests, while indecent material is patently offensive.)

Provocative programming aside, noncommercial radio fills other cracks between the formats that dominate commercial radio. Noncommercial radio provides services—including access and programming—to the young, the old, the poor and the lower middle class, and to ethnic minorities not large enough to attract commercial attention. Programs are broadcast in Eskimo and in Navajo; programs are broadcast for the blind. In these economically unproductive markets, which offer little promise of profits to commercial broadcasters, public radio is most valuable..

Noncommercial radio also has provided educational services, especially through a type of broadcasting known as SCA, for Subsidiary Communications Authority. SCA is a form of multiplexing that can be picked up only by special receivers. (The same capability permits Muzak broadcasts in department stores.) SCA broadcasts have ranged from adult education courses in rural Appalachia to continuing professional education for doctors and dentists. It also has been used in school for instruction in all grades from kindergarten up. Some of this instructional material has been broadcast on the main channel as well, but more and more of it in the past decade has been diverted to SCA. (However, a recent CPB study found that instructional material was more effectively delivered by nonbroadcast media, such as cassettes.)

To its advocates, noncommercial radio serves a more dramatic function as well. They wax poetic in stating the case, "Public radio is a monastery of liberal humanism in the dark age of mercantilism," wrote Larry Josephson, a CPB consultant, in the *Public Telecommunications Review*. "It is often the only broadcast source of the liberal tradition and its intellectual and cultural manifestations." These include opera, jazz, folk, and avant-garde music, public affairs, dramatic readings, and children's shows. Precisely because of this unusual programming, and because of the eccentric personalities who have emerged, noncommercial radio is a forgotten medium no longer. The field mouse has roared.

9

WHITHER RADIO?

The future of radio is tremendous. It will benefit in times of recession, when its cost to reach listeners and to serve advertisers is so much smaller than television's or newspapers'. I see radio as having a tremendous future for those operators who work at it.

—Gordon McLendon, 1979

The future of radio is bleak.... The FCC is terrible. It needs reform. It's always been the lapdog of the broadcasters; it has opposed every reform possible and protected the broadcasters. It's too bad for the nation.

—The Rev. Everett Parker, 1979

RADIO faces the 1980s with a bright future. It has conquered its world, and what remains on the agenda are refinements rather than great innovations. But there is no ready agreement on some of the tinkering that remains to be done.

Among the issues that radio will tackle in the next few years are:

AM Stereo. FM radio used its capability for stereo broadcasting to gain strength during the 1960s. In April 1980, with AM-FM parity at hand, the FCC approved stereo broadcasting in AM as well.

The FCC was first asked to approve AM stereo in the late 1950s, immediately after the development of stereo recording. In 1961 it said no, in order to protect some of the fledgling FM industry's advantage. More than a decade passed before the commissioners decided to permit AM stereo experiments on the air. Five similar, but technologically incompatible, systems were put on trial at various stations around the country. FCC engineers judged the system developed by the Magnavox Consumer Electronics Corp. to be superior, and on April 9, 1980, the commission approved AM stereo broadcasting and told broadcasters to use the Magnavox system.

The most immediate result of the AM stereo decision will be to increase Magnavox's revenue; the impact on radio programming and audiences is harder to measure. Broadcasters disagree about whether AM stereo is a significant development. At CBS, for example, network officials say they have little interest in the new system; at Group W, however, plans are being made to convert the group's AM music stations to stereo.

All-Channel Legislation. There has been a lobbying struggle in Washington for years over proposals to require that all radios be built with the capability to receive AM and FM signals. (The struggle mirrors the debate over whether to require all televisions to receive both VHF and UHF signals—which became law in 1964.) Supporters of the plan include all the major broadcast organizations. Opposition has been led by the auto manufacturers, who prefer to offer FM radio as an expensive option.

Satellites. All four major commercial networks and National Public Radio are planning to broadcast by satellite rather than telephone lines. Satellite transmission provides better sound quality, lower distribution costs, and the capability for more flexibility and diversity in programming. At this point, it's simply a question of getting enough satellites into orbit and building the receiving dishes to catch the signals. It will happen within the next few years.

Along with these advances in technology are likely to come more stations on the air. Clamor has continued for licenses even though the AM and FM spectrums are nearly full. The FCC began examining methods of adding more stations to the spectrum, and found two possibilities: extending the spectrum beyond 1600 kHz for AM stations, and reducing the spacing between frequencies from 10 kHz to 9. Both are subject to international negotiation.

The U.S. carried its plans to the World Administrative Radio Conference, an international group that convenes every 20 years to negotiate frequency uses and allocations. In late 1979 in Geneva, the WARC agreed to expand the spectrum to 1700 kHz (the U.S. had requested 1800 kHz). But use of the new spectrum space was delayed at least until 1985. The plan to reduce spacing to 9 kHz was taken up in March 1980 by the Western Hemisphere regional conference and a decision was deferred until late 1981 in order to permit additional engineering studies.

As another way to add more stations to the band, the FCC decided, in May 1980, to curb clear channel operations in the United States. The 25 clear channel stations were set aside in the late 1920s to ensure that every area of the United States would have some all-night service. The clear channel rule provides that no other station may be established on the same frequency as a clear channel station; as a result, the 25 stations have enormous reach. During the 1970s, the

FCC proposed to curb clear channel operations in order to get more stations on the air; it said room could be made for up to 125 more AM stations. Clear channel advocates clung to the original rationale and talked of the service they provided: For instance, WSM, Nashville, said its "Grand Ole Opry" could be heard in Canada, northern New York state, and west of Oklahoma. But the FCC decided the new stations—many of which might be earmarked for minority group ownership—outweighed the loss. The FCC decided to protect clear channel stations only within a 750-mile radius, which will continue to give them a much larger listening area than most stations.

Industry observers also agree that there will be changes in radio's content. They predict that formats will become more and more specialized. The demographic pie will be sliced more thinly and stations and networks will target those groups with music, news, and advertising. The 24 to 35 age market, for instance, now broken down only into males and females, will in the next few years be divided into singles and marrieds, and into narrower age groups. This refinement in formats will be based on rating reports that are a good deal more detailed. In addition to surveying the audience's listening habits, they will provide detailed information of purchasing habits as well.

The optimistic view in the radio industry is that the time the average person spends listening to radio will increase. In 1973, the average listener tuned in the radio three hours, 19 minutes a day. By 1985, the estimate is that the four-hour barrier will be near at hand.

All of this signals optimism. Station owners and investors expect their profits to grow as well. A study by the National Association of Broadcasters in 1977 predicted that industry revenues will increase 85 percent by 1985, and that the revenues per station will grow in every size market. No one has predicted that radio revenues or profits will decline.

By this measure, radio's future seems golden. Especially when compared to other electronic media. Communications industry observers have been speculating about a drastic fall off in the power of the television networks, spurred by the increase in satellite technology, cable television services, video recording devices, and other "home entertainment center" technology. These observers predict an end to prime time television as we know it. Radio most likely will be little affected by these changes.

It is even possible that cable TV will benefit radio: A substantial number of cable systems pick up radio signals and carry them as background on information channels that carry wire-service news, weather reports, race-track results, and local shopping information. So far they have been carrying music stations, but all-news radio would seem ideal on some channels.

Beyond technology and profitability are other, more abstract measures by which to evaluate radio. These variables include quality of programming, variety of programming, public service and station promise versus performance. What is saddest about radio's future (and indeed its present as well) is how few promises of substance have been made or kept that would fulfill radio's potential. Promises must come from those with the power to see them through—broadcasters and regulators. In the mouths of critics and philosophers, what might be promises sound instead like complaints. And with few promises made, the public has settled for a radio that, for the most part, replicates the industry view of what it should be. Yet we believe that radio could provide a great deal more than it does.

This vision of radio is admittedly unrestrained by day-to-day business practices; its ideas will be labeled pie-in-the-sky. These reforms won't come from within the broadcasting industry. They must come instead from the government regulators, who are appointed by the president and confirmed by other elected officials. This is where pressure must be brought to bear. And that is why we feel that some form of radio regulation is required if these goals are to be realized. Proponents of deregulation argue that having more than 8,000 commercial radio stations assures diversity, and that market forces can effectively regulate radio. But consider these market forces. Radio strives to deliver listeners to advertisers. These desirable segments of the audience do not mirror the public. Systematically excluded are those substantial elements of society that advertisers are not interested in reaching, most notably the poor and the elderly.

Stations tend to ignore programming for children and minorities—until the minorites can demonstrate middle-class economic clout.

Radio's potential for immediacy and diversity is not sufficiently realized. For every major city with an all-news station, there are dozens more with no such service. For all the varieties of music on the air, too much music is ignored. For all the massive audiences that radio draws, too many people are neglected. Deregulation will bring these goals no closer. Vigorous regulatory reform will.

New York City provides a useful case study. More than 70 radio stations can be heard there. Not one of these stations carries extensive programming for children. Not one carries substantial programming for the tens of thousands of Orientals who have settled there. (Other, longer-entrenched ethnic groups can hear short blocks of programming in their native tongues.) Is it naive to think that the "public interest" would be better served by reserving one of the 70-odd channels exclusively for children's radio? Is it wrong to think that some channels might be set aside for more ethnic programming (or even for bilingual educational services)? Can the situation be significantly better in other areas of the country, where there are fewer channels?

This is a national dilemma. We know that radio will not change overnight, nor indeed within a decade. We acknowledge that we are not the first to call for some of these reforms. But we believe it's time that radio's users paid more attention to what radio might do for them. We believe it's time for the government to effectively overhaul American broadcasting. And these are some of the reforms we would like to see:

A more diverse Federal Communications Commission. Many FCC procedures are cumbersome and drawn-out. They serve neither the public nor the industry. The most direct route to overhauling procedures would be to inject fresh blood and attitudes into the commission, starting at the top. In more than five decades of federal regulation, there have been only four women commissioners, only two blacks, and only one "citizen-activist." We believe the FCC should be made to reflect both the diversity of society and the diverse points of view on what broadcasting should be. It should no longer be dominated by white, male lawyers sympathetic to the broadcasting industry (and often employed by that industry when they leave the FCC). We believe it is essential that more women and minority members be added to the commission; their addition will have a ripple effect on attitudes throughout the industry. We believe at least two of the seven commissioners should be candidates of public-interest groups, to provide a balanced point of view on broadcast matters. These reforms should be pressed on candidates during political primaries and during party platform hearings. Concerned listeners must carry the issue to public officials, and to candidates.

More diverse programming. We are deeply concerned about the increasing use of automated formats provided by consultants; however efficiently they are produced, they cut deeply into local input. Banning automation is outlandish, but we believe it is reasonable to require any station using more than twelve hours of such programming daily to carry several shows a week of locally produced material. We are equally concerned about how few stations leave decisions on what music to play to their on-air personnel. We feel there is social value in diversity. The trend to limited play lists in many formats (and a tightening of those play lists) is unfortunate. We do not believe the commission should regulate this type of music selection, but we feel stations who commit themselves either to "free form" programming by their deejays, or to bringing a new format into a market, should be encouraged with longer-than-standard licenses. Licenses are currently renewed every three years, and there is talk in Washington of extending the period to five years. We think station operators willing to bring classical music, or big-band jazz, or bluegrass, or all-news to an area that has no such format, or who will experiment with more freedom of selection for deejays, should receive seven- to ten-year licenses, provided the promises are kept. The FCC has always been reluctant to judge programming matters. But in 1979 a federal appeals court instructed the commission to pay attention to preserving unique formats, and we believe the FCC should actively encourage them.

More diversity within the spectrum. With the AM and FM bands nearly full, applications and proposals are wedging in more stations continue. Commercial broadcasters seek profits; community stations and National Public Radio affiliates have combined to crowd out of the noncommercial area the small 10-watt operations. We believe there are two priorities in this area: increasing the size of the noncommercial band and imposing lower limits on multiple ownership. We do not suggest that in every instance a noncommercial station is more desirable than a new commercial operation. But we do believe that college and school broadcast stations and community access stations should be fostered. They increase awareness of radio, help train broadcasters, and provide localized service of a very special nature. License holders are currently permitted to own up to seven AM stations and seven FM stations (as well as seven TV stations). We would lower the limit to four each, and require those who exceed the limit to divest within ten years. This will bring more owners into broadcasting and we believe this diversity is the best long-range solution to the overcrowded spectrum. It will also increase the likelihood of women and minority owners having access to good properties.

Finally, we believe the FCC should be granted additional funding by Congress to open two new operations: an Office of Media Studies and an Office of Public Advocacy. Too often the FCC has been caught without enough data and has been forced to turn to studies conducted by the broadcasters it seeks to regulate. At the same time a wide variety of research conducted at campuses and think tanks gets no hearing outside academic circles. We have no simple solution for how to measure this research, nor do we welcome government *control* of media research. But by sponsoring and coordinating research projects, the FCC could provide cross-pollination within the field and gain access to new data at the same time. And bringing in more outsiders would help the FCC escape its dominance by the broadcasting industry. An Office for Public Advocacy would serve to foster more citizen participation in broadcast policy-making. It could provide legal and engineering counsel on starting broadcast operations; it could expedite license challenges (aiding not only the complainants but broadcasters as well, by avoiding drawn-out proceedings and harassment).

Commercial broadcasting has in many ways been beneficial to the American people. Because it was profitable it expanded; competition for dollars led to significant innovations. We do not believe these motivations should be proscribed—only mediated. There is substantial room for improvement in the quality of American radio, and the solution lies in bringing more people into the medium. This will require dramatic action, for recent trends have reduced the number of participants in radio decision-making. Radio's penetration into our lives makes it our most accessible medium. It must also be the most diverse and the most democratic to fully realize its potential.

In 1945, NAB President J. Harold Ryan told a group of broadcasters celebrating radio's 25th anniversary, "American radio is the product of American business! It is just as much that kind of product as the vacuum cleaner, the washing machine, the automobile and the airplane. . . . If the legend still persists that a radio station is some kind of art center, a technical museum or a little piece of Hollywood transplanted strangely to your hometown, then the first official act of the second quarter-century should be to list it along with the local dairies, laundries, banks, restaurants, and filling stations."

Ryan wasn't exaggerating, and broadcasters took his message to heart. That is certainly one view—an influential and predominant one—of radio. Our intent has been to suggest here the possibilities of another type of radio. A radio that can be a successful business, but at the same time be a bit of an art center, a technical museum, and yes, a little bit of Hollywood (or Nashville or Tin Pan Alley) transplanted into each of our hometowns. There is ample room for citizen participation in radio on several levels, and the medium—and its listeners—will be well-served by attention from more sources. It is high time that radio started making more substantive promises. . . and keeping them.

BIBLIOGRAPHY

Abarbanel, Albert, and Haley, Alex. "A New Audience for Radio." *Harper's Magazine* (February 1956), 57–59.

Abrams, Lee. "Tight Format Key to Reach." *Advertising Age* (May 29, 1978), R1–R26.

Adler, Renata. "The New Sound." *The New Yorker* (February 20, 1965), 63–105.

"The AM-FM Program Duplication Rule." *Broadcast Management/Engineering* (August 1966), 14–18.

Avery, Robert K., and Pepper, Robert. "Balancing the Equation: Public Radio Comes of Age." *Public Telecommunications Review* (March/April 1979), 19–30.

Barnett, Stephen. "Merger, Monopoly and a Free Press." *The Nation* (January 15, 1973), 76–86.

Barnouw, Erik. *The Golden Web: A History of Broadcasting in the United States 1933–1953*. New York: Oxford University Press, 1968.

_____. *The Image Empire: A History of Broadcasting in the United States From 1953*. New York: Oxford University Press, 1970.

_____. *A Tower in Babel: A History of Broadcasting in the United States to 1933*. New York: Oxford University Press, 1966.

_____. *Tube of Plenty: The Evolution of American Television*. New York: Oxford University Press, 1975.

Bester, Alfred. "The New Age of Radio." *Holiday* (June 1963), 56–73.

"Black Radio: Hard Swim Toward Main Stream." *Advertising Age* (May 29, 1978), R8–R33.

Braudy, Susan. "A Radio Station With Real Hair, Sweat and Body Odor." *The New York Times Magazine* (September 17, 1972), 10–18.

Broadcasting, 1948–present.

Broadcasting Yearbook 1979. Washington, D.C.: Broadcasting Publications, Inc.

Brown, Les. *Television: The Business Behind the Box.* New York: Harvest, 1971.

Brunn, Stanley D., Johnson, James H., Jr., and Zeigler, Donald J. "Preliminary Report on a Social Survey of Three Mile Island Area Residents." Department of Geography, Michigan State University (May 1979).

Carmody, Deirdre. "Challenging Media Monopolies." *The New York Times Magazine* (July 31, 1977), 19–24.

Carpenter, Edmund. *Oh, What a Blow That Phantom Gave Me!* New York: Holt, Rinehart and Winston, 1972.

Chapple, Steve, and Garofalo, Reebee. *Rock 'n' Roll Is Here to Pay.* Chicago: Nelson-Hall, 1977.

————, and Rogers, Joel. "The Rise and Fall of FM Rock." *Mother Jones* (May 1976), 55–61.

Chester, Giraud, Garrison, Garnet R., and Willis, Edgar E. *Television and Radio,* 4th ed. New York: Appleton-Century-Crofts, 1971.

Clark, Dick, and Robinson, Richard. *Rock, Roll & Remember.* New York: Thomas Y. Crowell Co., 1976.

Cole, Barry, and Oettinger, Mal. *Reluctant Regulators: The FCC and the Broadcast Audience.* Reading, Mass.: Addison-Wesley Publishing Co., 1978.

Donahue, Rachael. "Tom Donahue." *The AOR Story.* Los Angeles: Radio & Records, Inc., 1978. 6–13.

Donahue, Tom. "A Rotting Corpse, Stinking Up the Airways." *Rolling Stone* (November 23, 1967), 14–15.

Duff, Willis. "The Talk Radio Handbook." New York: unpublished, 1969.

"During the Nov. 9, 1965 Blackout." New York: Trendex, Inc., 1965

Ebert, Alan. "Monitor." *Electronic Age* (Spring 1965), 14–17.

Eisen, Jonathan, ed. *The Age of Rock.* New York: Vintage Books, 1969.

"Expanded Sample Frame." *Radio Research Primer.* New York: McGavren Guild Radio, 1979.

"FM Radio Has to Change Its Tune." *Business Week* (September 24, 1966), 173–178.

Fong-Torres, Ben. "FM Underground Radio: Love for Sale." *Rolling Stone* (April 2, 1970), 1–8.

"Foreign Language Radio Fighting Barriers." *Advertising Age* (May 29, 1978), R16–R37.

Fornatale, Peter. "Hey Radio–Help Me Make It Through the Night." *Scholastic Scope* (October 25, 1971), 32–34.

————, and Mills, Josh. "Radios That Receive TV Shows." *TV Guide* (August 20, 1977), 21–22.

_____ . "Static: Hey Mister, What's Free Form on the Playlist?" *Crawdaddy* (January 1978), 16–20.

Frank, Alan, and Bayer, Cary. "Network Radio Comes Out of the Trenches." *Broadcast Report* (October 9, 1978), 38–41.

Frank, Karen S. "Diversity: Lifeblood and Future of Public Radio." *Public Telecommunications Review* (March/April 1979), 67–69.

Freedgood, Seymour. "The Money-Makers of New Radio." *Fortune* (February 1958), 122–226.

Freedman, Max C., and De Knight, Jimmy. "Rock Around the Clock." New York: Myers Music, 1953.

Friendly, Fred. "The Campaign to Politicize Broadcasting." *Columbia Journalism Review* (March/April 1973), 9–18.

_____ . "Will Broadcasting Be Politicized?" *Current* (May 1973), 19–31.

Gillett, Charlie. *The Sound of the City: The Rise of Rock and Roll.* New York: Outerbridge & Dienstfrey, 1970.

Gordon, George N., and Falk, Irving A. *On the Spot Reporting: Radio Records History.* New York: Julian Messner, 1967.

Gould, Jack. "Around Country, FM Turns to Rock." *The New York Times* (May 20, 1970), 33.

_____ . "Radio *Has* a Future." *The New York Times Magazine* (April 17, 1955), 17–62.

Greenfield, Jeff. *No Peace, No Place: Excavations Along the Generational Fault.* Garden City, N.Y.: Doubleday & Co., 1973.

_____ . *Television: The First Fifty Years.* New York: Harry N. Abrams, Inc., 1977.

Hall, Claude, and Hall, Barbara. *This Business of Radio Programming.* New York: Billboard Publications, Inc., 1977.

"The Happening Sound." *Newsweek* (August 28, 1967), 84.

Head, Sydney W. *Broadcasting in America: A Survey of Television and Radio.* Boston: Houghton Mifflin Co., 1956.

_____ . Ibid., rev. 3rd ed., 1976.

Honan, William. "The New Sound of Radio." *The New York Times Magazine* (December 3, 1967), 56–76.

"Hooper Riding the Big Radio Boom." *Sponsor* (October 18, 1958), 42–44.

Hopkins, Jerry. *Elvis: A Biography.* New York: Simon and Schuster, 1971.

"How Radio Fills a Local Gap." *Business Week* (July 14, 1962), 50–56.

Hulleberg, Ellen. "Radio Rating Service Compared: Making It Easy." *Television/Radio Age* (February 26, 1979), 14–20.

Jacobs, Sam. "Ratings, Profits Roll In to Spanish Broadcasters." *Miami Herald* (December 25, 1977), 1F–2F.

Josephson, Larry. "Why Radio?" *Public Telecommunications Review* (March/April 1979), 6–18.

"The King of the Giveaway." *Time* (June 4, 1956), 100–102.

"KLIQ." *Sponsor* (April 25, 1959), 69.

"The Late Bill Lear, Invented Car Radio." *Billboard* (May 27, 1978), 41.

Lichty, Lawrence W., and Topping, Malachi C. *American Broadcasting: A Source Book on the History of Radio and Television.* New York: Hastings House, 1976.

"A Lot of Life in Radio Yet." *Business Week* (February 9, 1957), 132–135.

Lydon, Michael. *Rock Folk.* New York: The Dial Press, 1971.

Lyons, Eugene. *David Sarnoff: A Biography.* New York: Harper & Row, 1966.

MacFarland, David T. "The Development of the Top 40 Format." Unpublished dissertation, University of Wisconsin, 1972.

Mahler, Richard. "Community Radio: Its Day in the Sun." *Public Telecommunications Review* (March/April 1979), 70–75.

Marshall, Eliot. "FCC Cover-Up." *New Republic* (December 20, 1975), 6–8.

McLuhan, Marshall. *Understanding Media: The Extensions of Man.* New York: McGraw Hill, 1964.

Mendelsohn, Harold. "The Roles of Radio." *Radio and Television: Readings in the Mass Media,* ed. Allen Kirschner and Linda Kirschner. New York: Odyssey Press, 1971, 85–87.

"Metromedia," *The AOR Story.* Los Angeles: Radio & Records, Inc., 1978, 18–29.

Milam, Lorenzo. *Sex and Broadcasting: A Handbook for Starting a Radio Station for the Community, 3rd ed.* Dallas: The Dildo Press, 1975.

Miller, Jim, ed. *The Rolling Stone Illustrated History of Rock & Roll.* New York: The Rolling Stone Press, 1976.

Mitchell, Curtis. *Cavalcade of Broadcasting.* Chicago: Follett Publishing Co., 1970.

Mitford, Jessica. "Hello, There! You're on the Air." *Harper's Magazine* (May 1966), 47–53.

NBC: A History. New York: National Broadcasting Company, 1966.

"Negro Radio—Voice of a Growing Market." *Timebuyer* (December 1966), 36–39.

"Negro Radio Zeroes In." *U.S. Radio* (December 1959), 24–28.

Nelson, Lindsey, with Hirshberg, Al. "A Stadium Inside a Studio." *Sports Illustrated* (March 28, 1966), 38–45.

"Networks Offer More News to Listeners, Greater Flexibility to Affiliated Stations." *Television/Radio Age* (December 12, 1977), 63–77.

Niven, Harold. "Surveys of Colleges and Universities Offering Courses in Broadcasting." *Journal of Broadcasting* (1961–1972).

O'Hallaren, William. "Radio Is Worth Saving." *The Atlantic Monthly* (October 1959), 69–72.

Passman, Arnold. *The Deejays.* New York: The Macmillan Co., 1971.

"Profile of a Station: WOR-FM." *FM Guide* (February 1967), 10–13.

"Public Radio Perks Up." *Newsweek* (March 12, 1979), 84–85.

"The Pulse—In-Home Interviews." *Sponsor* (September 20, 1958), 30–68.

"Pulse Ratings on Spanish Language Radio Assailed as 'Confused, Inaccurate' by Coyle." *Media Agencies Clients* (September 14, 1964), 36–38.

Radio Facts. New York: Radio Advertising Bureau, 1979.

"Radio Gaining Strength as Local Service." *Business Week* (May 27, 1961), 111–114.

"Radio Splits Over Strategy Against TV." *Business Week* (May 31, 1952), 38–40.

"Radio's New Voice Is Golden." *Business Week* (March 5, 1960), 94–110.

"Recent Gallup Survey Indicates Strong Majority Preference for Network Radio Coverage of World and National News." NBC Radio Network press release, August 11, 1977.

"Religious Broadcasting—Big, Big Business." *Media Agencies Clients* (February 12, 1979), 11–17.

"The Return of Network Radio." *Forbes* (October 30, 1978), 152.

Routt, Ed, McGrath, James B., and Weiss, Fredric A. *The Radio Format Conundrum.* New York: Hastings House, 1978.

Rubin, David. "Tuning in Trouble at Arbitron." *MORE* (December 1977), 34–37.

Salzman, Ed. "The All-News Radio Station." *Saturday Review* (May 13, 1961), 65–66.

Sandman, Peter, and Paden, Mary. "The Local Media Feel the Heat." *Columbia Journalism Review* (July/August 1979), 56–57.

Sandman, Peter, Rubin, David, and Sachsman, Peter. *Media: An Introductory Analysis of American Mass Communication,* 2nd ed. Englewood Cliffs, N.J.: Prentice-Hall, 1976.

Schwartz, Tony. *The Responsive Chord.* Garden City, N.Y.: Anchor Press, 1973.

Settel, Irving. *A Pictoral History of Radio.* New York: Grosset & Dunlap, 1960.

"Sex Talk Radio: Is It Here to Stay?" *Media Decisions* (December 1972), 43–98.

Shaw, Arnold. *Honkers and Shouters: The Golden Years of Rhythm & Blues.* New York: Collier Books, 1978.

Simkins, Tania. "Public Radio: Coming Out of Hiding." *Issues in Broadcasting: Radio, Television and Cable,* ed. Ted C. Smythe and George A. Mastroianni. Palo Alto, Calif.: Mayfield Publishing Co., 1975, 355–366.

Smith, Desmond. "American Radio Today." *Harper's Magazine* (September 1964), 58–63.

Stephens, Mitchell. *Broadcast Journalism: Radio Journalism and an Introduction to Television.* New York: Holt, Rinehart and Winston, 1980.

"Striking It Rich in Radio." *Business Week* (February 5, 1979), 58–62.

"Sure. TV Is OK—but people still love radio." *Changing Times* (February 1954), 41–42.

Sweeney, Joan. "Radio Stations Dial 'A' for Automation." *Issues in Broadcasting: Radio, Television and Cable,* ed. Ted C. Smythe and George A. Mastroianni. Palo Alto, Calif.: Mayfield Publishing Co., 1975 394–400.

Thomas, Thomas J. "Tuning Up the Band: FCC Strikes a Chord." *U.S. Radio* (June 1958), 52-53.

"Tiny Key to Tomorrow's Radio." *U.S. Radio* (June 1958), 52-53.

Tobin, Richard L. "The Amazing Comeback of Radio." *Saturday Review* (May 12, 1962), 65–66.

Tolbert, Frank X. "Man Behind a Network." *Nation's Business* (March 1952), 56–60.

"Transistor Set Sales." New York: Radio Advertising Bureau, 1965.

Trow, George W. S. "Button, Button, Who's Got the WABC $25,000 Promotion Button?" *The New York Times* (July 28, 1974), II, 1–13.

"Uncle T and Boston AOR." *The AOR Story.* Los Angeles: Radio & Records, Inc., 1978. 9–16.

United States. Department of Commerce. "Facts for Industry" (May 14, 1957). 8–9.

———. Court of Appeals. *WLBT.* 425 F2d, 543 (1969).

———. Federal Communications Commission
AM-FM Broadcast Services. FCC 64-609, 29 FR 9492 (July 7, 1964).
Requests for Waivers. FCC 66-252, 2: FCC 2nd: 833. (1966).
Conglomerate Ownership. 34 FR 2131 (1969).
Licensee Responsibility. 28 FCC 2d 409 (March 5, 1971).
Minority Ownership. FCC 78-322 (May 5, 1978).

"What Boundaries for Federal Censorship?" *Publishers' Weekly* (May 3, 1971), 39.

"What's Communicaster Radio?" *Media Decision* (July 1968), 30–60.

Whiteside, Thomas. "Shaking the Tree." *The New Yorker* (March 17, 1975), 41–90.

Whitney, Frederick C. *Mass Media and Mass Communications in Society.* Dubuque, Iowa: William C. Brown Co., 1975.

Williams, Roger Neville. "The Future of Radio Is—You!" *The Village Voice* (July 5, 1976), 14–18.

Wilson, Earl. "Freed Tells Earl: I Never Asked, Took a Cash Bribe." *Newsday* (November 23, 1959), 5–98.

Witty, Paul. "Studies of the Mass Media 1949–1965." *Science Education* (March 1966), 119–126.

Wylie, Max. "Is TV Killing Radio?" *Science Digest* (February 1955), 1–5.

Yurdin, Larry. "Waves Upon the Ether." *Crawdaddy* (April 30, 1972), 30–35.

_____. "Waves Upon the Ether, II." *Crawdaddy* (May 14, 1972), 30–34.

INDEX

Abarbanel, Albert, 16
Abrams, Lee, 142
Action for Children's Television, 154
Adler, Lou, 105
Adult contemporary format, 68
Advertising, xxvii–xxviii, 4, 11, 22–23, 103,
  134, 140–41
Agnew, Spiro, 145, 147
"Alan Freed's Rock 'n' Roll Party" (show),
  40
Album-oriented rock (AOR), 141–42
All-channel legislation, 189–90
All-News format, 23, 57, 99–108
All-Radio Methodology Study, 64
Alternative radio, 168, 173–74
Amalgamated Federation of International
  FM Workers of the World, 132
"American Bandstand" (show), 49–50, 52
American Marconi Company, 19
American Radio Network, 55
American Research Bureau (ARB), 64–65
"Amos 'n' Andy" (show), 8, 16
Ampex, 97–98
Anthony, John J., 83
APRadio, 99
Arbitron, 65–66, 76
Armstrong, Edwin H., 119–21
Armstrong, George "Bud," 27, 31
ASCAP, 13, 43, 48–49
Association of National Advertisers, 61
Associated Press, xxiv, 99

Association of Public Radio Stations, 177
Authors League, 146
Autry, Gene, 81
Audits & Surveys, Inc., 66
Automated radio, 143–44
Avco Corporation, 100
Average quarter hour, 66

Backus, Jim, 55
Baez, Joan, 128
Ballance, Bill, 84–85
Ballard, Hank, 40
Ballgame radios, xvi
Baltimore Harbor Terminal, xv
Baptist Radio and Television Commission,
  89
Bard, Morton, xix
Bardeen, John, 17, 18
Barnouw, Erik, 4, 113
Bartell, Gerald, 20, 31–32
Bartell Group, 43, 45
Barter syndication, 144–45
Bartley, Robert T., 126
Beatles, the, 42, 57, 68, 145
Beaudin, Ralph, 111–12
Beautiful Music format, 23, 27, 77–80, 135
Bedroom radios, xv
Bell, Alexander Graham, 18
Bennett, Tony, 68
Berdis, Bert, 23

Berle, Milton, 3, 6
Berry, Chuck, 40, 49
"Big Bopper, The," 54
Big Brother and the Holding Company, 129
Billboard, 13, 19, 25, 37, 39, 42
Black format, 15–17, 69–73
Blackboard Jungle (movie), 41
Blackout of 1965, xxii–xxiii, 95, 104
Blacks for Soul in Television, 154
Blair, Frank, 23
Block, Martin, 12–13, 56, 69
Blore, Chuck, 26, 44, 74
BMI (Broadcast Music Inc.), 13, 48–49
Boone, Pat, 40
Bonneville Broadcast Consultants, 79
Boston Herald Traveler, The, 178, 151
Brando, Marlon, 41
Brattain, Walter H., 17, 18
Brewer and Shipley, 146
Brinkley, David, 110
Broadcast ownership, 148–59
Broadcast Ratings: The Methodology, Accuracy and Use of Ratings in Broadcasting (House Special Subcommittee on Investigations), 64
Broadcasting, xxv, 30, 67, 83 98
Broadcasting Rating Council, 64
Brown, Tyrone, 149
Brown v. Board of Education of Topeka (1954), 43
Buchanan, Patrick, 149
Burch, Dean, 85, 146–50, 154–55
Burger, Warren, 137, 152
Burke Broadcast Research, 66
Burckhardt, Kent, 142
Business Week, 6

Cable TV, 192
Cantor, Eddie, 7
Capitol Records, 40
Car radios, xv, 19–20
Carlin, George, 183

Carnegie Commission, 175
Carpenter, Edmund, xxv–xxviii
Carroll, John P., 42
Carter, Jimmy, xxvii, 85
Caruso, Enrico, 86
CBS Radio Stations News Service, 114
Census Bureau, 64
Chancellor, John, 110
Channel 5 (New York), 50
Chess Records, 40
Chris-Craft Industries, 150
Citizen participation, 153–56, 195–96
Citizens Communication Center, 153–54
Clark, Dick, 49–50, 52
Classical music format, 85–89
Classical Radio for Connecticut, 87
Clock radios, 20
College radio, 124, 131, 133–34, 167, 172, 182–83
Collins, Judy, 128
Colson, Charles, 148, 149
Columbia Records, 40, 41, 128
Community access, 168, 173–74
Companionship function, xvii–xix
Conglomerate ownership, 149–51
Conrad, Frank, 12
Consultants, 142–43
Control Data Corporation, 65
Cooperative Analysis of Broadcast, 61, 62
Corporation for Public Broadcasting, 174–78
Cossman, Edward L., 76–77
Country format, 80–82
Country Joe and the Fish, 129
Country Music Association, 81
Cox, Kenneth, 149–50
Cox Communications, 80
Cox Enterprises, 150
Crocker, Frankie, 71
Cronkite, Walter, 95
Crosby, Bing, 51, 52
Cross-ownership, 151-52
Crossley, Archibald, 61
Crossley ratings, 61, 62
"Cume," 66–67

D.I.R. Broadcasting, 144–45
Dali, Salvador, 56
Daniel, Dan, xxiii
Dean, James, 41
Debs, Eugene V., 72
Decca Records, 40
DeForest, Lee, 17
Denver, John, 68
Deregulation, 160-62
Diamond, Neil, 68
Diddley, Bo, 40
Digges, Sam Cooke, 8, 113
Disc Jockeys Convention (1959), 46
Disco format, 75–77
Disney World, xv
Doerfer, John C., 53
Domino, Fats, 40
"Don McNeil's Breakfast Club" (show), 55
Donahue, Rachel, 132
Donahue, Tom "Big Daddy," 52, 117, 131–33, 140–41
Doors, the, 128
Dorsey Brothers, 42
Drake, Bill, 73–74
Drug-lyric warning, 145–47, 149
Dumont, Allen, 5
Durr, Clifford J., 152
Dylan, Bob, xviii, 127–29

E. W. Scripps Company, 150
Easy Rider (movie), 130
Economic role of radio, xxi
"Ed Sullivan Show," 42, 129
Eddy, Duane, 50
Educational radio, 168–72
Eisenhower, Dwight D., 53
Eisgrau, Mike, xviii
Elektra Records, 128
Ethnic formats, 69–73
Everly Brothers, 54
Expanded Sample Frame (ESF), 65

Federal Communications Act, 53
Federal Communications Commission (FCC), 3, 5, 12, 15, 51, 53, 61, 70, 74, 85–87, 89, 101, 119–27, 145, 189–91, 193–95
Federal Council of Churches, 89
Federal Trade Commission, xxviii, 51
"Feminine Forum" (show), 84–85
Fessenden, Reginald, 12
Field reporting, 97–99
Fisher, Eddie, 38
FM radio, 117–35
Ford, Mary, 37
Ford, Tennessee Ernie, 8
Foreign-language programming, 71–72, 132
Format (formula) radio, 13
    See also specific formats
Fornatale, Peter, 133–34
Fortune, 31
Franzbalu, Rose, 105
Freberg, Stan, 22
Freed, Alan, 35, 38–40, 45–46, 49–51
Freedom Rides, 128
Freeman, Robert, 88
Frost, David, 114
Fuqua Industries, 150

GAF Corporation, 87
Galvin, Paul, 19
Galvin Manufacturing Company, 19
Gamache, Tom, 133–34
Gatekeepers, 142–43
General Cinema Corporation, 86
General Electric, 20
Georgia Association of Broadcasters, 26
Gibbs, Georgia, 40
Gila Monster, The (movie), 28
Glaser, Milton, 131
Godfrey, Arthur, 69
Golden Age of Radio, 3–8, 15, 19, 21
Goldmark, Peter, 40

Goldstein, Richard, 134
Goldwater, Barry, 149
Gould, Jack, 18, 42, 130
Graduate, The (movie), 130
Graham, Bill, 132, 133
"Grand Ole Opry" (show), 80
Grateful Dead, xvii–xix, 133
Gray, Barry, 55
Great Adventure, xv
Griffin, Merv, 55
Guthrie, Arlo, 128

Haley, Alex, 16
Hancock, Hunter, 38, 39
Hardy, Ashton, 161
Harper's, 16
Harris, Oren, 48
Harvey, Paul, 112
Hatfield, Henry D., 170
Hauptmann, Bruno, 13
Head, Sydney, 113
Hill, Lewis Kimball, 171
Hindenburg disaster, 96
"Hit Parade" (show), 26
Holly, Buddy, 54
Holt, Sam, 179
Hooks, Benjamin, 154, 156, 157
Hooper, C. E., 62–64
"Hooperatings," 62
Hoover, Herbert, 5, 165, 169
"Hot Line" (show), 71
House Special Subcommittee on Investigations, 63–64
Howard, Bob, 27
Hunt, George P., xxiv

Ingram, Dan, 56
Institute of Radio Engineers, 120

Jamie Records, 50
Jarvis, Al, 12

Jazz format, 87–89
Jefferson Airplane, 129, 133, 145
Jewish Daily Forward, The, 72
Johnson, Lyndon Baines, 45
Johnson, Nicholas, 70, 146, 149, 152, 153
Jolliffe, C. B., 120–21
Josephson, Larry, 185
Journal of College Radio, 180

KABC (Los Angeles), 83
KABL (San Francisco), 27, 78
KADS (Los Angeles), 28
Kaufman, Murray "the K," 57, 131
KBON (Omaha), 28
KBOO (Portland, Ore.), 174
KBRT (Los Angeles), 90
KCBQ (San Diego), 32
KCBS (San Francisco), 115
KCOR (San Antonio), 72
KDAY (Los Angeles), 52, 71
KDKA (Pittsburgh), 45, 83, 96
KELP (El Paso), 44
Kennedy, John Fitzgerald, 128
Kennedy, Robert F., 95, 177
KFAB (Omaha), 28
KFAX (San Francisco), 100, 101
KFSG (Los Angeles), 88
KFUO (Clayton, Mo.), 88
KFWB (Los Angeles), 12, 74, 104
KGBS (Los Angeles), 84
KGFJ (Los Angeles), 71
KHJ (Los Angeles), 73
Killer Shrews, The (movie), 28
King, Ed and Wendy, 83
"King Biscuit Flower Hour" (show), 145
"King Biscuit Time" (show), 145
Kinney, Richard, 103
Kirksmith, Jim, 25
Kitchen radios, xv
KIXL (Dallas), 78
KLAC (Los Angeles), 83
Klein, Herb, 148, 149
Klein, Stewart, xxiii

KLIF (Dallas), 24, 26–27, 98
KLIQ (Portland, Ore.), 100
KMOX (St. Louis), 110
KMPX (San Francisco), 119, 131–32
Knauth, Victor, 100
KNET (Palestine, Tex.), 24
KNOB (Long Beach, Cal.), 87
KNOE (Monroe, La.), 32
Koch, Edward, 169
Kops, Daniel, 100
KOST (Los Angeles), 78
KOWH (Omaha), 27, 29–30, 98
KPFA (Berkeley), 171, 173
KPFK (Los Angeles), 172
KPFT (Houston), 172–73
KPPC (Pasadena), 88, 132
KRAB (Seattle), 174
Kramer, Albert, 153
KRBB (El Dorado, Ark), 53
KROW (San Francisco), 78
KSAN (San Francisco), 132, 140, 141
KSFX (San Francisco), 75, 77
KWBW (Hutchinson, Ka.), 28
KWIZ (Santa Ana), 74
KXLW (St. Louis), 71
KYA (San Francisco), 52, 132
KYW (Philadelphia), 104

Labunski, Stephen, 30
Laine, Frankie, 37
Laquidara, Charles, 141
Latino Media Coalition, 155
Lavergne, Nelson, 73
Lear, William, 19
Lee, Peggy, 68
Lennon, John, 68
Lewis, Jerry Lee, 40, 46, 54
Liberty Broadcasting System, 25
Life, xxiv
Little Richard, 40, 54
Localization of programming, 11–15, 61
Lorenz, George, 38
Los Angeles Forum, xvi

Los Angeles International Airport, xv
Low-frequency extenders, 115
Lower, Elmer, 112
Lutheran Church of America, 89
Lymon, Frankie, 46

McCartney, Paul, 68
McCuller, James, 155
McGannon, Donald, 45
McGavern Guild, 63
McGovern, George S., 177
McIntire, Carl, 148
McKernan, Phil, 38
McLendon, Gordon, 9, 24–32, 43–45, 71, 74, 78, 79, 98, 101–4, 126–27
McLuhan, Marshall, xvii, xxv–xxvii, 17
McMahon, Ed, 23
McNeill, Don, 112
McPherson, Aimee Semple, 88
Magnavox Consumer Electronics Corporation, 189
"Make Believe Ballroom" (show), 13, 56
Malcolm X, 128
Mankiewicz, Frank, 177
Marx, Groucho, 7
Mass media, functions of, xx–xxi
Maynard, Ken, 80–81
Media Statistics, Inc., 66
Mediastats, 66
Mediatrends, 66
Mendelson, Harold, xvi–xvii
Mercer, Bill, see Rosko
Mercury Records, 40
Meyrowitz, Robert, 144
MGM Records, 40
Midas International Foundation, 153
Middle-of-the-Road (MOR) format, 56, 57, 67–69, 109, 135
Milam, Lorenzo, 165, 173–74
Miller, Justin, 152
Miller, Larry, 132
Miller, Mitch, 45
"Milton Berle Show, The," 42

Minidocumentaries, 110

Minority hiring, 159–60

Minority ownership, 156–59

Mitchell, Bobby, 52

Moby Grape, 129

"Monitor" (show), 23

Monroe, Vaughn, 81

"Moon Dog Coronation Ball, The" (concert), 39

"Moon Dog House Rock 'n' Roll Party, The" (show), 38

Mormon Church, 79

Morrison, Herbert, 96

Motorola, Inc., 19

Muni, Scott, xviii–xix, 131

Murrow, Edward R., 96–97

Mutual Black Network, 111, 114

Muzak, 78

N. W. Ayer Advertising Agency, 62

National Advertising Bureau, 64

National Association of Broadcasters, xix, 14, 70

National Black Network, 111

National Citizen's Committee for Broadcasting (NCCB), 151–52

National Educational Radio, 175

National Organization for Women (NOW), 154–55

National Public Radio, 111, 167, 175–81, 195

National Religious Broadcasters, 89

NBC News and Information Service (NIS), 105–6

Neal, Hal, 55–56

Nelson, Barry, 23

Nelson, Harriet, 40

Nelson, Lindsey, 28

Nelson, Ozzie, 40

Nelson, Ricky, 40

New York Herald, The, 19

New York Times, The, xxiv, 18, 42, 46, 70, 130, 147

News broadcasting, 26, 95–116

Niagara, Joe, 52

Nipkow, Paul, 5

Nixon, Richard M., 114, 141, 148, 149

Nobles, Gene, 38

Noe, James, 29

Noncommercial radio, 167–85

O'Brien, Tom, 112, 114

Ochs, Phil, 128

Office radios, xvi

Oh, What a Blow That Phantom Gave Me!, xxvi

Oldies format, 74

Olsen, Ray "Cat," xviii–xix

Orkin, Dick, 23

Outdoor radios, xvi

Oxford, George, 38

Pacifica Foundation, 171–74

Page, Patti, 37, 38, 68

Paltridge, J. Gil, 100

Parker, Everett, 144

Paul, Les, 37

Pauley, 114

Paxton, Tom, 128

Payola, 47–54, 131–32

Pearl Harbor, attack on, 97

Peter Paul, and Mary, 129

Pittsburgh Symphony, 45

PLNX, 114

Politz, Arthur, 21–22

Potter, Peter, 43

Poulsen, Valdemar, 97

Presley, Elvis, 40, 42–45, 54, 57

Primitive cultures, impact of radio on, xxvi

Progressive FM format, 109, 130–35, 139–41, 143, 145, 182

Promotions, 27, 29–30, 56, 98, 103

Psychological Corporation, 62

Public Broadcasting Act (1967), 175

Public Telecommunications Review, 185

Pucinski, Roman, 102
Pulse, Inc., The, 62-65
Punch, 5

Rabbitt, Johnny, 27
Radio Advertising Bureau, 66
Radio Information Center for the Blind, xx
Radio Luxembourg, 46
Radio & Records, 132
Rafshoon, Gerald, xxvii
RAM Research, 66
Ratings, 61-67
Ray, Johnny, 37-38
Rayburn, Gene, 23
RCA, 5, 40, 119-21, 128
Rebel Without a Cause (movie), 41-42
"Record Rendezvous" (show), 38
Reeves, Jim, 55
Reid, Charlotte, 154
Religious format, 88-91, 109
"Request Review" (show), 38
Responsive Chord, The, xxvii
Reuters News Service, 113
Rhodes, L. Ray, 100
Robert F. Kennedy Memorial Foundation, 153
Rock 'n' roll, 37-46, 48, 52-55, 57, 104, 127, 128
Rogers, Roy, 81
Rolling Stone, 117, 132
Rolling Stones, 127, 129
Rollins Broadcasting Company, 39
Roosevelt, Franklin Delano, 97
Rosko, 131
Roslow, Irma, 62
Roslow, Sydney, 62, 63, 65
Ryan, J. Harold, 196
Rydgren, John, 134

Satellites, 115, 190
Saturday Night Fever (movie), 75
Schorr, Daniel, 148

Schulke, Jim, 79, 135
Schwartz, Tony, xxv, xxvii–xxviii
Sears, Zenas, 38, 39, 70
Seeger, Pete, 128-29
Segall, Lee, 78
Seitz, Frank A., 19
Senate Communications Subcommittee, xxviii
Sex and Broadcasting: A Handbook for Starting a Radio Station for the Community, 173-74
Share, 67
Shockley, William B., 17-19
Shriner, Herb, 7
Simon, Carly, 68
Simulcasting, 122, 124, 126, 131
Sinatra, Frank, 7, 26, 57, 68
"$64,000 Question, The" (show), 48
SJR Communications, 76
Sklar, Rick, 56
Small Business Administration, 137
Smith, Bob, 37
Smothers Brothers, 129
Soft-rock stations, 68
"Sound Stage" (show), 42
Spanish-language radio, 72-73
Specialized audiences, 15-17
Sponsor, 100
Sporting News, The, 25
Sports broadcasts, 24-25, 108
Springsteen, Bruce, xxvi
Stanton, Frank, 149
Starch, Daniel, 64
Starr Broadcasting Group, 87
Stephens, Mitchell, 109
Stereo broadcasting, 125-25, 130, 189
Stereo Radio Productions, 79-80, 135
Stevens, John Paul, 184
Stewart, Bill, 27
Storer Broadcasting Company, 53, 84-85
Storz, Robert, 9, 31
Storz, Robert Todd, 9, 27-32, 43, 45, 46, 51, 83, 98, 127
Straus, R. Peter, 55

Subsidiary Communications Authority, 184
Sullivan, Ed, 3, 129
Sultans of Swing, 38
Sun Records, 40
Supremes, The, 68

"Take It or Leave It" (show), 7
Talk shows, 82–85
Tape recorders, 97–98
Taylor, James, 68
Teen culture, 37–57
Television (periodical), 5
Television/Radio Age, xxv
"Tell It Like It Is" (show), 70–71
"Texaco Star Theater" (show), 3
Texas Instruments, 18
Thayer, Jack, 6
Thomas, Tom, 174
3M Company, 97–98
Three Mile Island nuclear accident, xxii, 95
Time, 29–30
Titanic, sinking of, 96
"Toast of the Town" (show), 3
Top 40 format, 23, 26–27, 29, 54–57, 68, 73–75, 104, 109, 127, 131, 144, 146
Torin, "Symphony" Sid, 38
Toscanini, Arturo, 86
Trac-7, 66
Transceivers, 115
Transistors, 17–19
Travelers Insurance Company, 150
Tribal drum theory, xvii
Tripp, Peter, 52
Troggs, the, 131
Trout, Robert, 97
TV radios, xvi
"Two for the Money" (show), 7

Underground radio, 129–30
Understanding Media (McLuhan), xxv, 17
United Church of Christ, Office of Communication of, 87, 144

United Press International, xxiv, 99
UPI Audio, 99

Vacuum tube, 17
Valens, Ritchie, 54
Van Deerlin, Lionel, 161
Variety, 12, 43, 44
Video-display units, 115
Village Voice, 131, 134

WABC (New York), 50, 55–57, 75, 77
WADO (New York), 73
WAER (Syracuse), 172
Wagner, Robert F., 170
WAKR (Akron), 38
Wall Street Journal, The, 44
Wallace, George, 95
WAOK (Atlanta), 70
"War of the Worlds" (show), xxiv
Washington Post, 147–49, 177
WAVZ (New Haven), 100
WBAI (New York), 172–73, 183–84
WBBM (Chicago), 114
WBCN (Boston), 133, 140, 141
WBEZ (Chicago), 86
WBLS (New York), 71, 75, 77
WBOR (Boston), 133
WBUS (Boston), 77
WBZ (Boston), 110
WCAU (Philadelphia), 77
WCCO (Minneapolis), 110
WCHB (Detroit), 71
WCKO (Fort Lauderdale), 77
WCKY (Cincinatti), 98
WCMQ (Miami), 72
WDAF (Kansas City, Mo.), xxi–xxii
WDAI (Chicago), 77
WDBN (Cleveland), 80
WDIA (Memphis), 43, 69
WDSU (New Orleans), 27
WEAT (West Palm Beach), 79
Weavers, the, 37

WEFM (Chicago), 86
Welles, Orson, xxiv
WEVD (New York), 71–72
WFAB (Miami), 72
WFUV (New York), 133
WGCI (Chicago), 75
WGDY (Minneapolis), 29
WGES (Chicago), 71, 102
WGLD (Oak Park Ill.), 85
WHB (Kansas City), 29, 30, 32, 83
Whitehead, Clay, 147
Whiteman, Paul, 8
Whole Earth Catalogue, The, 174
WHOM (New York), 76
WIBG (Philadelphia), 131–32
Wild One, The (movie), 41
Wiley, Richard, 155–57
Williams, Andy, 68
Wilson, Earl, 50
WINS (New York), 35, 39–40, 46, 56–57, 104–5
Wire recorders, 97
WJW (Cleveland), 38, 39
"WKRP in Cincinnati" (show), xxv
WKST (New Castle, Pa.), 38
WKTU (New York), 56, 66, 76–77
WKYS (Washington), 75
WLBT-TV (Jackson, Miss.), 153
WLIB (New York), 71
WLS (Chicago), 96
WMAL (Washington), 113
WMAQ (Chicago), 107
WMBI (Chicago), 88–89
WMCA (New York), xvii, xxiii, 55, 57
WMGM (New York), 52, 57
WNBC (New York) 107
WNCN (New York), 87
WNCN Listeners Guild, 87
WNEW (New York), xxiii–xxiv
WNEW-FM (New York), xviii–xix
WNIB (Chicago), 86

WNJR (Newark), 39
WNOE (New Orleans), 29, 32
WNUS (Chicago), 78, 102–4
WOCN (Miami), 72
Wogan, Bob, 23
WOKY (Milwaukee), 31, 45
WOOD (Grand Rapids), 79
Woodstock (movie), xxviii
WOOK (Washington), xx
WOR (New York), 82, 131, 133
World Administrative Radio Conference, 190
"World's Largest Make-Believe Ballroom, The" (show), 12
WOWO (Fort Wayne, Ind.), xxi
WPAT (Paterson, N.J.), 78
WPFW (Washington), 172–73
WQAM (Miami), 30
WQBA (Miami), 72
WRHC (Miami), 72
WSH (Nashville), 80, 191
WTIX (New Orleans), 27, 29
WTWR (Detroit), 77
WVON (Chicago), 69
WWDC (Washington), 98
WWRL (New York), 70
WXEL (Cleveland), 38
WXUR (Media, Pa.), 148
WXYZ (Detroit), 55
WYNR (Chicago), 102
WYSL (Buffalo), 78
W2XMN (Alpine, N.J.), 121

XEAK (Tijuana), 101
XETRA (Tijuana), 27, 78, 100–4

"You Bet Your Life" (show), 7
Young, Roland, 141
"Your Hit Parade" (show), 15